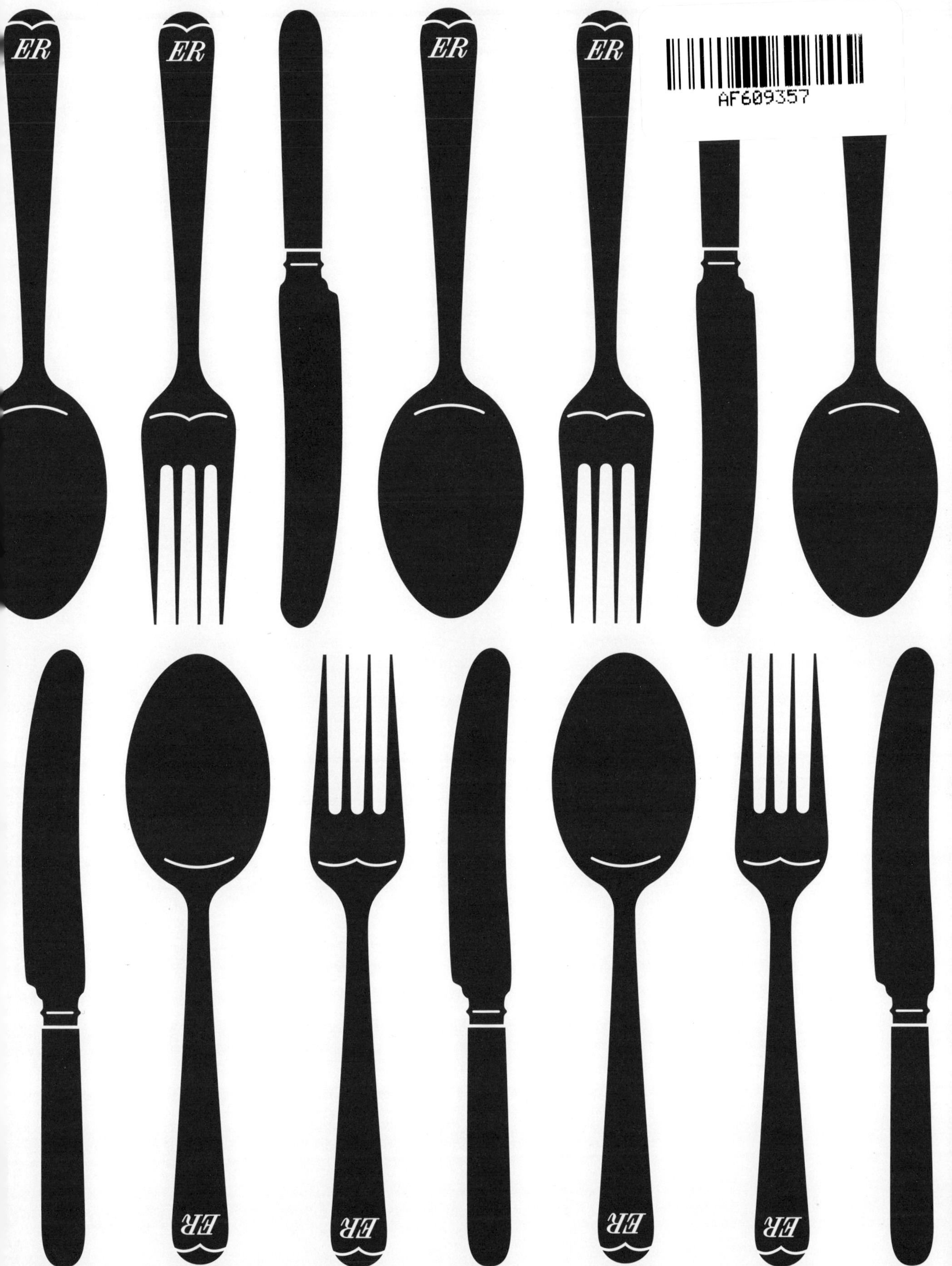
ER

The Kitchen Book

Ella Risbridger is a writer and journalist from London. With bylines in the *Financial Times, Guardian, Observer, Vogue* and many others, her books span from cookery to picture books, poetry to essay collections. Her bestselling debut, *Midnight Chicken (& Other Recipes Worth Living For)*, won Cookbook of the Year at the Guild of Food Writers Awards, and was named a book of the year in multiple publications on both sides of the Atlantic, including the *Sunday Times, New York Times, Daily Mail* and *Washington Post*. Her books are sold across six continents; and have been translated into many languages, including Russian and Chinese.

She was described by the *Times* as 'the most talented cookbook writer of a generation', which is always nice to hear. Ella is also the creator of *You Get In Love And Then...?*, her bestselling newsletter; an amateur painter, potter and candlestick maker; and the part-owner of one very fat orange cat. She divides her time between London, and the sea.

The Kitchen Book

GOOD FOOD FOR EVERY DAY

Ella Risbridger

Photography by Yuki Sugiura

4TH ESTATE • *LONDON*

4th Estate
An imprint of HarperCollinsPublishers
1 London Bridge Street
London SE1 9GF

www.4thEstate.co.uk

HarperCollinsPublishers
Macken House, 39/40 Mayor Street Upper,
Dublin 1, D01 C9W8, Ireland

First published in Great Britain by 4th Estate in 2026

Design by Luke Bird

Always follow the manufacturer's instructions
when using kitchen appliances.

A catalogue record for this book is
available from the British Library

978-0-00-871913-5

Typesetting
GS Typesetting

Printed and bound by GPS Group

FOR MY FAMILY:
THE ONE WE STARTED WITH,
THE ONE WE CHOSE,
AND THE ONE WE MADE

A NOTE ON OVENS

The recipes in this book have been made and tested in six or seven different ovens. Some of them – my oldest friends – even more than that. Here is what you need to know: every oven, almost from the moment you install a fresh new baby out of the box, behaves differently. Every oven is different. Learn to know yours. Learn to love yours, and if you can't love it, learn to live around it. (And what is love but learning to live around another?)

The oven in the kitchen where I write this is substantially hotter on the left-hand side than on the right. The oven in the kitchen where we made the farinata was running a good fifteen degrees cooler than the temperature on the dial. One oven I'm fond of has a faulty door latch, meaning that it will only click closed with a vigorous full-body hipcheck, but *also* only operates happily on either Gas Mark 7 or Gas Mark 2. Luckily this is familiar to me: I grew up cooking first on a Rayburn – which also was the only source of heating – and then an AGA. Hot oven, cold oven, maybe a warming oven. (I still kind of default to cooking everything at 180°C. That's Hot-ish Oven, baby!)

My parents' oven – seven wide feet of turn-of-the-century French enamel, inherited from previous tenants of their mountain farm – works great, provided you are happy to cook entirely at the whims of the fire. Throw a new log on for hot, let it die back for cold. Simple, provided it doesn't get *so* hot that the wooden structure of the house doesn't simply catch alight from sheer proximity. Then again, the presence of eight bold *sapeurs-pompiers* and the light-up red Land Rover (with horse trailer!) did add a certain *je ne sais quoi* to Christmas '24.

The temperatures in this book have been standardised to an **electric fan oven**.

They are guidelines. You might need to go a little hotter, or a little colder. You might need to turn your roast chicken or your coconut-cherry breakfast bars or whatever half-way through cooking. You might need just to keep an eye on it. The more you cook, the more you will feel fine about this. The more you cook, the more you will feel fine about everything.

A NOTE ON HOBS

I don't know what I'm doing with an electric hob, and have refused to rent flats because I was too afraid of the electric hob that came with them. The recipes here have been made mostly with my **gas hob**, but have been tested with **induction hobs** (how fast can that water boil!!) and those hot plate bits on the top of AGAs, Rayburns and other enormous range beasts. Gas hobs are, apparently, cigarette-level bad for you. Unluckily, much like cigarettes, they are also undeniably cool and fun. I will be very sad when we all have to quit gas hobs.

Contents

Introduction

This book is a list of things I love.

Mainly it is a list of things I love to eat, and things that I think you will also love to eat. Some things – peanut butter jalapeño bagels, etc. – I have included even though I have no idea if you will love them or not because I love them *so much*, and this is a book about loving things. It is a book about the beautiful and useful things I make all the time: the things that make my life better and easier and nicer just because I know how to make them. Now you can also make them.

Every recipe in this book is here because knowing it improved my life. I think they will also improve your life. They are the things I make all the time; the things that I think are delicious or magic or cool or fun or – dare we say it? – chic, in a way I constantly strive for and at which I almost always fall down. There is something very funny to me about striving for chicness in the twenty-first century. Why not shoot for the moon, you know? Why not pretend to live in the past? The key eras of chic have been eras of great global trial: thus I attempt elegance. Thus we can attempt elegance together. Being chic is out; *trying* to be chic is the new chic. Trying is chic! Bothering is chic! Putting in the work is elegant and stylish and I will die on this hill!

(Deciding what's chic or not chic: very chic. Also very funny. For example: matches, especially promotional matches = chic. Lighters, excluding Zippo lighters, but *not* excluding those bendy ones for igniting a gas hob = *not* chic. Coffee pods? Not chic. Italian stovetop Moka pot? Very chic. French press? Chic in summer, not so much in winter. I don't make the rules! I make all the rules. Play it yourselves with any random item or thought; write in with the answers.)

I love to try to be chic because it's so funny to try and be chic. I love when things are funny and I love when things are silly and I love when things are beautiful and I love when things are useful.

I love to make my life nice in ways that it doesn't need to be nice. I love to make things nicer than they need to be. I love to make things just, like, ten per cent more lovely than the bare minimum. I love to use heavy cutlery and beautiful Japanese ceramics to eat dinner on the sofa watching twenty-year-old cop shows. I love to buy flowers and make butter and buy bread. I love to make noodles at lunchtime in five minutes flat. I love to know that it's possible to make noodles at lunchtime in five minutes flat. I love to eat brown-butter cornbread straight out of the skillet. I love to serve supermarket cherry pie with too much soft whipped cream. I love to stamp out smoked salmon sandwiches in the shape of snowflakes and unfurl the sharp silvery top of a smart tin of anchovies. I love to stand at the counter with my laptop on the toaster and blitz white beans into

A · HAND · TURNED · UPWARDS · HOLDS · ONLY

a smooth fat swirl so I can dunk in a scissored wedge of plump pale pitta. I love to spatchcock a chicken and eat it hot with friends and cold from the fridge. I love to take bright green herbs-and-beans soup to a neighbour and her newborn. I love to wake up to a cannelé, squidgier and crispier and uglier than anything from a shop. I love to make mayonnaise and damson vodka and the scallion sauce that costs £3 a tiny tub from the takeaway. I love to drink a martini (two at the very most). I love to drink a Manhattan. I love to make pints of palomas in an ice-cold jug. I love to make pickles, and I love to eat pickles from the jar. Like Baby All Gone, I love to eat cherries from the jar. I love to eat a rack of lamb and a cucumber-tahini fattoush on a Tuesday night for no reason. I love to come home late with a furious headache and make a dozen perfect cookies in the dark.

I love to be in the kitchen and I love to be eating and I love to be cooking, and I hate that I have to do it every day, and if I have to do it every day it has to be so much better than just eating toast.

I love to cook; I love to eat; I hate to wash up.

I love when dinner is fantastic and I hate when the kitchen is a horrible hole. I love to eat an elaborate meal and I hate the rag that hangs around the sink. I love food and I hate to use more than two pans, tops.

I love to try very hard and I hate when things aren't worth it. This is a book of things that are worth it.

Every single thing in here is worth it to me, a person with a low tolerance for faff, a great love of nice things, and not a huge abundance of spare time or energy. I think they will be worth it to you too. I think you will love these things, and I hope you make them so much that you barely need to open this book to do it.

My dream for this cookbook is that you almost never look at it. My dream for this cookbook is that you absorb it so thoroughly into your life that you don't need it any more: that the recipes you love – and I'm pretty confident there will be recipes here that you love – slip so neatly and effortlessly into your regular rotation that you kind of forget where they come from.

Ideally, people would ask you for the recipe, and you would write it down and give it to them; and then they would make it for other people and tell them it was your recipe, and write it down for those people, etc. The dream, of course, is that one of those people, somewhere down the line, makes the thing for me, and I get to feel gently and distantly glow-y with pride.

This isn't an *economically* fantastic dream for me to have, obviously, but the heart wants what the heart wants. I want to give you recipes that feel like yours.

These are the recipes of my life; and I want them – even, like, two of them! – to become the recipes of yours. I want them to feel like yours from the start. I want you to do anything to them: amend them; edit them; make them work with what you have. I will help you do it! I will help you fuck around with these recipes until they fit your life so exactly it's like they were tailored! I believe you can do this with what you have, and who you are.

People love to ask me what kind of food I write about, and I never know what to say. The answer, I suppose, is home cooking, but home cooking done beautifully and cheerfully and in ways that make you feel better. I want you to like your life! I want you to feel good about your whole deal! I want this to work for you, and I think that it will, and I think we can figure it out. This is what this book is about: I think we will have a nice time here, and by the time it's finished your whole deal will feel just slightly better than it did before.

When you sell a cookbook, people like you to be able to explain the 'promise'. I never meant to sell (or write) this cookbook, which was supposed to be just for me – my own personal recipe collection, my own personal best-in-show, my private real contenders – but there's a promise here, nonetheless.

The promise of this book is this: however bad your day has been, however good your day has been, having something nice to eat has the power to improve it by a solid ten–fifteen per cent.

Listen: I am actually staggeringly keen not to over-inflate this promise. I am very tired by cookbooks – and other non-fiction books, in fact, the kind of thing primarily grouped under 'lifestyle' – which promise radical change as a result of following their simple steps. Mostly things are not simple; and real change happens incrementally, in small ways.

But then perhaps this can be a small way, a very small way, for things to change. At least, for things to change by ten or fifteen per cent. Net. After the washing-up is deducted. I have arrived at this number through a lot of thought. It's not a total transformation; it's not even most of a transformation. Your day will largely remain recognisably the same. The dinner is not magic: it has no power to fix anything that came before.

But it is also not an insignificant amount, is it, ten per cent? I mean you would notice ten per cent: you would notice fifteen per cent. It's a tangible difference, no? You would be able to see and recognise that the day had improved by ten to fifteen per cent.

The interesting thing is that a bad dinner, or no dinner, can comprehensively ruin the day. It doesn't have to – I mean it can be avoided, with enough goodwill banked and income disposable – but it can. And does! It does! There is nothing to eat. You have failed in your animal task. Prehistory growls. The evening becomes shapeless and untrammelled. The night creeps in with wild abandon. You become hungry, and then irritable. The snap descends. Result: misery.

In some ways, then, I suppose the net gain – factoring in what you stand to lose – might be more than ten percent. But let's stay with it for the time being. I feel confident in that ten. I feel like I can promise you that ten.

This book will improve your life, on a small and daily basis, by ten to fifteen per cent. It will do this by improving the meals you eat – mostly dinner, often snacks, sometimes lunch, rarely breakfast – by ten to fifteen per cent too. It will do this by meeting you exactly where you are, wherever you need it to find you: big flavours, new ideas, classic feelings. Dinner solutions.

I believe you can make your own personal life pointlessly, deliciously, ten per cent more lovely with this book. And I believe you will.

This is a list of things I love, and I hope you love them too.

MAX
500ml

ELLA

The Big List

I always like the part of a cookbook where there is a list of things. I like it for the same reason I always turn to the acknowledgements first in novels: I like seeing inside people's lives, like those magazine features where you get to look inside a celebrity's handbag. It's like a shortcut into knowing someone: like someone taking you backstage and showing you all the props before we go all in, like unhooking the front of the doll's house and swinging it open. It's a cross-section of a world, and this is mine.

This is not a list of things you should have. I don't even think it's a list of things *I* should have, necessarily. If I were starting from scratch, with an unlimited budget, would I choose everything I've ended up with? It's very hard to say. I do, almost without exception, love all these things I own, but is that because they are the things that I own or because they are the best things of their kind? Again, hard to say. Most of these things I have had for many years, and they have not failed me.

I suppose I tend towards something along the William Morris rules, although possibly even stricter: everything beautiful and useful, and if not beautiful exactly then at least deeply beloved. (Could anyone call an orange silicone spatula with a bit missing beautiful? No, but without it the scrambled eggs are doomed.)

I think it's useful, though, and nice, to know the kinds of thing I'm talking about when I say 'shallow casserole' or 'egg pan'. Partly nice so that you can feel familiar with these objects, which reoccur through this book like trinkets in a doll's house; but partly nice so that you can find in your own kitchen the thing that most closely replicates the thing I want you to use. Also, I like to show you around my kitchen.

My kitchen *is* these objects! I have carried them around to many physical kitchens, and many houses – renting in this country being a lesson in abject disappointment – and wherever they are I am, and that's where home is. A KitchenAid stand mixer is made of solid, unwieldy metal, weighs almost two stone, has many equally unwieldy attachments and must be packed – being very expensive – in a whole Sunday newspaper and change. It is a commitment, is what I am saying. It is a commitment kind of like owning a beautiful and temperamental racehorse, and it is similarly difficult with which to travel. And yet – perhaps like the horse! – when I open the box and let it free, and stroke its lovely smooth glossy neck, I feel a sense of rightness that can't be denied. This is my kitchen and my kitchen is my home.

The fridge! The freezer! The cupboards! The Kilner jars! I give you free rein to look around them all. Rifle away.

COPPER SAUCEPANS

I have three of these, from quite small to quite big (nothing extreme on either end). All three have lids, and they are very beautiful and reasonably impractical as they do not stay shiny if you cook with them every day. They are lined with some kind of tin, but I am unclear as to what exactly. They work on gas but probably not on induction, unless you choose very carefully. Please don't write in to explain why yours have stayed shiny. Mine haven't.

SHALLOW CASSEROLE WITH LID

My most-used pot: a wide, shallow Le Creuset-type thing that can fit horizontal spaghetti, toast spices, roast a chicken, make a chilli, and even, in a pinch, bake a cake.

BIG CASSEROLE WITH LID

Nevertheless, the big casserole – a classic guy – remains in play. Mostly, bread lives in it: good sourdough, probably seedy. A perfect bread bin. A great day job for this guy.

WOK

The wok is kind of my enemy. It's such a faff to keep it nice! It's such an unwieldy shape in the cupboard! And yet! For the things it's good at – e.g. beef and broccoli – it's so good that we will never get rid of it.

SKILLET

The cast-iron skillet is also my enemy for 'faff to keep nice' reasons, i.e. that you cannot wash it with soap, but it's so good at making things crispy, and so good at evenly heating up, and so good at enriching things with iron that it stays. For now. You probably need this or the shallow casserole, if I'm being honest. The arrival of the shallow casserole really put the skillet on the back burner. Then again, as soon as there's a steak to sear, a cornbread to bake, anything really that an old-timey cowboy might eat...the skillet is king once more. Hello, old pal.

EGG PAN

The egg pan is a small, 20cm non-stick egg-poaching pan for which we have lost almost all of the egg-poaching parts. It is about 3cm deep. It is the perfect pan for all things egg-related: omelettes, fried eggs, a little scramble. (We used to own a very expensive French pan, specifically designed for frying a single egg. It is long gone and nobody misses it.)

SIEVE, COLANDER

The sieve is an ordinary fine-mesh sieve. The colander is like an ordinary colander except extremely beautiful, enamel in white and purple and blue and pink and yellow with a gold rim, and I'm only telling you about it because it makes me happy to think about it.

SLOTTED SPOON

Our slotted spoon has gone missing. It is so useful and I yearn for it constantly. I'm going to replace it with a wire skimmer, designed for fishing things out of deep-fat fryers, but useful for extracting all kinds of objects from sauces and drippy pans.

WOODEN SPOON

Why mess with a winning formula? I use a wooden spoon every day of my life and I always feel good about it.

SILICONE SPATULA

There is literally nothing like a silicone spatula for scraping every last scrap of something out of something else. Every bit of sauce! Every bit of batter! Plus you can wiggle a silicone spatula – flexible and strong – underneath pretty much anything stuck to the bottom of a pot.

From a microplastics perspective, it seems like silicone is an ok option, if you're the kind of person who worries about microplastics. If you're not the kind of person who worries about microplastics, would you mind writing in and letting me know your secrets? Thanks.

An unshakeable rule in my kitchens: orange silicone for savoury, pink silicone for sweet. This is because I find that silicone picks up strong flavours, and while I don't think you can necessarily always taste it in the finished product, I can always taste it on the spoon. And I am always tasting what I'm cooking off the spoon.

LADLE

I used to know a man who lived in a thin, tall house full of objects: a pair of boots that had once belonged to a Spice Girl; an enamel Thunderbird 2; eight hundred empty egg boxes. The boots were real, but the Thunderbird was a replica. He sold meat from the back of a pub, and drank ice-cold martinis, and did the crossword very fast, and gave me a silver soup ladle. I don't know what became of him, but I use the ladle all the time.

BIG SPOON

I don't know where the big spoon came from but it's useful.

BIG TABLESPOON

The big tablespoon I stole from my parents, who dug it up from the garden of our English house when I was a kid. It's hefty, it's ancient, it is exactly the right size for adding an extra bit of flour to a too-wet cookie dough.

THERMOMETER

If I didn't have a meat thermometer I would never have learned to cook meat at all. You can also use it for the inside of bread. I have a list of internal temperatures, cut out of a magazine, taped up on the kitchen wall. 71°C for pork! 74°C for chicken! 52°C for rare steak, and 90°C for bread!

PEELERS

Regular potato peeler – metal, one piece, not the one shaped like a Y – which I almost never use for potatoes but usually for peeling courgettes into ribbons or thin slivers of fancy cheese. The julienne peeler is for cutting vegetables into little strips, which I use a lot for making small tiny carrot pickles, elegant matchsticks of apple for salads, slaws, that kind of business.

GARLIC PRESS

Where is our garlic press? Where has it gone? In the absence of a garlic press, I mostly use a very fine grater, but you know, the garlic press was pretty handy.

GRATERS

Box grater! Coarse grater! Medium grater! Microplane! We could probably get rid of the box grater at this point, but it's such a faithful friend, even if nobody knows what three out of four sides do. (Don't tell me the little nobbly one is for Parmesan: it's a death trap and impossible to wash up.) I'd feel lost if I didn't own a box grater. Coarse grater for Cheddar; medium grater for most things; Microplane for lemon zest, chocolate and nutmeg.

KNIVES

I have a big Chinese cleaver, which lives in the box it came in, scares the shit out of me, and is absolutely magnificent for chopping every single thing in the world if you can be brave and dextrous. I also have a big chef's knife, wrapped in old cardboard, a pair of fancy Japanese knives – a santoku and a utility blade – which have driftwood handles and leather scabbards, and a bread knife. The main thing with knives is to keep them sharp. In the absence of a knife sharpener, you can do it on the unglazed rim of a ceramic mug – swipe the blade along the edge away from you, fast, one two three – and be careful once you've sharpened them because they will move differently.

BLENDERS AND MIXERS AND WHISKS

Oh boy, do I have a humiliating number of blenders and mixers and whisks! What happens is, every time we move house, I do a purge, and give away a load of them e.g. the manky smoothie-maker that seemed like such a good present, or the hand blender that we *really never use anymore*, or the electric whisk *because I never make cakes*. Then I start cooking and realise that I need *all those things*. You do not need all these things.

I have a KitchenAid stand mixer, which was a present for my 21st birthday, and is fantastic for dough. It is not extremely practical in any other way.

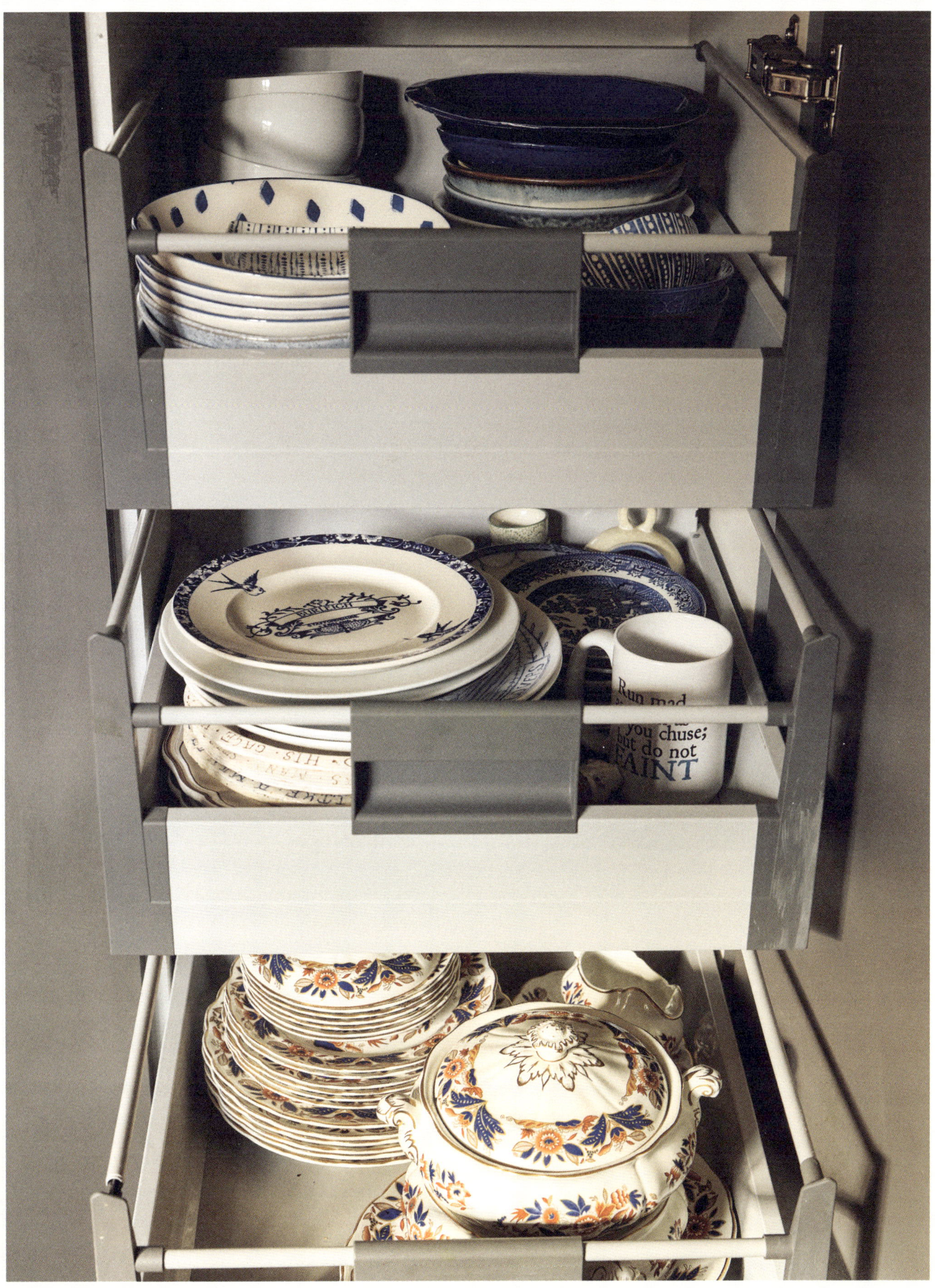
Run mad
you chuse;
but do not
AINT

I have a Magimix food processor, which has basically been rendered obsolete by the Nutribullet. The Nutribullet lives on the countertop permanently, and I love it. It is my most beloved bit of kitchen kit I have bought in the last 5 years. I use it for grinding nuts, seeds, breadcrumbs; making sauces, dips, pastes, anything that needs blending or chopping or mixing. The heat makes green sauces very green without blanching, which I like a lot, and you can make a bean dip (my most frequent lunch? Fancy white beans; olive oil; salt; Nutribullet; pitta bread) in 2 minutes with everything going directly into the dishwasher. The dishwasherability is mainly what it has over the Magimix. I hate washing up the Magimix more than anything in this life or at least in this kitchen.

I have an electric whisk for making cakes and mayonnaise. It's the *Goodbye to Berlin* of kitchen equipment: always giving it to the charity shop, always replacing it because, you know, what's a home without Christopher Isherwood? What's a home without homemade mayonnaise? Don't answer that.

The current electric whisk has dough hooks attached which I have never used even once; just as the hand blender has a whisk attachment that I never, ever use. This duplication is wholly unnecessary. And yet: if I give one of these two items away, I know I will simply end up replacing it. I cannot explain this. I just know it's true.

What it actually is, I think, is that I fear the hand blender. I got my finger caught in one a decade ago, requiring neat little stitches and leaving a permanent crook to the tip of my left index. It aches in wet weather. I don't like the hand blender but if you haven't got a Nutribullet and/or an electric whisk you can probably get a lot of use out of it.

I also have a regular balloon whisk with not one single bell or whistle. It is probably the most useful!

PESTLE AND MORTAR

I use this all the time. A big granite one is the best: rough enough to release all the lovely oils, smooth enough to avoid absorbing their lovely smells. Ours is a small granite one. It's annoying! But it's better than using a big porcelain one, or a wooden one, which – in my opinion – are worse than useless. Using a bad pestle and mortar is immensely annoying, and owning a bad pestle and mortar is even more annoying because it is always out on the kitchen side, dusty and unloved and looking like something out of an apothecary's shop. Get a good one and use it. It is a fantastic present to ask for. A proper Mexican molcajete is on my birthday list.

DIGITAL SCALES

Ideally you would get a set of good digital scales on which you can set any bowl or saucepan. Scraping things from the bowl of the scales into the bowl of the…bowl…drives me insane. I hate to transfer things because I hate to wash up. I used to have a set of heavy Victorian cast-iron scales with little weights (where did they go?) that were very beautiful and exactly like the one we had when I was little. It was very inaccurate, gathered dust like a bad pestle and mortar, and I hadn't actually noticed that it was gone from my life until I wrote about it. Get a good digital scale.

MEASURING CUPS

Stuff I measure in American cups: rice. All kinds of rice. Here is how to cook rice: ½ cup of rice per person, 1 cup of boiling water per person. Add, for example: a stock cube. Salt. Butter. Oil. Teabag. Lemongrass stick. Whatever. Lid on tight. Low heat. Twelve minutes. Heat off. Wrap lid in clean tea towel. Lid back on pot. Leave for 5–10 minutes until all water absorbs. Fluff with fork.

Other stuff I use American measuring cups for: fast, flexible baking where I don't mind too much about the outcome. Banana bread. I also use them on the daily as, for example, a vessel for vinaigrettes, or small chopped ingredients I'm about to put into something else, or general prep.

MASURING SPOONS

Mine came free with an Ocado delivery about thirteen years ago and are objectively horrible. Cheap plastic! Gaudy colours! The markings have rubbed off so nobody except me knows what they are measuring. And yet! Listen to me: in this book, when I say teaspoon, half-teaspoon, tablespoon, whatever, I am talking about the measurements given by measuring spoons. I do not mean the spoons in your spoon drawer. If you use those, which I bet almost everybody will, the recipes will not be as accurate. Like, it will probably be fine. But they will not be accurate.

PYREX JUG (BIG)

It doesn't have to be Pyrex, but it does have to be heatproof, and transparent (do not get a ceramic one and try and guess the measurements from top down), and the Pyrex one is a timeless classic. I usually put this on the digital scale for extra accuracy.

PYREX JUG (SMALL)

You think you don't need both, but our small one got smashed (flagstone floor, last house but one) and I miss it a surprising amount.

Everything looks better if you light a lot of candles and turn the big light off.

Don't buy napkins you have to iron. In fact, save napkins for fancy, and instead commit to owning ten billion tea towels in varying states of distress. Wipe mouths, wipe spills, hold hot things, dry wet things, boil wash. I love tea towels. I have nice ones for looking nice and some that are essentially rags at this point. All useful, and better for the planet than kitchen paper.

If you insist on having nice linen napkins (why do I do this to myself?), they will stain if you have napkin-happy friends, so soak with bicarb for an hour before you wash. Teaspoon of bicarbonate, bowl of cold water.

Salt gets out most bloodstains. Bicarb gets out almost everything else. If you bulk buy Tide pens from America, you can be the hero of so many spills.

Life is too short to forage fruitlessly for Tupperware lids. May I recommend ruthlessly binning every piece of Tupperware or faux-Tupperware or old takeaway containers that currently linger lidlessly in your cupboard, tumbling out with gay abandon whenever you open the door, and making instead the small powerful investment in a brand-new set of glass storage containers with identical clip-lock, sealable lids? I have six big ones and six small ones and it has changed my life. *Write down which brand you buy. Never buy another brand. It is vital that all lids match all boxes.* They are constantly in use: storing picked herbs, storing leftovers, freezing bits for chicken stock, freezing made chicken stock, freezing ancient brown bananas for banana bread, plus generally for pastas, grains, rice, etc. that don't yet have a Kilner jar.

I have so many 2-litre Kilner jars full of grains and rices and flours. The highlights:

The rices I actually use: jasmine, arborio, white basmati, brown basmati.

The flours I actually use: plain flour, gram flour, bread flour, cornflour.

The sugars I actually use: light brown, dark brown, golden caster.

The grains I can't stop buying: barley, bulgur, spelt, freekeh, farro, whole oats and porridge oats and those quick-cook five-grain mixes.

This is not all of my Kilner jars but it is most of the useful ones. Kilner jars are not a wholly practical way to store dry goods, although they are airtight and BPA-free, which is how I justify it to myself when I am packing thirty-five Kilner jars into IKEA bags and wrapping them in duvets for yet another move. Storage! Putting flowers in! It's all to play for!

Mrs Elswood Haimisha Gherkins come in 670g glass jars. The pickles are delicious. The jars, dishwasher-safe, are endlessly useful. They are the exact amount of water, for instance, that I like to drink. They are fantastic for making cheat's iced coffee in. (Nescafé; ice; water; half-teaspoon of sugar; lid on; shake. Top up with oat milk.) They are just the right size to comfortably hold the half-bag of rice or sunflower seeds or orzo that is too small for a Kilner but that cannot go back in the cupboard because the plastic got ripped and the bits will go everywhere. They hold flowers in a beautiful and chill way, and also, if you forget about the flowers and the water goes horrible, you can simply bin the lot. These pickles are a blessing.

Stovetop cooking is generally done on a gas hob.

Flowers: you can make a supermarket bunch of roses look expensive by cutting them short, sticking them in a jam jar, and adding in a few grass stems or bits from the garden, graveyard or roadside. Cow parsley! Ferns! Long grass! Greenery, generally, makes cheap flowers look more expensive, or at least more chic. The ideal flowers:greenery ratio is about 1:3. A big bunch of eucalyptus is a good buy if you want greenery to last through a variety of £3 cheapies. Rough up supermarket roses a bit; cut their stems short and at an angle; pull off their guard petals and put them in the sun to loosen up. Let tulips sprawl. Stocks make everything look like an English country garden. Sweet Williams last forever. Think loose, think easy, think relaxed. Think any colour but red: red is hard. Pinks, whites, a fun splash of orange or purple. Plus all your green. Chuck out any single flower as soon as it looks sad, and replace the water as often as you remember. If you're giving flowers as a present, they will instantly seem more expensive if you take off the cellophane and wrap them in brown paper.

The Fridge

OAT MILK

One of the great trials of my life is that while I have the digestive system of a weak and feeble woman, I have the heart and hunger of, if not a Tudor king, then at least a hearty Tudor wench.

I seek, you know, a roughly kneaded loaf, a wheel of yellow cheese, buckets of raw milk with the cream on top, freshly churned butter. I seek the wholesome and simple fare of an inn in a fantasy novel. I seek, in fact, to run an inn in a fantasy novel. The main problem with this is that, like many people, if I lived in that world I would probably die quite quickly due to my inability to adequately digest lactose at quantity.

Almost all of the recipes in this book – aside from a few baking bits – which call for milk or yoghurt were made first with oat milk or coconut yoghurt. I save all my lactose tolerance up for butter: *il faut souffrir,* etc. My agonies are a small price to pay for the really good salted butter. For this book, I've put the dairy back in because it's mostly more delicious, but I've flagged where you can easily switch it back to dairy-free, for everyone else in Fussy Club. I mostly use Oatly Barista full-fat as a milk substitute.

YOGHURT

Full-fat Greek yoghurt is so perfect a foodstuff that it's hard to emulate.

Goat's yoghurt is lactose *lighter*, though not lactose free, and obviously works as a one-to-one swap; but coconut yoghurt with a pinch of citric acid stirred in, to cut the sweetness, is probably the closest I have come to a plain vegan yoghurt which is good to eat on its own. The very plain Greek-style soy stuff is an ok swap; be very careful with swapping in oat yoghurt, as texturally it can go a bit odd.

Sometimes I just suck it up because good Greek yoghurt is so, so delicious.

BUTTER

Life is too short for bad butter. Life is also too short, in my opinion, for almost all fake butters. (Avocado oil makes a pretty good swap on toast.)

PEANUT BUTTER

The fantastic peanut butter is the kind that you get ground fresh at a health-type shop. Sorry to say: worth it. Put it on toast; put sweet jalapeño pickle on it; thank me later.

GINGER PURÉE

Ginger purée is not as nice as fresh ginger. It is, however, very fast and I use it all the time. A teaspoon of grated ginger = a teaspoon of ginger purée.

GARLIC PURÉE

Garlic purée is not as nice as fresh garlic. It is, however, very fast and I use it all the time. A teaspoon of grated garlic = a teaspoon of garlic purée = a couple of cloves. Both ginger and garlic purée I buy either from the enormous Tesco or the international supermarket. (Worth the trip.)

TOMATO PURÉE

You already have tomato purée in your fridge.

ROASTED GARLIC PURÉE

You can make this yourself (see p. 242). You can also buy a very nice one from Belazu. Other brands are available but that's the one I go for. I always, always have it in. An instant little boost for anything that needs umami.

MISO

Another shortcut umami trick. Red miso (or brown, which for the purposes of this book is the same vibes under a different name) is darker and richer and saltier. White miso is sweeter and smoother and lighter. Red gets a longer ferment for a bigger flavour. White is what you want for caramels or creamy things, red for intensity and big slow braises. This is all true, and I have both always, but you can pretty much swap them out for whatever you can get to at any given moment.

GOCHUJANG

You're seeing a lot of fermented things in this fridge. This is because fermented things are both great for you and extremely delicious. Gochujang is a Korean fermented chilli paste: deep, funky, spicy, rich. It makes a phenomenal pasta, a thick rub for pork, a crisp skin for chicken, a quick hit in a salad dressing with pickled carrots and prawns.

CHILLI CRISP

Lao Gan Ma is the brand of my heart. Sorry to 100 indie crisp makers; it's the big hitter for me. And I buy it in the 750g jars, so you know I'm serious. Salty! Sweet! Spicy! Texturally irresistible! Apply to all noodles, rices, even toast. On its own with a spoon while thinking.

PICKLES

Mrs Elswood Haimisha Gherkins, or whatever big dill pickles look best at the Polish shop.

PICKLED JALAPEÑOS

Cornershop pickled jalapeños (red and green) are always in my fridge. Also always in my fridge: hot sweet chopped jalapeño relish.

HOT SAUCE

A constantly shifting rotation. Right now: sriracha, always. Dunn's River Jamaican-style hot sauce. Aye Pickled kimchi hot sauce from a little Edinburgh brand. Encona African Peri-Peri yellow hot sauce. Aunt May's Bajan Pepper Sauce. Tabasco, mostly for hangovers.

KIMCHI

My fridge is absolutely never without kimchi. Often there are several jars of it in varying stages of consumption. The kind I love is always almost empty; other, less-favoured jars, gently decaying in their abandonment. This is because kimchi, in my experience, is all about experimentation: one brand you might hate, another brand you might adore. One brand you might absolutely love with an authentically Korean meal, but find a bit much at 8am; another brand might knock it out of the park at breakfast but feel blandly salty when up against a big hitter. What I'm saying is: if you don't already love kimchi, may I recommend you keep trying? May I recommend you just buy a bunch of different kinds, and see what works for you?

SAUERKRAUT

Have it hot! Have it cold! Have it with bacon, with potatoes, in a salad, in a sandwich, on a bagel with peanut butter. (Trust me.)

LAOGANMA
香辣脆油辣椒
Crispy Chilli in Oil
Net Weight: 670g
tajin

LEMONS

If you buy unwaxed lemons, which you should, they will need to be kept in the fridge. I often can't bear to do this because they come with leaves on and look so pretty in a bowl, but they do go blue much quicker than the waxed kind. You can unwax a waxed lemon with a scrubbing brush, very hot water, and dish soap.

HERBS, GENERALLY

The best thing you can do with soft herbs is wash them, dry them, and pick the leaves off the stems into a Tupperware lined with a folded damp paper towel as soon as you buy them. This makes them about a million times more usable. Throw into salads! Blitz into sauces! No fuss, big flavour. I usually have rosemary and thyme for the tough stuff and coriander, parsley and Thai basil for soft. I also love to have a huge bouquet of basil and dill on the table, like cut flowers, but that's a niche interest I know. About 15g is a small bunch. About 30g is a medium bunch. About 100g is an enormous bunch and if you need that much I will tell you specifically.

Growing Vietnamese coriander and Thai basil in pots on the inside windowsill is easier than you think and much cheaper in the long run. Growing supermarket basil is very difficult unless you are great at separating out the rootball, because supermarkets cram twenty plants into one pot to make it look temporarily fantastic.

Growing rosemary, in huge sprawling Italian-style bushes, is a lifelong dream. I'll let you know if I ever make it.

GREENS, GENERALLY

Cavolo nero is my mainstay and my guide. Also, a metric ton of broccoli. Usually, you can swap cavolo for regular kale or even spinach, chard or another cruciferous green. I just love cavolo the best – I love how it keeps its shape, I love how it goes crispy, I love how it wilts – so that's what I use.

MEAT, GENERALLY

Please try to buy meat from a nice butcher if you can. The flavour is better. The morals are better. The whole thing is better. Ideally, get it from someone who got it from someone who knew the animal. Eat less, but better. Then again, I have bought a million supermarket chickens in my life, and I have not bought my last one yet. I buy supermarket sausages on the way home and feel bad about it, but I eat them anyway. It's a balancing act. Do what you can.

FISH, GENERALLY

It seems to be basically impossible to buy fish ethically. Or, at least, to be sure you're buying fish ethically. You can look it up on the Marine Stewardship Council database. Best bets: mussels, clams, anchovies. Salmon and prawns are my real problems: I love both so much. MSC blue label, for wild caught; or the Aquaculture Stewardship Council teal label for farmed. There are not a ton of fish recipes in this book because I don't feel like I've got a decent handle on how to buy it right.

Tomatoes do not live in the fridge. Unless they are the cheap ones and you are making tomato sauce, in which case, do what you will. Good tomatoes live in a paper bag on the kitchen side, far away from any bananas. (Bananas will push all other fruit to ripen. Great for a too-hard avocado, terrible for a perfect tomato.)

As Nigella says: *all eggs are large, all butter is salted, all milk is whole*. Unless I tell you otherwise.

The Freezer

FROZEN SPINACH

A game changer for health at speed. I prefer it when it comes in those little pucks in a cardboard box because then the little pucks of frozen spinach stay put.

PARATHAS

Always a lifesaver. Anywhere you need a flatbread, a naan, a pitta, a wrap: frozen paratha, flipped in a hot pan for 2–4 minutes. The most delicious bread/pastry product! Like if a croissant was a wrap.

FISH FINGERS

I love them. Always have a box of twelve for emergencies.

NUGGETS

Fun fact: the Quorn ones are the most delicious of all the freezer nuggets!

DUMPLINGS

A blessing from God. I buy mine from the Chinese supermarket and I like to keep a variety in for impromptu dim sum. We're talking kimchi gyoza; we're talking leek potstickers; we're talking my beloved all-time faves: soup dumplings. Steam them.

ICE CREAM

Dark chocolate sorbetto for me; roasted-strawberry shortcakes for everyone else. Calippos just in case.

BERRIES

Frozen mixed berries = instant crumble.

COOKIE DOUGH

Baking sheet; greaseproof paper; 2 teaspoons of dough per cookie; fill baking sheet as if baking; freezer (instead of oven) until solid. Slide cookies (not baking sheet) into Ziploc bag. *Never freeze cookie dough in a block unless you love struggle*. Bake from frozen, 10 minutes, 180°C (p. 310).

MARTINIS

Little tins.
Or: gin, splash of vermouth, shake, freeze (p. 180).

Lasagne n.189
COLLEZIONE
Barilla
BELAZU
BORWICK'S
SAINT LOUIS
1kg

STOCK

I would like to be a person who made homemade stock every time. I think I used to be? I remember that person with a sense of admiration and distance. I use the Knorr jelly stock pots for chicken and fish; I use Marigold bouillon powder for vegetable – it's really *very* good, much better than the pots; and I tend to buy the fancy cans or pouches they have at the butcher for beef or lamb because I use them so much more rarely, and think it's harder to get that flavour *right*. (I almost never use pork stock for anything but if I did I think I would probably slow-simmer a ham and use the broth from that. Now I want to slow-simmer a ham! Yet I have no use for it.)

CHICKEN SPINES

I spatchcock almost all the chickens I buy, for speed. I freeze their horrible spines. I make amazing chicken stock from their horrible spines. I use homemade chicken stock only for things where chicken stock is going to shine. A broth! A soup! Maybe a risotto! Spines, bones, rosemary, olive oil, salt, celery, shallot. Cover with water. Simmer for many hours on a low, low heat.

Eggs also live in a bowl on the countertop! Ideally, brown and white, for beauty. Get the good kind with the golden yolks. Don't cheap out on eggs: eggs are the best of all things.

I love Marmite.

TAHINI

The good tahini is not the stuff in small expensive jars from the supermarket that becomes claggy and cement-like. It is the silky, sexy stuff in the beige tubs with the green lids that comes from Lebanon. It usually has a drawing of a palm tree on it and the writing will be at least partially in Arabic. It says to keep it in the fridge. I hate keeping it in the fridge so I don't, but maybe you should. Do you keep peanut butter in the fridge? Keep it where you keep peanut butter.

SMOKE

I try to have at least one of these things around for an instant hit of good smoky flavour. Smoked water is one of those ingredients that people laugh at right up until they use some, when it becomes invaluable: unlike, say, 'liquid smoke', it is not made of one million foul chemicals, and the flavour is so good. The water evaporates; the smoke remains. Magic. Smoked butter I buy from a small smokehouse in Brighton called Curing Rebels and is wonderful stirred into, for example, smooth polenta. Smoked salt I buy from Maldon and use mainly on cookies or in crispy toppings for savoury things; smoked water I buy from Halen Môn in Wales and use for everything.

Olive oil, sesame oil, the fancy olive oil; red wine vinegar, white wine vinegar, rice wine vinegar. Other, less important, kinds of oils and vinegars that I buy on a whim and have to throw out because I can't figure out how to pack them in a box.

Knife-cut noodles are the only kind of noodles I can successfully cook. I don't know why this is! They are frilly and beautiful and a little chewy and glossy and delicious. I love them so much, so if they are the only kind I can cook, that's an ok deal by me!

I love all forms of frilly pasta. Mafalda corta pasta is the frilliest and silliest. Use whenever you would use something boring, like penne. It catches sauce in all the little frills! I also think that spelt casarecce is fantastic for a change of pace and wholesome vibes. Great with fish. Great with peas. Linguine forever.

You can buy dried sour cherries in 2kg bags.

The Spice Drawer

Whole seeds, toasted dry in a frying pan over medium heat for 2–4 minutes, then ground in a pestle and mortar (or spice grinder! or coffee grinder!) have the best flavour and the best aroma and they make everything better. They are, however, kind of a faff.

When I say 'ground coriander', for example, you can either toast and grind the seeds yourself…or you can buy it ground. I have both and use both.

Things I wouldn't be without:

• Anise, whole stars • Bay leaf • Black cumin • Caraway, whole seeds • Cardamom, pods and ground • Citric acid • Chilli, flakes, powder, and whole dried • Chocolate • Cinnamon, stick and ground • Coriander seeds • Cumin, seeds and ground • Fennel, seeds • Garlic powder • Ground ginger • MSG • Nutmeg • Oregano, Mexican • Paprika, sweet smoked • Paprika, hot smoked • Peppercorns, black • Peppercorns, Szechuan • Peppercorns, white • Poppy seeds • Saffron • Sesame, seeds, black • Sesame, seeds, white • Turmeric, ground • Za'atar.

I love whole dried chillies. Think ancho, think cascabel, think chipotle, think guajillo. Beautiful, chocolate-coloured, rich dark coffee-scented chillies that will make you happy every time you look at them. And every time you cook with them.

MSG is a secret weapon. Deploy it with care and to pack an enormous, delicious, finger-dipping, one-last-lick-ing punch. Have no fear.

Citric acid is especially good for making vegan yoghurts taste more funky, sour and fermented. It's also useful when you want to use lemon juice or vinegar, but you want no more wet: crispy stuff, roast potatoes, little dips. A pinch of pick-and-mix sour to lift without changing the vibe.

My house is full of chocolate. Jagged hunks of plain chocolate from Mexico. A cardboard tub of white chocolate chips for cookies. A chunky and uneven bar of 60% caramel sea salt for long days; a slim grown-up bar of dark for after dinner. A bag of Minstrels for tossing with freshly popped popcorn and a big pinch of sea salt for movie night.

I buy my sea salt in 2kg tubs from Maldon. I get through it.

I don't have a microwave, so feel free to e.g. melt butter, chocolate, coconut, condensed milk in

Knorr
Responsibly Sourced
Fish
4x Pots
BISTO
AJWAIN
MEXICAN OREGANO
DRIED HERB
20g
PEPERONCINI
Bodrum
Thyme
Green peppercorn
Bodrum
48g
PIMENTÓN DE LA VERA
Denominación de Origen Protegida
DULCE · SWEET

yours if you do. I would really like one because they seem like an excellent way to cut down on my main enemy, unnecessary faff.

Most of the recipes in this book, especially the dinners, take forty-five minutes.

This is because that is simply how long dinner takes to make, start to finish, from thinking of the idea to having it on the table.

It is possible to go faster than this if you are exceptionally rich or exceptionally well prepared, like a Boy Scout, but basically, in almost all circumstances, dinner is a forty-five-minute process. Quite a lot of cookbooks will tell you that it is possible to go faster than this. Maybe! Maybe so! But then: is this because they often tell you to start with, for example, '2 onions, finely chopped', and do not factor in the hunt for the onions, culminating in a single red onion manky on one side; and then the hunt for the big knife, which someone has inexplicably put in the dishwasher and now it has kind of a thin sandy patina of dishwasher grime across the blade; and then the actual time it takes to chop something finely, and so on, in such a way as to put you *at least* ten minutes behind before the recipe has even started?

There *are* fifteen-minute meals. There *are* short-cuts. Frozen dumplings! Fish fingers! Eggs, of all kinds! There are two chapters dedicated to these kinds of meals! But an actual dinner, I think, takes on average about forty-five minutes.

I could lie to you! I could tell you that I accomplish having a feast on the table every night in fifteen minutes flat, and my kitchen is always spotless. But it would be stupid, like when you read a restaurant cookbook and they have halved all the quantities of fat and salt so that you won't freak out about eating in their restaurants. Then you make the food and it doesn't taste as nice, and you think you fucked up, but you *didn't*. You didn't!

Here is the truth: I accomplish a pretty fantastic dinner in about forty-five minutes about five nights a week, sometimes four, and I am fairly happy with that as a ratio.

Actually, please judge everything for yourselves. You can make these things; you *can* figure stuff out. You will be fine. We will do it together, and we will be fine!

Diversions
CROSSWORD 18,196 by ROSA KLEBB

On the Sofa

No-Knife Potato and Prawn Curry

Yoghurt Pot Naan

Pumpkin and Raisin Roasted Rice

Turmeric Satay Salmon and Greens

Banh Banh Sheet Pan Chicken

Rich Rich Noodles

Sticky-Crispy Korean Tofu

Beef, Broccoli, and Other Takeaways

Yoghurt, Honey, and Walnut Chicken

Crisp Soup

Dukkah Buckwheat Bowls

Tomato Pasta

Pistachio Chilli

Heaven Is a Bowl of Garlic Soup

Chicken and Egg Meatballs

Cumin Lamb Noodle Ragù

Proper Weeknight Dinners for All Comers

If I were a different person I'd have called this chapter something like 'At the Dinner Table' but my dinner table is covered in junk, and I'm eating this from a bowl on the sofa. I'm already in pyjamas. The day is almost at an end. I have not cleared or laid the table, because the table is heavy with papers and pencils, and I'm done. I'm done!

You have to know yourself to like yourself. You have to know your life to like your life. My life is an eating-on-the-sofa life. My life is a TV-dinner life. My life is eating something delicious, in my pyjamas, with candles lit and a blanket, and I like it so much.

I wish, in a way, that we were the kind of people who always ate at the table. But we're not. *Spiritually*, we're dinner-at-the-table people, you know? In my heart, we're *dinner-at-the-table people*! We have cloth napkins and beautiful Japanese crockery and old junkshop silverware that's correctly heavy in the hand! But alas our kitchen table is small, rickety, and doubles as my desk. I am not a tidy writer. I like to write surrounded by evidence of my own presence: stacks of books, strands of thread, pencil shavings, and the cat. And I like to come back to things where I left them. Which means that the kitchen table, basically, is out of commission on a daily basis. Weekends? Maybe I'll clear away; maybe we'll get all dolled up. Monday to Friday, it's one bowl, one spoon. Big-time cosy. Easy wins, not too much washing-up, things you can eat with a blanket on your lap and the candles lit. Weeknight dinners with a minimum of fuss, and nobody moving my papers. Weeknight dinners that feel special even if you eat them on the sofa: regular rotation real contenders.

One day, maybe we'll have the kind of dinner table I dream of. Maybe someday I'll have a desk and a door that shuts! Maybe you already do, in which case, feel free to black out the title of this chapter and write *At The Ordinary Dinner Table* instead, or something that conveys in your life the place you eat most of your Tuesday night suppers.

But for now, here we are. Telly on. Coffee table. Everyday dinners for everyone around.

A little strawberry ice cream, maybe, after the washing-up. A Hobnob.

A custard cream and a cup of tea and an episode of *House*.

No-Knife Potato and Prawn Curry

My friend B says the number one thing he seeks in a recipe is *knifelessness*: no chopping board required, just everything in a pot and leave it alone until it's done.

This is because B has two very small children, and there is always something else that needs doing as well as cooking dinner. And yet! Dinner at B's house is always delightful. When I was thinking about this book, I knew I wanted to make recipes that would work there: the kind of dinners that work for the whole family, but can be made while the whole family are tugging at your sleeve. The kind of dinners that feel like a treat after a long day: the kind of dinners that require almost nothing of you, but give you everything back, the kind of dinners that have a kind of alchemy to them; the kind of dinners that are more than the sum of their parts. A good recipe has to be that, I think. It has to feel a little like magic. This one feels like that to me.

You fry spices, puréed garlic and ginger and tomato. You blister a punnet of cherry tomatoes and a little bag of whole, tiny, new potatoes. You pour over coconut milk and add a fish stock cube. You add a dollop of mango chutney, then you walk away until the tomatoes have almost disintegrated into sharp-sweet sauce, and the potatoes have softened into that fudgy-perfect softness that you only get from cooking them in their skins, and soaked up all the umami-depth of the broth. You toss in a bag of spinach, and a thing of prawns, until the spinach is wilted and the prawns blush pink. You take the pan to the table, and serve.

You have nothing extraneous to wash up. You have a beautiful, cosy, lively dinner. You have something, I hope, much more than the sum of its parts.

Notes and Queries

Do try your best to find the tiniest new potatoes you can: they will cook more quickly and more evenly than bigger ones sliced in half, but that would work too. Supermarkets now sell 'miniature potatoes' year-round, and greengrocers will likely have some beautiful extremely teeny-tiny friends in teeny-tiny potato season.

Happily, you can use the worst cherry tomatoes you can find, if you like: cooking them like this, first in the hot pan then poached in broth, will bring out all their latent great qualities. The mango chutney brings out their sweetness, the splash of vinegar their sharpness.

Spices can and must be tweaked to suit delicate palates. Feel free to leave out the chilli altogether, and to swap the garam masala for a sweet garam with less chilli.

Pre-cooked chicken instead of the prawns, plus chicken stock, will also work if you don't have fish stock. Do not try to poach raw chicken in 5 minutes.

☞

SERVES 4

1 tablespoon garlic purée
1 tablespoon ginger purée
1 tablespoon tomato purée
1 tablespoon neutral oil
1 tablespoon mild chilli powder
2 teaspoons turmeric
1 teaspoon ground cumin
2 tablespoons garam masala
500g cherry tomatoes
500g tiny new potatoes
400ml tin coconut milk
1 tablespoon mango chutney
1 tablespoon fish sauce
1 teaspoon red wine vinegar
½ coconut-milk-tin double-strength fish stock (for now: one fish stock pot + 200ml water)
200g baby spinach
160g raw peeled prawns

rice, to serve (May I introduce you to... the microwave pouch?)

In a big heavy-bottomed pan with a lid, mix together the purées, the oil, the chilli powder, spices and the garam masala. Cook for 2 minutes over a low heat.

Add the tomatoes, and cook for another 5 minutes, scraping up any stuck bits of purée from the bottom. Add the potatoes, coconut milk, mango chutney, fish sauce and red wine vinegar. Stir the fish stock pot into a half coconut-milk can of boiling water (careful of fingers), and add that too. Stir.

Two choices: lid on for a soupier vibe (helpful for colds); or lid off for a thicker, currier vibe, and walk away for 45 minutes, taking the lid off after the first 15 minutes then leave for another 30.

Lift the lid off (if on), turn the heat right down, and fold the spinach through in handfuls. It will look like much too much. It isn't! It's the right amount! Handful, wilt, handful, wilt, handful, wilt. When all the spinach is in, add the prawns. The nice thing about cooking prawns is that they go from blue to pink when cooked, like a built-in temperature gauge. It will take 5 minutes to do both of these things.

Season generously with salt and pepper. Maybe also chilli flakes? We tend to do this with hot sauce at the table, to accommodate as many palates as possible.

Yoghurt Pot Naan

My mum has been making these little yoghurt flatbreads my entire life. Are they naan? Technically? Probably not. Are they delicious? Wholesome? Easy? Oh yes.

Listen, here are the official measurements. This official recipe makes 12 little naan, and relies on you both needing 12 naan at once and also having a full, untouched pot of Greek yoghurt. I never need 12 naan, and I never, ever, have a pot of yoghurt someone hasn't had a spoon out of.

The smell of these, plus Madhur Jaffrey's green coriander chicken (p. 79 of the *Ultimate Curry Bible*), is the smell of Friday nights when I was a kid: the pinnacle of hosting, the Platonic ideal of entertaining. An open house; a pot of curry; flatbread spitting and sizzling on the AGA hotplate. Children asleep in corners. Coats on the sofa. Good music. Kitchen dancing. Cumin, black cumin, and a sink full of glasses and grains of rice. Feel free to freeze (rolled out, greaseproof paper), also.

SERVES 4

350g self-raising flour
+ 2 teaspoons for dusting
3 teaspoons ground cumin
1 teaspoon salt
500g Greek yoghurt (coconut yoghurt is a great sub here)
2 garlic cloves, minced
4 tablespoons ghee or butter
2 tablespoons black cumin (nigella seeds)

What I do is I put a shake of flour, a teaspoon of ground cumin, and a pinch of salt directly into the half-empty yoghurt pot and stir. Then I add more flour. Then I add more flour. Then I keep adding flour, until the dough is no longer tacky.

Then I knead lightly, and set aside for an hour. In that hour, I fry the garlic in half the butter, until golden. (Low heat, big shallow casserole or pan that you can also cook the naan in.) Turn off the heat, siphon off the garlic butter, but don't wash the pan.

After an hour has passed, dust a work surface with the extra flour. Re-knead the dough, and divide into plum-sized balls. Turn the heat back on under the pan. Add a little butter.

Flatten one ball at a time into a round, using either a rolling pin (if you can be bothered) or the palm of your hand. Flour on both sides, and slip into the hot butter. Repeat until the pan is full, without any overlapping. This for me is two at a time.

Once they puff up, flip them. They should be golden brown, maybe even a little burnt in places. When puffed and browned on both sides, lift out of the pan. Repeat for all balls of dough.

Paint with garlic butter then scatter with black cumin. Serve with curry, serve with dhal. Serve with a crispy fried egg on top.

LODGE

Pumpkin and Raisin Roasted Rice

I had been trying to do something with pumpkins and raisins for probably several years before I found the right answer. One hundred failures! Then this! It's like that sometimes with cooking. (*See also:* life itself.)

Call it a pilaf, call it a biryani, it's neither of those things but carries something of their jewelled-rice gorgeousness: grains more defined than a risotto, but with the creaminess of risotto rice soaking up generous glugs of golden oil, and a jug of rich, deep, salty stock. The sweetness of pumpkin, roasted with salt and herbs, and the sweetness of raisin; the char of pumpkin in a skillet, plus the plump, taut-skinned burst of a roasted raisin. The crispness of the edges of both, plus crisp sage, and crisp rosemary. Salty and sweet; crispy and soft; unbelievably easy. Goat's cheese on top, optional, but outrageously nice. One pan, all in. If you buy pre-chopped squash, you don't even need a knife. A perfect side dish, for a bigger crowd, for sure – but a perfect one-pot family dinner as is. And fantastic as leftovers, even cold.

SERVES 4

2 tablespoons olive oil
small bunch sage
3 sprigs rosemary
2 big shallots
1 small pumpkin or squash, peeled and chopped into chunky dice – about 550g
75g raisins
small bunch tarragon
250g arborio rice
750ml stock
75g soft goat's cheese (optional)

Pre-heat the oven to 180°C.

Optional, but very nice, first step: crispy sage leaves! These are crispier and more delicious than if you do them in the oven, but fine either way. Heat the olive oil in a heavy-bottomed skillet or shallow casserole dish over a medium heat until shimmering. Add the sage leaves and the rosemary, and fry until crispy, then set aside.

Peel and halve the shallots, then thinly slice. Tip into the oil and cook for 5 minutes over a low heat, probably while you peel and chop the pumpkin. Add the pumpkin cubes and raisins then shake to cover in the oil. Tuck the tarragon and crisp rosemary down in there too.

If you opted out of extra-crispy sage, simply toss everything – rosemary, shallots, pumpkin, raisins, tarragon, sage, olive oil – together into the skillet.

Either way, slip the skillet into the oven, and roast for 25 minutes. Add the rice and stock, and roast for 20 more.

Top with crispy sage leaves, if using – also little splodges of goat's cheese? – and serve straight from the skillet.

Turmeric Satay Salmon with Greens

Oh, man, the takeaways I have loved and lost!

Nobody talks about this casualty of the UK rental market: never being a regular anywhere. Or, worse, becoming a regular for half a minute and then being swept away on the tide. Sometimes I look at these places on Google Streetview. Sometimes they are still open, full of people who aren't me. Sometimes they are just gone, swept away too. (Same problem.)

One of my great losses is a Thai restaurant by the sea,[†] which sold this incredible thing they called – simply and amazingly – 'I Love Salmon'. And listen: it would be impossible not to love salmon by the time you've finished eating this. I spent a long time trying to recreate this recipe: a bright gold, creamy, coconutty sauce, thickened with peanuts, and salty-deep with fish stock, bright with spices and given a boost with cavolo nero or whatever wilty greens you have to hand. It is so incredibly easy. It tastes like a takeaway while being perfectly healthy and full of nourishment. It takes about half an hour with minimal skill and minimal washing-up. Everyone loves it. I love it. I love salmon! It is the easiest win I have ever achieved.

It is not exactly like the original, but it is – dare I? – maybe even better: more of a dinner, more substantial, bright with turmeric (exceptionally good for you!) and greens (also fantastic!). It is so easy!

And, best of all – you can make it wherever you happen to be.

SERVES 4

2 tablespoons coconut oil
4 garlic cloves
10cm ginger
1 big shallot
4 tablespoons red curry paste
3 teaspoons ground turmeric
2 limes
400ml tin coconut milk
2 tablespoons peanut butter
1 tablespoon light soy sauce
1 tablespoon brown sugar
1 fish stock cube
4 salmon fillets
2 teaspoons sesame oil

Melt the coconut oil in a large heavy-bottomed pan over a medium-low heat.

Peel and grate the garlic, ginger, and also the shallot. Tip into the melted coconut oil, and soften for 15 minutes.

(This is a good point to pre-heat the oven to 180°C.)

Stir through the red curry paste and cook for a couple of minutes. Add the turmeric, stir,and cook for another minute or so.

Juice one of the limes. Add the coconut milk, peanut butter, light soy sauce, brown sugar, lime juice, a coconut-milk tin of hot water (400ml) and the fish stock cube. Stir to fully dissolve the stock cube and sugar. Simmer for 20 minutes.

[†] *Chilli in Hove.*

☞

100g shelled, roasted peanuts
small bunch spring onions
200g cavolo nero
rice, to serve

Brush the salmon fillets with sesame oil and season well. Roast for 20 minutes, or until just flaking apart.

At this time, it is helpful to cook the rice (we do plain jasmine) and do the washing-up. There is not much! It's a gem of a dinner, this one. For garnish, finely chop the peanuts and the spring onions.

When you're 5 minutes away from serving, wash and tear the cavolo nero into strips. Toss into the sauce until wilted.

Rice into bowls. Salmon atop the rice. Generous ladleful of turmeric-coconut-peanut sauce, plus wilted greens, over the top of everything. Scatter with peanuts and spring onions. A squeeze of lime. Heaven.

Notes and Queries

Cavolo nero keeps its shape really well, which is why I like it so much. Feel free to toss in basically any cruciferous green: broccoli will need steaming, so pop a lid on; spinach will add water, so it's lid off and heat high.

I just use whatever shelled, roasted peanuts are available. The salted kind tend to be easier to get hold of in corner shops. Salty! Delicious!

Reheating thoughts: it will be weirdly solid at fridge-temp. Don't worry about this. It will be fine.

Banh Banh Sheet Pan Chicken

A second, staggering, takeaway loss: Banh Banh Kitchen in South East London, and in particular, the chicken rice bowl from Banh Banh Kitchen. I don't think I ever, once, in four years and three houses, ordered anything else. A small brown box, neatly packed: sticky, fish-sauce-brown-sugar, crisp-skinned chicken thighs; pickled carrots; slivers of cucumber; vivid little lettuce leaves; fragrant jasmine rice stained generously with the drippings from the chicken. It was – and I am sorry to reveal this about myself – the perfect *midweek takeaway*: the dream for something delivered to your door that felt like a real dinner, shame-free, wholesome, correctly balanced. And such perfect lunch leftovers the next day! Alas: lost.

From memory, however – and since I had ordered it a frankly staggering number of times, the memory was exceptionally clear and vivid – I set out with hope in my heart. And oh, how that hope was fulfilled! The really humbling thing, often, with trying to recreate a takeaway at home is how easy it is. The rice was easy. The pickles were easy. The chicken, above all, was incredibly easy. A spoon of this; a spoon of that; a sheet pan in a pre-heated oven. Almost no bother at all.

Not as little bother as calling someone to bring it to your door, obviously, but as easy as things get without that. And substantially cheaper, also! I am aware that 'it is cheaper and easier to cook from scratch' is both a very boring and often incorrect position to take but, in this case, I think it is probably true. (It is certainly true if you have moved out of the delivery postcode.)

There is a marinating time here and it really is worth it.

SERVES 4

For the marinade and chicken:
25ml fish sauce
25ml oyster sauce
50ml soy sauce (mostly I use dark, it will be fine either way)
50g light brown soft sugar
1 tablespoon garlic purée
1 tablespoon ginger purée
1 lime
1 teaspoon sesame oil
1kg chicken thighs and drumsticks (skin-on, bone-in)

In a big bowl, mix the marinade ingredients together with the juice of half a lime; tip in the chicken pieces, and coat thoroughly. Set aside for at least 30 minutes, but the longer you leave it up to about 24 hours, the more delicious it will be. If you can remember to make this in the morning, or indeed the night before, it will be knockout.

The same is true of the carrots: in your second biggest bowl – this will be the bowl in which you make the salad, and this pickle juice the dressing for the rest of it – mix together the vinegar and caster sugar (or sushi vinegar) with the fish sauce and the juice of the other lime half. Add a teaspoon of salt. Stir until the sugar and salt dissolve. Finely shred the carrots, ideally with a julienne peeler. Chop the red chilli into hoops, discarding the seeds. Set most of the chilli aside for garnish then mix the rest with the carrots into the brine, and set aside for 15 minutes to 24 hours.

☞

For the carrot pickle:
2 tablespoons rice wine vinegar
1 tablespoon caster sugar
(or swap the vinegar and sugar for 2 tablespoons sweet sushi vinegar)
1 tablespoon fish sauce
3 big carrots
1 red chilli

For the salad:
2 Little Gem lettuce
smallish bunch (about 25g) mint
smallish bunch (about 25g) Thai basil
smallish bunch (about 25g) coriander

3 spring onions

When you're an hour short of eating, pre-heat the oven to 200°C.

Set a shallow casserole, or ovenproof skillet over a medium heat. Lift the chicken thighs out of the marinade, and sear – starting skin-side down – to seal on all sides.

Pour the remainder of the marinade (a rubber spatula helps here) over the chicken and roast for 25 minutes, or until a thermometer inserted into the thickest part of the thigh reads 72°C. It should be blistered and glossy and sticky-looking.

While the chicken is roasting, finely shred the Little Gem lettuce and strip the herb leaves from their stems. Add to the bowl with the carrot pickles and toss with your hands to combine and coat thoroughly in the hot-sour-sweet brine.

Finely chop the spring onions for garnish; scatter over with the reserved red chilli. Rice if you want it; bread, ideally soft, if you're lazy. Either way, don't waste the sauce.

Notes and Queries

This is a lunchbox hero: maybe even better cold, fantastic in sandwiches (especially baguette, plus pâté, for ad-hoc bánh-mì making), fantastic in a Tupperware for a picnic. Keep the salad ingredients prepared but separate for maximum crispness, and since the pickle brine dresses everything else it becomes the fastest assembly job in the West. I debated putting this in a later chapter, about cooking for the week ahead, but I decided I couldn't wait: I wanted you to make this now, tonight. I don't want you to wait either! But the leftovers will change your life.

One thing that absolutely makes it cheaper, easier and excellent for lunch leftovers is making lots of it: a kilo of chicken thighs, plus the best part of a whole bag of carrots, pickled. I practically always have a Tupperware of these chicken thighs in the fridge, for eating whole, or shredding into salads, or slicing into sandwiches. I make lettuce cups for lunch the next day: a whole little lettuce leaf stuffed with a spoonful of rice, and a little shredded chicken (and chicken skin), and a few little pickles on top. Portable and perfect.

Rich Rich Noodles

Imagine if cacio e pepe was dandan noodles.

It's a lot to consider, but in terms of vibe, that's just where we are. Let miso depth stand in for the pasta's Parmesan, swap the peppercorns from black to Szechuan, and fall hard for these rich, creamy, garlicky noodles; crisp pork; tangly, loopy greens. A vote of confidence for this one: it is my *most texted recipe*: I simply searched my WhatsApp history for 'Rich Rich noodle sauce', and here it was, all ready for me.

The name, I grant you: dumb as hell. Sometimes – not for 'Dan', but for Rich, you get it, you're there – these things stick, and renaming them is harder than you'd think.

This dinner takes literally as long as it takes crumbled sausages to become crisp – so perhaps 15, 20 minutes from the start. Mix up a few spoonfuls of nice big flavours from a few nice little jars; cook some noodles; let some greens cook in the sausage fat. Arrange in bowls. Voilà! Dinner!

SERVES 4

4 handfuls cavolo nero, de-stemmed and shredded (by hand is fine)
2 teaspoons toasted sesame oil
6 Lincolnshire sausages
4 nests knife-cut noodles
2 tablespoons rice wine
2 teaspoons or so sesame seeds, to garnish
a couple of spring onions, greens only, chopped, to garnish

For the dressing:
2 tablespoons tahini
2 tablespoons white miso
2 tablespoons roasted garlic purée (p. 242)
4 teaspoons Szechuan pepper
4 teaspoons rice wine
4 teaspoons rice wine vinegar
2–4 tablespoons noodle water

In a large skillet-type pan over a medium heat, crisp up your greens in a teaspoon of toasted sesame oil. I do this by heating the oil, then washing the greens under the tap, throwing them into the oil still wet, and sticking a lid on for 3–4 minutes.

While the greens are crisping, skin and crumble your sausages (slit down one side and peel).

Lift the greens out of the pan, and set aside. I usually do this in one of the bowls I will serve in.

Add the sausage meat and the other teaspoon of sesame oil to the skillet and stir. Cook until golden, which should give you enough time to make the dressing and the noodles.

Mix together all the dressing ingredients, except the noodle water, and set to one side for a minute.

Following packet instructions, cook 1–2 noodle nests per person. When the noodles are done, drain, reserving 2–4 tablespoons of noodle water. You will probably want to rinse the noodles in cool water.

☞

Stir the dressing, adding the noodle water slowly until it comes to a smooth double-cream consistency. Pour equally into four bowls. Divide the noodles into four atop the sauce.

Are the sausage crumbles golden? Deglaze the pan, still on the heat, with the two tablespoons of rice wine. Scrape up any nice bits with a spoon. Push the sausage (and nice bits) to one side and toss the greens into the other side of the skillet to warm through.

Add greens to the four bowls, followed by sausage. Top with sesame seeds, chopped spring onion greens and – if you like – crispy chilli oil. Bonus points if you get the kind with crispy garlic.

Notes and Queries

Greens: it's cavolo nero for me! Spinach tastes fine but won't crisp; if you can get hold of any beautiful Chinese greens, say if you have a Chinese supermarket, do that instead.

Lincolnshire sausages tend to have white pepper and nutmeg, which works extremely well. I have made this with basically all kinds of sausage now, and I think the only one I would truly advise against is anything with Bramley apple. I have also done this with pork mince, and you know what, with a generous bit of seasoning, it's fine, but not as good and takes longer.

Noodles: knife-cut noodles are the only noodles I've ever reliably been able to cook without them sticking. This recipe has been done very successfully by other people, *not* me, with thick udon noodles, regular egg noodles, and a variety of other cupboard staples. Me, though: I miss the frill of the knife-cut king. I buy them at the Chinese supermarket. (See introduction for more notes.)

Sticky-Crispy Korean Tofu

This is tofu for people who think they don't like tofu. Is that you? Maybe! It's also tofu for people who like their dinners to taste just a little bit decadent, in a get-a-lot-of-paper-napkins type of way, but *also* in a fancy-platter lot-of-herbs type of way.

Here's the deal: we press and crumble extra-firm tofu into chunks and nuggets and little friable bits. We toss green beans in sesame oil, turn the heat up high, *don't touch them* and burn the shit out of the beans. Blacken them! Burn them! Char them so the skin blisters and splits! Then we fry the tofu fragments until crisp (same pan, so easy); make an unbelievably fast brown-sugar rice-vinegar Korean-adjacent sauce; stir it all together; shred a whole bunch of Thai basil and fresh green herbs; and serve it on a heap of rice, or wedged into a pitta bread, or whatever carb your little heart desires. It is also the gateway drug, or was for me, to tofu in all other forms. A good beginning!

If it helps any tofu haters get over any ancient prejudices, it's sort of based on a pork dish, and it's *significantly better than the original.* Sometimes you eat something somewhere and you know, you just know, you're never going to be able to recreate it. That's how I feel about the pork-and-green-bean stir-fry from Chinatown Olympiades in Paris, in the summer of 2018. My God it was good. It was sticky, it was crispy, it was burnt in just the right places. I was solo in the city of lights with my friends and a stack of good books and I could see that the car crash of my twenties was going to start, any minute, to recede into the rubbernecking distance of the rear-view mirror. Was that it? Was that why? Extra solitude, please, waiter, and hold the chaos for just five minutes while I eat my pork. It's hard to measure relief on a kitchen scale. *Maybe it could have been any meal*, I thought, wildly! *Maybe I would have remembered any meal as fondly!* Then I realised that I have forgotten almost every other meal I ate in the summer of 2018, so it can't have been just that. It must have been pretty good, even unseasoned by suffering. I don't even like pork much, and it was still so good!

It was this revelation, obviously, that tipped me off. What if it was the *pork* that I was getting wrong? What if it was the pork that was getting in the way of the perfect bean-based high I'd been chasing all this time? Then I discovered tofu and friends, it was all over for the humble pig. Double bean all the way.

☞

SERVES 4

400g extra-firm tofu
250g green beans
2 tablespoons toasted sesame oil
40g basil leaves, picked
20g mint leaves, picked
20g coriander leaves, picked
1 teaspoon soy sauce (usually dark, could easily be light)
2 tablespoons cornflour
2 tablespoons sesame seeds

For the sauce:
50g gochujang
50g dark brown soft sugar
50g rice wine vinegar
2 tablespoons soy sauce
4 garlic cloves
30g ginger

Take a baking sheet with a lip; line it with kitchen paper. Slice the tofu into thick slices, about 2cm, and lay out on the kitchen paper. Top with more kitchen paper and another flat baking sheet. Top this symmetrical sandwich with two or three heavy cookbooks. Leave for at least 20 minutes. This step feels like a faff, and it is a bit, but it's worth it if you want crispy tofu. Pressing tofu gets the water out, making the tofu ready to receive other – more exciting – flavours in its place.

(If you're going to serve this with rice, which I recommend, this is a fabulous time to set the rice cooking. See p. 288.)

Trim the stringy ends off the green beans (feel free to use scissors). Set a big frying pan – ideally with a lid – over a high heat. Switch on your extractor fan or open the window, and heat 1 tablespoon of the sesame oil for thirty seconds. Toss in the beans, put the lid on if you have it, and shake the pan to coat the beans. Take the lid off (that's done now) and walk away. I mean, don't walk far; there's still fire involved. But don't touch the beans any more. Do not stir them. They will take 15 minutes in total, but you're going to shake the pan again in about 8 minutes. They will become kind of blistered and split, black and sticky in places, and those burnt places will simply drink up the soy and the rice vinegar and the spice.

While the beans are burning, whisk together the gochujang, dark brown soft sugar, rice wine vinegar and soy sauce. Mince the garlic and grate the ginger. Set to one side.

Your tofu, by now, will have yielded up a lot of that water to the kitchen paper. Bin the kitchen paper, put away the baking sheets, return the cookbooks to the shelf, and crumble the tofu into a big bowl. You will break it into little nugget-y bits with your hands.

Lift the beans out of the pan. Toss with all the leafy herbs, tearing the herbs as you go. Reserve maybe a pretty leaf or two to garnish. Tip onto a – warmed, please – serving platter or big plate. Drizzle with 1 teaspoon soy sauce.

Put the same pan over a high heat and add the rest of the sesame oil. Toss the cornflour vigorously with the tofu then tip it into the hot pan. Do not hesitate at all, or be tempted to add the cornflour ahead of time. The tofu will simply soak up the cornflour, and what we want is for the cornflour to hit the hot oil and become incredibly sizzly and crisp. Cook for 5 minutes, then use a wooden spoon to

☞

break up the mass of tofu into nuggets again. Turn the nuggets as best you can. Cook 5 minutes more. The tofu should become golden and crunchy. If it is a little burnt in places, don't worry. Return the tofu to the big bowl from whence it came.

You may want to switch off the heat here, and cook the sauce in the residual heat. Maybe not! But my pan keeps enough heat in that I usually do. Toss the garlic and ginger into the hot pan and stir-fry briefly, about 30 seconds. Add the whisked-together sauce and cook for a couple of minutes, stirring continuously until glossy and thick – you want it to cling to the spoon, like if you drew a line with your finger down the back of the spoon the line would stay. *Do not do this! This is hot sugar!* Toss the crispy tofu into the sticky sauce. Decant onto the platter, on top of the beans and herbs. Scatter over the sesame seeds and the little pretty leaves.

Serve with rice, and perhaps also some pickles (p. 243) or – ideally – kimchi.

Notes and Queries

Feel free to chop a courgette into uneven chunks and toss that in alongside the beans. Maybe two courgettes! Courgettes love to be burnt, and they love to soak up a sauce.

If you can get hold of Thai basil, please try to get hold of Thai basil. Also worth getting hold of if you can – but hard enough to find for it not to make it into the recipe title – Vietnamese coriander. Holy basil and hot mint: double trouble. If you can't: standard basil, standard mint, standard coriander. Big generous handfuls of soft green herbs.

Spice fiends, stick with gochujang. For a family-friendly version, seek out the Korean paste doenjang! We buy it at the Asian supermarket. It is just like gochujang – you will probably find it on the same shelf or the same website – but not at all spicy. It fulfils the exact same textural purpose. If you do this, though, just use a single tablespoon of soy.

A blob of coconut yoghurt is so good here.

Extremely pushed for time? Quorn chicken nuggets (or indeed, regular chicken nuggets, but I genuinely prefer those little Quorn guys) made according to box instructions will sit unbelievably well on a bed of soft white rice, thoroughly soaked in sticky, spicy sauce.

Beef, Broccoli, and Other Takeaways

I like to tell people I don't like stir-fry, because when people can't cook they always make you stir-fry. You know this? You know this. It is also not a name for a dinner: it is a cooking technique!

(Weirdly, I am realising I also don't love 'a roast' or 'a traybake'. Famously – in my family, anyway – I don't like 'casserole' either, so perhaps this is the problem? Don't tell me how: tell me what! Tell me what's so good about it!)

Stir-fry, to me, is one of life's most depressing meals. It's so good done right, no? But even the most ardent defenders of the stir-fry form have to admit it's so grim done wrong; and it is persistently done wrong. One of my sisters won't ever eat easy peelers because she likes them too much and is consistently disappointed: me with stir-fry. You have to protect your heart in these circumstances!

Slimy pre-cut vegetables cooked to a uniform unpleasantness, and nothing cooked how you'd choose it to be cooked by itself – too crunchy, too wet – with a heavy, salty sauce that tastes mostly of the packet it came in. Burnt wet rice, or noodles stuck together in a fat sticky clump and all chalky in the middle, which is better I suppose than the chicken, which – if not bone dry – is straight-up *bloody* in the middle. I don't know who to blame for this. I just know there is an epidemic of bad stir-fry and I hate it.

Actually it isn't bad stir-fry I hate so much as average stir-fry; because more than that, it's everything that distinctly average stir-fry represents: quick food done badly but who cares, it's only fuel. The stir-fry is the heart of bad, boring weeknight cooking, which sucks, because what a perfect meal it can be. What a perfect meal it should be!

Listen: I am a soy sauce fiend, an oyster sauce aficionado. Rice is my favourite food. I love anything you can throw fistfuls of greens into and call it dinner. This is my stir-fry intervention and you should make it right now. I nearly didn't write this recipe up because we eat it so much it felt like you probably also knew how to make it. Then I remembered: we are different people and you don't know what *I* know, which is how to make this Chinese-American beef-and-broccoli stir-fry in such a way as will make cheap meat taste like the finest butcher's cuts, and with a sauce that you can use for literally every stir-fry for the rest of your life.

We make this recipe, like, once a week. It is a real staple for us and I bet it will be for you too.

☞

SERVES 4

¼ teaspoon bicarbonate of soda
4 tablespoons cornflour
500g frying steak, thinly cut
2 heads broccoli
1 tablespoon sesame oil
1 tablespoon garlic purée
1 tablespoon ginger purée
2 tablespoons rice wine

For the sauce:
125ml chicken stock
70ml oyster sauce
30ml light soy sauce
30ml dark soy sauce
25g dark brown sugar
1 teaspoon black pepper
1 teaspoon sesame oil
splash rice wine vinegar

For garnish:
sliced red chilli
chopped spring onions
toasted sesame seeds
chilli oil

In a bowl, mix together the bicarb, cornflour and 2–3 tablespoons water. You should have a smooth white paste, kind of like water icing for a fairy cake. Add the steak and stir. Set aside to tenderise for 30 minutes. Get some rice on to cook, however you do that, and chop your broccoli into florets.

The sauce is immensely easy: stir together everything from 'chicken stock' down to 'rice wine vinegar'. Set aside.

Take your wok (or deep sauté pan) and put it over a high heat. Get the wok nice and hot and add the sesame oil until it sizzles. Throw in the beef to brown – this will seal in delicious juices and tenderness – including the cornflour marinade. When crispy, add the garlic and ginger purées. Fry for about 2 minutes.

Drizzle the rice wine around the hot inner edge of the wok, so that it drips down into the garlic and ginger. This cooks off the alcohol and also, we think, stops it spitting.

Add the sauce. Turn the heat down to a simmer to reduce the sauce. This will take about 5 minutes, in which time you can boil and drain your broccoli.

Add the broccoli to the sauce and beef. Shake all together. Garnish generously with sliced red chilli, spring onions, sesame seeds, chilli oil and serve.

Notes and Queries

Use whatever steak is cheapest. We get those thin-cut rump 'frying steak' guys for this, but also, *whatever is cheap*. Cheap in steak terms, anyway.

You can probably make this work in a normal frying pan! But a wok is much, much better. A wok is one of the differences, I think, between a sad stir-fry and a great stir-fry.

Yoghurt, Honey, and Walnut Chicken

Big green salad, lots of fresh herbs, oregano, basil, dill, crispy little potatoes, unbelievably tender golden chicken with a honey-walnut-fennel seed crust...and an addictively salty, creamy, allium-y dip-slash-drizzle. Which also, unbelievably, serves as a marinade for the chicken itself. (Divided in half, obviously, do not eat anything that has touched raw chicken.) Handy!

This extremely delicious and wholesome dinner has, like most of us, two parents. The father was a recipe in *The New York Times* for 'ranch-dressing chicken'; the mother, a faint memory of breakfast on a Greek island a long time ago. Unlikely lovers, for sure. But you can't fault the results.

I was about fourteen, and aiming for sophistication by breakfasting solo several tables away from my large and loudly cheerful family. Just coffee and yoghurt for me, please! And yet, a mind-blowing experience: thick-set, lactic yoghurt; honey tinged with thyme and basil and that faint body-ish smell of sunshine on earth; chopped walnuts. How was it so good? How could this be? Why was I just experiencing it for the first time at my great age?

A similarly mind-blowing experience, aged thirty-two: reading Ali Slagle's recipe for ranch-dressing chicken. Ranch dressing was new to me. (I know, I know, I was a rube.)

I loved it double with the buttermilk switched out for Greek yoghurt. Easier to buy, for sure, but also yoghurt marinades for meat are basically universally a good idea: there's a reason they pop up on pretty much every continent. Bulgaria! Zimbabwe! Lebanon! Pakistan! Persia! Heaven. Consider, for example, tandoori chicken: tender, complex, crisp on the outside and yielding within. Plus, unlike other acid-type marinades, you can leave them comfortably overnight without the acid getting carried away. A make-in-advance sauce that worked twice as hard as usual? Sign me up.

But I wanted more. I wanted to make it in the oven, for a start, because it kept catching on the stovetop. I wanted crispy skin on the chicken. I wanted some sweetness in there somewhere. I wanted not to waste a drop of the lovely chicken juices. I wanted more crunch, and more complexity, and I wanted a complete meal. I wanted greens! I wanted – and the heart wants what the heart wants – little crispy potatoes. I wanted the flavours of Greek breakfast, but the irresistible double-dip of Pringle-flavoured ranch dressing. I wanted something addictive and wholesome all at once. I wanted this, and I got it.

☞

SERVES 4

For the dressing:
2 small garlic cloves
zest and juice of 1 lemon
20g chives, finely chopped
1 teaspoon sea salt
1 teaspoon garlic powder
1 teaspoon onion powder
¼ teaspoon MSG, if you have it
4 tablespoons mayonnaise
200g Greek yoghurt

For the chicken:
8 chicken thighs (skin-on, bone-in)
100g walnuts
2 tablespoons fennel seeds
4 medium potatoes
2 tablespoons neutral oil
2 tablespoons honey
sea salt (for seasoning)

For the salad:
1 handful basil, leaves picked
1 handful dill, fronds picked
handful oregano, leaves picked
4 sprigs thyme, leaves picked
2 big handfuls rocket
2 big handfuls lamb's lettuce

Start with your dressing: grate 2 garlic cloves, and the zest of your lemon, and mix them with chives, salt, garlic powder, onion powder – and, if using, your MSG. MSG gets a bad rap, but a pinch of it is genuinely fantastic at lifting flavours. You can, of course, just use fresh garlic, but you won't have that *thing*. You know the thing? I know you know the thing.

Stir in the mayonnaise and the Greek yoghurt. Taste. Resist the urge to eat it all immediately. Take about two-thirds of the dressing and the chicken thighs, and toss them together in a large bowl. Cover and leave in the fridge for at least 1 hour and up to 24.

Pre-heat the oven to 200°C. With a pestle and mortar, roughly bash the walnuts and fennel seeds together to make a crumb for the chicken.

Peel and dice your potatoes: keep them nice and small to ensure they cook through. Shake them across a baking sheet and drizzle with the oil. Shake again to coat. Slip into the oven for 15 minutes, to give them a head start.

Press the yoghurt-y chicken (skin side down) into the walnut and fennel crumb; set atop the diced potatoes, skin side up; drizzle with the honey and scatter with sea salt. Turn the oven down and roast for 20 minutes at 180°C, or until the chicken is cooked through and the crumb is golden and crispy.

Toss the herbs and leaves together with the lemon juice. Arrange on a platter. Toss through the crispy potatoes and top with crispy walnut chicken. Remaining dressing on the side (for dipping).

Notes and Queries

Dairy-free friends, soy yoghurt is better than coconut here.

It's very difficult to resist dipping a whole bunch of vegetables in this dip. Make it even without the chicken and salad, why not? Cucumbers! Peppers! Carrots! An easy way to consume a lot of vegetables. I feel like children will enjoy dipping into this because, once again, it tastes like Pringles.

Crisp Soup

If the concept of 'crisp soup' doesn't make you happy, I think you might be a lost cause. I'm sorry! I don't know what to tell you! It's a soup full of crisps, my God. (If you count tortilla chips as crisps, which we always do.)

It is also nutritious, warming, wholesome, cosy, deeply-flavoured and richly-layered, and I think it is possible that even your fussiest eaters will like it because one good trick for feeding fussy eaters is to make something *customisable by design*: add your own toppings! Add your own sauces and sour creams and bonus spices! Add crisps you can dip, and thus consume nutrients almost without notice! Do not skimp on the avocado, and also do not get freaked out by the addition of cold avocado into a hot tomato soup. It is so perfect a combo, and if you consider it even briefly you will get it immediately: a crisp little golden tortilla chip, a smooth cool avocado, a dollop of sour cream, a confetti of chives, a rich, deep, spiced tomato broth. Unreal. I think it is...possibly...not a classic Mexican dish, maybe more like Tex-Mex? Maybe not even? Hilariously, I think I might have met this idea originally through Gwyneth Paltrow's Goop. Wherever it comes from, this is the way I do it, and the way I think you're going to make it on your regular rotation going forwards.

SERVES 4

For the soup:
1 red onion
1 dried ancho chilli
4 garlic cloves
1 small cinnamon stick
400g tinned tomatoes
1L good-quality stock (vegetable or chicken work best)
¼ teaspoon black pepper
¼ teaspoon chilli flakes
1 teaspoon smoked paprika
1 teaspoon ground cumin
½ teaspoon ground coriander
1 teaspoon smoked water (optional)

Halve the onion and the ancho chilli; put half of each to one side.

If you would like to be fancy, you can char the half-onion: hold it firmly with a pair of tongs and turn it over a lit gas hob until it blackens. If this sounds like too much hassle, you can simply toss the half-onion and the half-chilli into a lidded saucepan over a medium heat. Without peeling, bash your garlic cloves with the flat of your knife, and toss those in too. Add the cinnamon stick.

Strain the tin of tomatoes – sieve over bowl – and set the solids to one side. Pour the tomato juice into the saucepan and add a tomato-tin's worth of stock. Bring to a simmer. Turn the heat off, stick the lid on, and let alone to infuse for an hour while you do everything else.

If you make the tortilla chips first, you save on washing-up. Extractor fan on, or window open. Oil into skillet. Heat until shimmering. Slip tortilla into hot oil, and fry for 2-ish minutes, or until golden on one side. Flip and repeat. Lift out, slice into strips and set on kitchen paper to dry. Sprinkle with salt while still hot. Repeat for all four tortillas. Set to one side.

☞

Toppings:
1 tablespoon oil + 4 tortillas (alternatively: big bag of tortilla chips)
2 avocados
handful chives
cheese
sour cream
extra chilli flakes? Everything seasoning? Lime wedges? It's all to play for

Throw the tomato solids into the hot tortilla oil, and let sizzle. You want them to burn a little bit for smokiness. Finely chop the remaining half-onion and half-chilli and add to the pan. Stir, and cook for 10 minutes. Add in your spices, smoked water and the remaining stock, and stir. Cook over a low heat for 30 minutes.

Lift the cinnamon stick, half-chilli and half-onion out of the broth, and discard. Blitz together the broth (including the garlic) and the tomato mess until completely smooth. Taste for salt; this will depend on what stock you used. If you have time, return the smooth soup to the heat for as long as you've got (up to about an hour). If you don't, good news! It is already so nice.

Halve and slice your avocados; chop some chives finely; grate some cheese, especially if you have kids about; set out the sour cream plus everything else on the table. Tortilla chips, crisp and golden.

Ladle soup into bowls. Top each bowl lavishly, with everything, or as desired.

Notes and Queries

Feel free to leave out the chilli; feel free to tweak the spices down to your preferred level. This is pretty punchy, because that's how I like it, but you run this show.

I think it's worth making the chips yourself, one of those kitchen transformations you have to see to believe: a real doll of a level-up, the kind of easy win that you can't believe you haven't been doing all along. They are so crispy! They are so good! They are, actually, fantastic as a snack or in a salad (!) or, as here, in soup. They make things feel fancy.

Any leftovers, before you add toppings, make a fantastic chilli base. I make double, freeze the other half, and defrost it hard in a pan to reduce by about a third on busy nights. Then I put in browned beef mince or a big jar of black beans, fried with an onion and a green pepper. Voilà! Instant chilli!

Alternative use for leftovers: bring the frozen soup back up to a simmer, shred in rotisserie chicken, melt in grated mozzarella, top with torn-up toast or shop-bought croutons and Parmesan. It's a whole new meal!

Dukkah Buckwheat Bowls

Here's the elevator pitch: honey-cumin carrots and chickpeas and cherry tomatoes, roasted until charred and sticky; tossed with toasted buttery buckwheat grains, big fistfuls of soft green herbs, and gorgeous sweet-sharp slippery chunks of salted heirloom tomato, plump and firm and cool as a baby's cheek; and topped with punchy garlic yoghurt, and a scattering of sunset-yellow hazelnut-fennel spices.

Whenever I hear 'warm salad', I think of bad picnics and failed cool boxes and soggy leaves. If I didn't, though, I might use it here. If this were served cold (which it mostly isn't) it would be a salad, no question.

Something about it, though, feels heftier than that. It can't just be the heat. It is, potentially, the double-carb of the chickpeas and the buckwheat. Plus, of course, carrots.

I made this first because I had inexplicably signed up for an impossibly expensive vegetable box. The first week they gave us peaches and tomatoes and beautiful fresh peas. The next week they gave us a sack of potatoes and a bunch of carrots. The week after that, they gave us a sack of potatoes and a bunch of carrots. The week after that – well, you get the idea. It has been a salutary reminder that this country does root vegetables no matter the weather, and if the earth keeps on burning we'll all have to get a lot better at making those knobbly little roots into something spectacular.

This, in spite of the fact that I have grown three carrots in my life, and not one of them larger than a thumb. They were very sweet, both in size and flavour, but pound for pound (taking into account the compost and the pot and the water and the time and the rent on the garden) probably more expensive than gold. Sometimes I think I grow things just to remind myself that food should be more expensive than it is. Someone had to grow that carrot! And that one! And that one! And they are all such good carrots! Which is, I suppose, both why I buy the impossibly expensive vegetable box, but also a useful thing to remember when whinging over the credit card bill. Good food costs money. Flying peaches all around the world is insane. Carrots, treated with care, are outrageously delicious.

☞

SERVES 4

1 garlic clove
2 tablespoons Greek yoghurt
1 pinch saffron
6 medium carrots
400g tin chickpeas
200g cherry tomatoes
2 tablespoons honey
3 tablespoons olive oil
500g buckwheat grains
knob of butter
1 sprig rosemary (optional)
2 heirloom tomatoes
2 teaspoons flaky sea salt
small bunch flat-leaf parsley
small bunch oregano
small bunch mint
small bunch coriander

For the dukkah: *(optional)*
70g whole roasted hazelnuts
2 tablespoons fennel seeds
2 tablespoons black sesame seeds
1 tablespoon cumin seeds
1 tablespoon coriander seeds
2 teaspoons smoked paprika
2 teaspoons flaky sea salt

You want to give the yoghurt time, so either do it well before (like, the morning) or make it the first thing you do when you start cooking. Very easy: grate, or finely mince, the garlic. Swirl the yoghurt, minced garlic, and 1 teaspoon salt together. If you're using saffron – which is a knock-out colour and has a slightly bitter, rich depth of flavour – mix your pinch of saffron threads with 2 teaspoons of water separately, to bring it out. Stir that straight into the yoghurt. (You can just stir 2 teaspoons of water in with everything else if you're not using saffron.) Set aside.

The dukkah, also, is great to make in advance – if you're making it at all. You do not need to make it! You will be fine with shop bought! Tip everything except the salt into either an electric spice grinder or a pestle and mortar. Blitz or bash to a bright, chunky powder. Stir through the salt.

Pre-heat the oven to 180°C. Peel and chop the carrots into batons. Drain your tin of chickpeas. Halve the cherry tomatoes. Arrange the carrots, tomatoes, and chickpeas in a (mostly) single layer on a baking tray, drizzle with the honey and oil, and toss to coat with your hands. Scatter over 2 tablespoons of the dukkah, if using, and toss again. Roast for 30 minutes.

While it's cooking, rinse the buckwheat in a sieve. Tip into a dry, lidded saucepan, and toast for about 3–4 minutes – until the nice smell hits you: earthy and nutty and sort of intoxicatingly wholesome. You'll probably want to stir to stop it catching. Cover with water (about 1 litre in my saucepan, but check yours), add the knob of butter (about a teaspoon) and the rosemary, if using. Bring to a simmer, cover, and cook on a medium heat for 15 minutes.

Roughly chunk the heirloom tomatoes. Tip the tomatoes into a sieve, set the sieve over the sink, and add the flaky sea salt. Toss with your hands, and leave to sit. This draws the moisture out of the tomatoes, and intensifies their flavour.

Finely chop the parsley, oregano, mint and coriander.

Drain the buckwheat, and add to the baking tray. Toss together – not with your hands this time; it will be hot. Add the plump, cool tomatoes and green herbs. Stir briefly and spoon into bowls. Top each bowl with a dollop of the garlic yoghurt and a heavy sprinkling of the dukkah (if using).

☞

Notes and Queries

Those bags of little baby carrots you can buy are a wasteful but very speedy substitute here, if you don't have time to chop or peel. Or don't peel, if you can't be bothered, or want the extra nutrients.

Any tomatoes! Use 300g of any tomatoes you want – the heirlooms have a better flavour and are prettier, but salting them in this way brings out the flavour of pretty much even your standard corner-shop offering. If the tomatoes really suck, squeeze over half a lemon, and add a pinch of caster sugar with the salt.

I almost always stick a chicken stock cube or stock pot in with the buckwheat grains. This makes it, obviously, not suitable for vegetarians, but I love the flavour.

I almost always cook double this amount of buckwheat, because it's very versatile and useful to have it ready-made in the fridge for salads and snacks and lunches.

Buy the dukkah! You can get it online, in Waitrose, or in any decent world foods-type shop.

Tomato Pasta

The nerve to call something 'tomato pasta'! But I believe this one is the real one: the truest form.

We were at my parents' house for dinner with no idea what to make for dinner.

This often happens to me (not knowing what to have for dinner) but it's difficult at my parents' house because they live at the top of a mountain. Their neighbours are goats, and, once a day, the girl who climbs the mountain to feed the goats. There are no shops for many miles. There can be no spontaneous cooking unless you get good at raiding the garden, the nesting boxes, and the dry goods in the pantry.

(In winter you get good at meal planning, and having a full freezer from the summer.)

Also, we were all home, on this occasion, so there were almost a dozen of us.

Also also, we were *all* home, so it was a celebration.

What to make for 11 people that feels like a celebration? What to make for 11 people that feels like a celebration and a reunion under the high blue sky of the mountains in summer?

We were lucky: it was August, everything was ripe and perfect; the *tomatoes* were ripe and perfect.

There is, genuinely, only one thing to make with tomatoes in August: *pasta alla cecca* à la Nora Ephron, à la my friend Kate Young. It is perhaps the most perfect summer tomato dish; it is certainly the most perfect summer pasta dish. It is unbelievably light; totally full of flavour; and the tomatoes truly sing. You blanch them to skin them; that's all. Don't be alarmed. You can do it! It is the only bit of cooking-cooking in this recipe, and then you use the same water for the pasta. It is truly the most simple and beautiful recipe, and what it loses in points for requiring you to skin tomatoes it fully makes up for in one-pot everything else.

You peel them and chop them with garlic and basil and black pepper and you toss them through hot pasta, just as they are. The pasta is hot; the tomatoes are cool and slippery and aromatic.

I get so sad in summer to cook a tomato. They are perfect for such a fleeting little minute! They are perfect so rarely! When something is perfect for as short a time as a summer tomato, you have to find a way to love it just in that fleeting little minute; you have to find a way to let it be itself just as much as it can.

If all celebrations are about celebrating a moment in time, this is the best celebration dinner because it is so completely *about* that singular moment in time: it is about the ripeness of the tomato and the freshness of the basil and the people for whom and with whom you make it. For me, it is always about August in the mountains, with the sun sinking very slowly and pink behind the distant hills, and for those moments, rarer and rarer every year, when everyone is in one place.

This recipe comes from Nora Ephron's *Heartburn*, but it was my friend Kate who made it for me first; and it was also Kate who told me how to make it for my family; and it's Kate's recipe I am always basically thinking about when I make it.

☞

SERVES 4

750g ripe tomatoes – shapes and colours welcome
100g basil
4 tablespoons extra-virgin olive oil
1 teaspoon chilli flakes
1 garlic clove
400g dried pasta
also: ice

First, the tomatoes. Actually, really, *only* the tomatoes: that's all the cooking there is.

Do not be alarmed: blanching is very easy and not at all complex and it is absolutely worth it in this recipe. Take an enormous pan and fill it full of water. Put it over a nice high heat, and bring it up to a simmer. While it's coming to a simmer, slice a neat little X in the base of each tomato. This is so you can just slip the skin off. Fill your biggest bowl with cold water and ice.

If the water is now at a simmer, drop in your tomatoes a few at a time, and 'let them bob along for a minute', as Kate says. You can see when they are ready because the little Xs at their bases will start to flap away from the lovely tomato underneath. Scoop out with a slotted spoon, and drop into the iced water to cool. Repeat until every tomato is in the cold water. Add salt to the tomato water, and bring it back up to a rolling boil. This is for the pasta!

Peel the cooled tomatoes, and chop roughly. Chuck out the iced water, and toss the tomatoes into that big bowl. De-stem and chop the basil, and add that too. Add all the lovely olive oil, the chilli flakes, 3 teaspoons sea salt, and 3 big twists of black pepper. Peel and smash the garlic clove with the flat of your knife, and add that too. Give it a delightful stir, and set aside for 10–15 minutes while you cook the pasta in the water.

Drain the pasta, taking a cupful of the cooking water just in case, and toss the hot pasta through the tomatoes. If it looks dry (it shouldn't!), add a splash of the pasta water.

Serve in the big bowl; tongs to twirl into individual bowls. A perfect moment.

Notes and Queries

Tomato pasta in winter: 2 x 400g tins of tomatoes, one tomato can of red wine, 2 sprigs of rosemary, 4 garlic cloves (peeled, smashed, but basically intact) and half a peeled onion. A big bit of butter and a big glug of good olive oil. Salt and pepper. Simmer for hours.

Traditionally, this pasta is made with linguine – at least that's how Nora and Kate do it. I love to use orecchiette: I love the little ears; I love the way they hold sauce; I love to make them! But I think you could have a wonderful time with almost anything in your cupboard.

Pistachio Chilli

When I first had a blog, a thousand years ago, a lady from Texas used to send me furious emails because I never said what kind of chilli to use in my recipes. Joke's on you, Texas lady! I didn't even know there *were* different kinds of chilli. I thought it was just red and green, like a stunted traffic light.

In my defence, Stepney Green is kind of a long way from Mexico (9,000km!). Anyway, I know better now. Now I know there's one million fantastic chillies out there, none of which are sold in any of my local supermarkets. Crushing, made double crushing by this truly fantastic book – probably the book, actually – on Mexican cooking, *Tu Casa Mi Casa*, by Enrique Olvera and friends. It is reasonably difficult to get hold of, and the ingredients it seeks are even more elusive. I am hoping that this sentence dates badly, like when you read Elizabeth David talking about 'olive oil' and 'garlic', but at the time of writing, the chances of me reliably being able to find, for example, *hoja santa* or seepweed in the supermarket are slim to none. (Actually: just none.)

All this means that when I became obsessed with this pistachio chilli, I knew I was going to take monstrous liberties with Olvera's original to make it work. And I knew I had to make it work. The picture in the book was the greenest green pistachios blended with herbs and warm water to a beautiful silky sauce, exuberant in its greenness, studded with coriander flowers and the pink-purple stems of amaranth, the shapes of summer squash just visible underneath. Vegan! Gluten-free! Summer, winter, autumn, spring! Reheatable! I had to have it. It was love at first sight. Tomatillos are like if a tomato was one of those round yellow fruits in the papery skin you find on top of expensive patisserie: savoury, green versions of a cape gooseberry. They were also £28 for 2, sagging gently, skins already wrinkling, at Borough Market. Nope!

Instead I found them online: tinned, but available next-day delivery. I imagine that Olvera et al would also think that this is not at all the same as theirs anyway, and lacking as it does the *hoja santa* and the *chile güero* and the amaranth, etc., and, *¡Madre de Dios!, what is the fennel doing in there, why are all the proportions different*? but you know what? I love this version. I love this rainy English version of this beautiful Mexican thing!

I add the fennel because I tried to find out what a *hoja santa* leaf would taste like and do something vaguely reminiscent of that: impossible, as it turns out. People kept comparing it to sassafras. I didn't know what sassafras tasted like either. Like root beer, apparently, but I didn't know that either. Anyway, someone told me that *hoja santa* was a little like anise, and a little like mint, and a little like tarragon. I tried various combinations. This one, I think, while probably nothing like *hoja santa* or sassafras, was the nicest. This recipe makes the most vivid green sauce, and you can pour it over basically anything: roasted squash, roasted courgette, poached chicken, pan-fried salmon. A bowl of plain rice if you want it all to yourself. Tortillas to dip.

☞

CROSSWORD

SERVES 4

1 tablespoon oil
2 shallots
50g fennel
1 green chilli (sorry, Texan lady)
2 garlic cloves
150g tinned tomatillos (drained)
125g roasted, shelled, unsalted pistachios
40g spinach
40g coriander (stems fine)
10g tarragon (stems fine)
10g mint (no stems)
if you can find them: coriander flowers, edible flowers, micro-coriander

Up to you:
rice + protein/roasted squash/ roasted courgettes/roasted veg + tortillas to serve

In a heavy pan, over a low flame, bring the oil up to temperature. Peel and trim then finely chop the shallots and fennel, and slip them into the oil. Gently soften without browning too much.

Finely mince the green chilli (de-seeding if you don't want too much heat) and the garlic. Toss those into the oil too, and give it all a stir. It will smell amazing in mere seconds. Cook for about 5 minutes.

Chop the tomatillos and add them to the pan. Let them sizzle for 5 minutes. Add the pistachios and 125ml of water, and simmer for 10 minutes more.

Pack the spinach and herbs into your blender. Pour over the simmering sauce to wilt the greens right down, and let it cool a little before blending. Season to taste.

Coriander flowers, very pretty and easy to come by if you grow coriander as it is constantly trying to bolt and bloom, for exquisite little garnish. Edible flowers make a very pretty substitute. Micro-coriander is pretty cute too.

Serve with rice, roasted veg, plain chicken, whatever. Tortilla chips to dip, even.

Notes and Queries

Roasted squash! Roasted courgette! Wedges of pumpkin! Plain poached chicken breast, the kind that men love to make themselves for lunch! Cumin-marinated chunks of lamb! Pan-fried salmon! All of these will be improved by this glowy green sauce. Do what you want! Let me know how it goes!

Keeps well, reheats well. I kind of like it cold.

Swap tomatillos for green or yellow tomatoes, blanched and skinned as in the Tomato Pasta recipe on p. 62. It will not be the same. Sorry! But nice anyway.

Thin with stock. Voilà, pistachio soup! Squash: wedges, cumin, olive oil, salt and pepper, 180°C for 30 minutes.

Heaven Is a Bowl of Garlic Soup

This is not really my recipe, but it's pretty difficult to find out who the credit belongs to originally. I probably came across it first on Deb Perelman's outrageously good *Smitten Kitchen*, some time in the early noughties (2006?); Deb, herself, gives credit to a 1999 edition of *Bon Appétit*. That edition is long gone and, in any case, other places give other sources. One website just calls it 'the infamous soup of the blogosphere', which is such a delightfully noughties phrase it makes me nostalgic just thinking about it. The blogosphere! Remember that? Remember when the internet felt like a new and hopeful home instead of the inaccurately documented collapse of civilisation?

Anyway, I don't know whose idea this was originally. What I do know is that any book about what I'm cooking would be wildly incomplete without it. I thought about leaving it out, honestly. But whenever I told anyone about this book – anyone I had cooked for in, say, the last three years – they would nod knowingly and happily, still gently glowing, and say 'Oh yes, of course, *the book about the garlic soup*'.

'But you must,' said my friend's mum, wide-eyed, fully sincere. 'You *must* include the garlic soup.' Then she leant forwards, as if what she was about to say was vital information. 'Ella, if Heaven exists, on the other side of the pearly gates is a cup of that magic brew.'

It was very hard to argue with. Who could? And she's right! It *is* magic! What I like best about it is that it has that proper alchemy you get in all great recipes: that sense of transformation. There are 44 cloves of garlic in this soup, around four full bulbs, and not a single one of them is overkill: it's not too much, I promise, and not even too garlicky. Some of the cloves are confit-ed in olive oil; some are sautéed lightly in butter with onions and thyme. It's creamy and spicy without a single dash of cream or spice; it brings out every complex, subtle, delicate, deep flavour that garlic has to offer. I cannot tell you whether they eat it in Heaven. I really hope they do. I would like to think of all the people I have loved and lost up there, somewhere in the sky, eating a large bowl of golden soup.

☞

SERVES 4

44 garlic cloves – about 4 bulbs
2 tablespoons olive oil
4 sprigs thyme
2 tablespoons butter
1 onion
1 litre chicken stock

Pre-heat the oven to 180°C.

Add 26 garlic cloves, unpeeled, to your smallest ovenproof dish, with all the olive oil. The olive oil should just about cover them, with their little tips poking above the surface. Tuck the thyme sprigs down under the oil. Season generously, and cover tightly with tin foil. Roast for 45 minutes. Your house is about to smell amazing. You are welcome.

Let the garlic confit cool until you can touch it comfortably then peel the roasted garlic cloves, keeping the oil and thyme stalks, but discarding the skins. (If you are tempted to suck the last little delicious fragments from them before putting them in the bin… who's watching?)

In a large, heavy-bottomed pot, melt the butter over a medium heat. Let it foam up gently.

Peel and thinly slice the onion and slip it into the foaming butter. Turn the heat down and cook for 10 minutes. Peel all the remaining garlic cloves and toss them in too. Throw in the roasted garlic, the garlic oil and the leaves from the thyme. Pour over the stock, turn the heat back up to medium and simmer (lidless) for 30 minutes.

Blitz until perfectly smooth – a stick blender is least trouble here. Divide into bowls; grate over a little Parmesan; maybe a squeeze of lemon. Plenty of black pepper. Something hearty and maybe a little sweet. Eat.

Heaven is a bowl of garlic soup.

Notes and Queries

Try to get the big garlic that comes unwrapped rather than the multipack, as the cloves are bigger and easier to handle.

Fantastic with, like, a walnut bread? A date and walnut-type dark sweet loaf?

If you can be bothered to make proper chicken stock, or you happen to have some, this is a really great place to use it. Do I? Not often! But it's always amazing when I do.

Chicken and Egg Meatballs

This is the perfect January dinner.

It is pretty great year-round, to be honest, but in January – the wrong side of Christmas, thermostat still falling – it excels itself. It walks that impossible line between brightness and cosiness: something, anything, to remind you simultaneously that you're alive and life is worth living. Lemons. Egg yolks. Handfuls of elegant, beautiful dill. A sunset yellow, creamy (but creamless!) pepper-speckled sauce, plus plump, delicate, fennel-flecked chicken-and-rice meatballs. A fat, warm little pitta bread to mop it up with, if you like, or possibly just a commitment to licking the bowl clean all by yourself.

What if avgolemono, the Greek egg soup, was instead a dill-heavy Swedish-adjacent (or Russian? Polish? Eastern European?) take on classic Italian meatballs? What if, instead of a vat of soup, you reduced the broth right down and kept the glossy yolks and fluffy whites the same? What if the sauce just coated the meatballs? And also, what if the meatballs also contained the carb, and the vegetable, so the whole thing could be as easy to eat as humanly possible?

It's an instant mood-lifter: the 5k run of dinners, the kind of minor triumph that makes you feel disproportionately fantastic, wholesome and glossy and righteously sleepy. Men are weirdly obsessed with this one: I don't know why. It is very impressive to them. And listen: they are right to be impressed.

SERVES 4

1 bulb fennel
2 shallots
2 big handfuls dill
4 tablespoons extra-virgin olive oil
2 lemons
500g minced chicken
125g short-grain rice
500ml chicken stock
3 eggs
2–4 handfuls spinach (optional, for bonus health)

Peel, trim and finely dice the fennel and shallots. Then dice them even finer. Big bowl.

Strip the dill leaves from the stalks. Set aside the stalks (a big, heatproof measuring jug is ideal, as you will use them to flavour the cooking broth), and about half the dill leaves, which you will stir in just before the end.

Finely chop the remaining leaves, and mix with the fennel and shallots. Stir in two tablespoons of the olive oil, the grated zest of both lemons, and 1 teaspoon of salt. It will look weirdly pretty! It will also taste lovely, and you will wonder why you don't have this as a salad more often.

Mix in the chicken mince, and the uncooked rice. Do not taste it after this point, obviously. Form into 13 chunky meatballs (or 25 small ones: the choice is yours!).

☞

A tablespoon of oil in a shallow casserole (with a lid) over a medium heat; brown the meatballs until lightly golden (shake the pan a couple of times to turn them).

Add (or make up) the 500ml chicken stock to (or in) the jug with the dill stalks. You may also want to splash in a couple of tablespoons of white wine, if you have some on the go, but don't worry if not. Pour the stock over the meatballs and cover. Cook for 25 minutes.

At about the 20-minute mark, take a large bowl, and whisk the eggs until fluffy and golden. Slowly add the juice of both lemons and keep whisking.

Remove your tester meatball from the pan: check the chicken is cooked and the rice is tender. If so, turn off the heat, but leave the pan where it is. Fish out the dill stalks.

Take a ladleful of the cooking stock from the meatball pot (stock probably now flecked with rogue grains of rice and shallot) and drizzle it slowly into your eggs. Whisk. Repeat until the stock is all incorporated and you have a thick, golden sauce. Pour back over the meatballs, into the still-hot pan, and shake to cover. (If your pan has cooled down completely, you may need a very low heat. I don't, because my pan is cast iron, but consider.) Stir for 2–3 minutes in the hot pan and add all the remaining dill. Spinach can go in now, if extra health is needed.

Bring to the table.

Notes and Queries

I think this would be really nice with pork mince.

Basmati works ok here! Short-grain is best – ideally, like, sticky jasmine? – but if long-grain is what you have, it will be fine. Try not to use brown rice unless you are very competent at cooking: it takes ages, and it's hard to get the timings right.

Brown rice is hard mode. I do it, and love it, but it is slightly more faff.

Try to make this just before serving. The egg sauce, while still delicious the next day, is not reliably beautiful after a night in the fridge.

Cumin Lamb Noodle Ragù

A lamb ragù, made with the soft, tender little fillet of the neck, and smokily and earthy scented with more cumin than is usually possible: cumin, and black cumin and Szechuan pepper. No tomato; only finely diced fennel and spring onion. A glass of rice wine to deglaze; anchovies for salt; a splash of vinegar to cut through the rich meat. Noodles. The meat falling apart, the spring onion tops scattered across. The toasted cumin-and-sesame seed crunch on the top. Something comforting.

Don't be scared by the words 'lamb neck': it's actually amazing. While the 'scrag end' (get a better marketing team, scrag end!) needs hours of cooking, the fillet falls apart with tenderness and a mere ninety-odd minutes of cooking; it clings gently to noodles; it obviously loves anchovies, as all lamb does, but it also balances out the deep earthiness of cumin in a way that simply works. You think the cumin will be too much. It's just enough.

SERVES 4

3 tablespoons cumin seeds
1 tablespoon black cumin seeds
1 tablespoon fennel seeds
1 tablespoon ground Szechuan pepper
2 tablespoons garlic purée
2 tablespoons ginger purée
2 tablespoons tomato purée
2 tablespoons sesame oil
500g lamb neck fillet, chopped
200g spring onions
1 small bulb fennel
75ml rice wine
500ml lamb stock
2 tablespoons rice wine vinegar
4 anchovies

1 tablespoon sesame seeds
noodles (or rice?), to serve

In a large casserole-type dish over a low heat, toast 2 tablespoons of cumin, black cumin and fennel seeds, then grind roughly in a pestle and mortar. Add the Szechuan pepper.

Mix the purées with 1 tablespoon of the sesame oil in a bowl. Stir through the toasted spices and add the lamb. Set aside.

In the same dish, toast the sesame seeds and 1 tablespoon cumin seeds. Cook until the sesame seeds turn golden. Set aside.

Chop the spring onions and fennel finely, reserving a few green tops for garnish. Heat the remaining tablespoon of sesame oil over a medium heat, and fry the spring onions and fennel for 5–10 minutes.

Throw in the meat to brown, with all the marinade, and cook for a further 10 minutes, turning once to brown the other side. Deglaze with a splash of rice wine, scraping up all the nice bits, then add the rest of the wine and the lamb stock.

Cover with a lid, turn the heat down to a simmer, and leave for an hour. Whip the lid off. Taste. Splash in the vinegar. Taste again: maybe season? Can you cut the neck fillet with a spoon? If not, keep simmering.

Serve as you would a classic ragù: noodles, meat sauce and sesame-cumin seeds (lightly bashed) where the Parmesan might be. Spring onion tops in place of basil.

At the Kitchen Counter

Radishes for Company

Feta, Dill, Crisps

Brown Butter Cornbread

Miso Soup with Thumbprint Dumplings

Egg and Bacon Date Wraps

Hetty Lui McKinnon's Tomato Dumpling Salad

Tajín Salad

Herby Mango Salad

Maple Pumpkin with Burrata

Kale Caesar! Salad Sandwiches

Tahini

Tahini Tomato Toast

Tahini, Dill and Cucumber Salad

Green Chickpea Quesadillas

Caraway Beans on Toast

Courgette and Brown Butter Tagliatelle

The Toast Matrix

Marzipan Apricots

Baklava

Frozen Grapes

Solo supper. Low-key lunch. Swift bits for one or two

Listen, you know when you would like to have something that is nice, but not so nice that you feel like you have to lay the table? Also, you know when it's just you? Maybe you and one other person? A sophisticated little bit? We're talking both standing up at the counter, we're talking laptops pushed to one side. We're talking big ideas and small plates. We're talking quick, we're talking elegant, we're talking useful.

We're talking meals that still feel like a treat, but sit smack-dab in the middle of something else: work, your evening, whatever. We're talking private little bonus joy. We're talking fork in the mixing bowl, spoon in the saucepan. Kindle propped up on knife rack. Laptop on toaster. Half an eye on the inbox, sights set firmly on something delicious.

A small flash of joy! A small flash of something so much better than it needed to be! A lunch that feels like something: a supper that feels like everything.

Radishes for Company

Say you have one friend for lunch; say you have, for example, a working lunch, or some other at-the-kitchen-counter lunch date. An immensely chic thing to do is to bring out a bowl of very cold radishes in very cold water.

You need a couple of rough napkins, ideally linen, and either butter, homemade mayonnaise, or some other kind of high-fat dip. If the butter is unsalted, you also need a little dish of sea salt. Remove radish from iced water; dry roughly with linen; swipe through butter; swipe through salt. Bite.

The leaves are also lovely: peppery and lively. Eat them too.

You should always store radishes in water, if they have the leaves attached, which they should. You should also do this with carrots, if you want to buy and keep them with the leaves, and in fact any root vegetable that comes with the leaves on top. They are, after all, roots. They are for storing water in the event that the leaves need it later and now it's later, and the roots do what they do. By the time the radish gets to you, unless you are truly plucking and eating them direct from a well-watered raised bed, it has already started to lose water: to hollow out, to become bendy, to become less than perfect. So: we wash the radishes and their leaves well, plunge into cold water, and leave for at least 12 hours. Serve in the bowl of water.

The trick with radishes I learned, incidentally, from a Joan Aiken short story about a little girl and her mother with no money who live in a room in Southampton Row. Hot and dirty London presses up against their front door, but their floor is scrubbed and their curtains are drawn and they have radishes in a blue bowl of water. Their house is an oasis. They can see a fig-tree. They have a bed, a box, a table, a stool and a gramophone with six records. They have a blue bowl of radishes. They need nothing else. Nor do you with this.

Feta, Dill, Crisps

The best salt and vinegar crisps on the market are the Co-op Irresistible Hand Cooked Sea Salt and Chardonnay Wine Vinegar Crisps. They will take all the skin off the roof of your mouth, which is my chief criterion for salt and vinegar crisps.

You take a family-sized bag of these crisps. Or, I suppose, an equally zingy equivalent.

Other, less zingy, crisps are available.

You take a block of completely normal feta.

You crumble the feta into the bowl of crisps.

If you like, you roughly tear a little bunch of dill into fronds.

Toss feta, dill and crisps together.

Elegant! Deranged! Unstoppable!

Brown Butter Cornbread

K. and I were in a café talking about books. We needed a treat to inspire us to stop talking about books and start writing them: K. volunteered to trundle off to look for, perhaps, a croissant. She came back with this.

It was not a croissant! It didn't matter. We ate it in about four seconds flat.

Then we ordered it again.

It was light; it was cosy; it was a little bit spicy; it was a little bit sweet; it was warm; it was crispy; it was soft; it was sharp. It was unbelievably delicious. I couldn't believe it. I became consumed by the desire to eat this absolutely all the time, which was a shame for me, as the café was approximately two and a half hours from my house. I saw a future for myself that revolved entirely around five-hour daily commutes to the cornbread.

Then I remembered that my job is to find out how things are made, and make them. I devoted myself to the task, and I think this is – dare I say it? – even better.

I learned the baking powder and bicarbonate of soda trick from a chef named Joshua Bousel, and while I have absolutely no idea *why* it would make a difference, it really seems to. The texture is better? It's lighter? I don't know. It just works. I think adding the Cheddar – just a bit! – adds the sharp note that you get from buttermilk without making it all about the cheese. (You can make it all about the cheese, if you want to just add quite a *lot* more cheese. It will work great.)

100g butter
140g fine cornmeal
100g plain flour
2 teaspoons baking powder
¼ teaspoon bicarbonate of soda
1 tablespoon caster sugar
½ teaspoon salt
100g strong Cheddar
big bunch (8? 9?) spring onions – it comes to about 50g
60g chopped sweet jalapeño pickle
200g thick Greek yoghurt
2 eggs

Pre-heat the oven to 200°C.

In a cast-iron skillet, or other ovenproof round pan, melt the butter over a medium heat until it foams, and then browns.

Flick off the heat underneath once it's got to the smelling-like-hazelnuts stage.

In a big bowl, whisk the cornmeal with the plain flour, baking powder, bicarbonate of soda, sugar and salt. Grate in all the cheese, finely chop in the spring onions, spoon in the jalapeño pickle.

☞

In a slightly smaller bowl (or big jug!), whisk together the Greek yoghurt with 100ml water until it thins. If your yoghurt is already pretty watery, feel free to just use 300 ml thin yoghurt, neat. Whisk in the eggs and most of the browned butter from the skillet. Leave just enough to coat the pan – maybe a spoonful? – but whisk in the rest.

Mix the wet with the dry ingredients. Flick the heat back on under the pan until the butter sizzles; then scrape in all the batter. It will foam up round the sides, which is nice.

Bake in the hot oven for 25 minutes. Turn out onto a cooling rack (flip up the right way again using a plate) and serve with an absolute ton of butter. Maybe butter and Marmite. I don't know! I'm not your boss! I just know that I could eat so much of this and still long for more.

Notes and Queries

You need cornmeal, which is, weirdly, often not the same thing as polenta in supermarket terms. Most polenta, in supermarkets, is *quick-cook* polenta, which has already been cooked once. You will most likely find the right stuff in the world foods aisle – sometimes in the Indian section, sometimes in the Caribbean section. It will say 'fine cornmeal'.

Someone once told me that blue cheese cornbread is delicious. Not tried it! You should, though, and report back.

If you can't get hold of the chopped sweet jalapeño pickle, then regular pickled green jalapeños will be great. I buy the chopped sweet, hot pickle from the supermarket; I buy the pickled green jalapeños from the corner shop. Fresh green chilli is less interesting but still pretty good in a pinch. If you're using fresh or pickled whole jalapeños, chop them first. Also, feel free to leave it out! Feel free to skip it entirely!

Miso Soup with Thumbprint Dumplings

What was left in the fridge were some ageing mushrooms and the withered end of a packet of cavolo nero. Unpromising! I cleared a space on the countertops and started making something, aiming for the twin destinations of comfort and clarity, ideally by way of speed.

Happily, it exceeded all expectations: transcending humble fridge-drawer origins to become the perfect lunch, easy to pull together, feels fancy, tastes peaceful and zippy and wholesome at once. Miso-dashi broth, flecked with seaweed; sliced mushrooms, quickly roasted (lightly dehydrated?) with soy and vinegar; ribbons of cavolo nero wilted in the broth; and – best bit – homemade, extremely fast, chewy little dumpling-noodles. You mix a little flour with some of the broth to make a dough! You press the dough into little flattish shapes, or roll it into thick noodles, just with your hands! You drop them back into the seaweed-freckled broth for a couple of minutes, just while the greens wilt! It's a real keeper.

FOR ONE:

200g mushrooms
1 tablespoon soy sauce
1 tablespoon rice wine vinegar
1 x 5g dashi packet
½-1 tablespoon miso
1 tablespoon dried seaweed seasoning
100g plain flour
big handful cavolo nero (4–6 stems)

Turn the oven to 180°C. Slice the mushrooms into fairly chunky slices, and arrange on a baking sheet. Drizzle with the soy and vinegar, using your hands to coat if necessary, and slip them into the oven for 20 minutes.

While the mushrooms are roasting, combine 500ml water, the dashi powder, miso and seaweed in a saucepan over a medium heat. Bring to a simmer, stirring until the miso and dashi dissolve. (Miso according to taste: I like a whole tablespoon, but I love salt.)

Take 3 tablespoons (about 50ml) of the soup, and tip into a bowl with the flour. Stir until cool enough to handle, then knead lightly to make a firm and not-too-sticky dough. You may need a little extra flour if you're somewhere very moist; you may need a little more liquid if you're somewhere very dry. Pinch off pieces of the dough and form into little dumpling shapes. Sometimes I make little spheres, then pinch them flattish to make, like, squashed coins? Sometimes I make little noodles. All are nice!

☞

Strip the cavolo nero leaves from the thick stems, and tear into ribbons. If you are using the pre-chopped cavolo nero, just discard any gnarly-looking bits.

Chuck the dumplings into the broth, simmer for 2 minutes, then add the greens and simmer for 2 more minutes.

Pour into bowls; top with the roasted mushrooms, which will be ready right about now. Drink deep. Lovely little dumplings. Big hit of salt and umami to see you through the afternoon. I love this so much.

Notes and Queries

Buy some dashi. Accept no substitutes! It is a Japanese stock, traditionally seaweed or fish, but in this case, a little paper packet that I buy online in a box of 20. You can next-day delivery it! It will truly jazz up any stock or soup you're making! It is salty and deep and really great.

I also feel like this about the dried seaweed. You can buy it from most big supermarkets, and even if you never make anything but this one recipe, I think you will make it enough times to make it worth it.

Buckwheat flour, rye flour: great little swaps for bonus nourishment!

Egg and Bacon Date Wraps

The efficiency of this sandwich! Every bit of it is like the nicest part of other, inferior sandwiches. The bread is crisp; the egg is soft; the pan is extremely easy to wash up, and listen: bacon plus date is a phenomenal combo. I like to add coriander and hot sauce, also, which is really fantastic.

The trick with this sandwich is that the flatbread (or tortilla) is crisped in the bacon fat, and then the egg is cooked *inside* the crispy flatbread. You know how if you cook an omelette in a hurry, and you are not a French chef, it gets a kind of very thin, tough edge to it? This makes that *never happen.* It stays tender and yielding all the way through, kind of like a set scrambled egg, or actually like the whole of the egg is like the best part of the egg: the soft and silky inside of the omelette. Steamed egg is an exceptionally delicious Chinese dish, in which the egg kind of takes on the texture of custard, and I probably had that in mind when I first made this wrap: the whisked egg here steams between the bread and the lid.

There is one caveat and I am, genuinely, sorry to be demanding. But it will be worth it: the flatbread needs to be, basically, the same size as the pan, including the sides. A small pan is better than a big pan, and the pan has to have a lid. A large wholemeal tortilla (Waitrose own brand) is 26cm across. The 'egg pan', which started off life as a novelty egg poacher before we lost the bits, is 20cm across and 3cm deep. They are a perfect match. The concept is, essentially, line the pan with the tortilla, and cook the egg inside the tortilla.

Also, it is so much easier to wash up an egg pan where no egg has touched the pan at all.

FOR ONE:

2 rashers streaky bacon
2 eggs
1 tablespoon chopped coriander
1 tortilla or flatbread
1 nice big date (no stone)

Put two slices of streaky bacon in your appropriately-sized pan, and put the pan on a low heat. Don't be tempted to put the pan on the heat first, and don't be tempted to add any oil. We just want the nice bacon fat.

Whisk the eggs with salt, pepper, and chopped coriander.

When the bacon is crisp, lift out of the pan and pop onto your plate. Carefully splash 1 teaspoon of water into the bacon fat and swirl it so that it sizzles.

Equally carefully, press the tortilla into the pan to line it. Pour the egg into the tortilla-hollow and put the lid on. Cook for 5 minutes exactly.

Thinly slice your single date. Lift off the lid, arrange the bacon and date down the centre of the just-set egg. Drizzle with hot sauce, if you like. Roll up as best you can: it's sort of a question of folding it into a roll shape because it's so nice and crispy. Slice in half. Marvel at neatness of egg layer.

Hetty Lui McKinnon's Tomato Dumpling Salad

Hetty Lui McKinnon makes this salad which is so simple you will not believe you've never done it before, and you will also not believe how life-affirmingly brilliant it is. I could not believe it! I still can't. Here is the deal: you chop up a bunch of tomatoes, ideally nice heirloom tomatoes. You pan-fry about the same weight of freezer dumplings until crispy (use more oil and more water than you think you need).

And then you make this extraordinary vinaigrette, of which I cannot get enough. The gist is: one part rice wine vinegar, two parts dark soy sauce, and two parts chilli crisp.

You toss the tomatoes with a clove of grated garlic and a fistful of torn-up basil and plenty of black pepper. You gently toss in the warm, crispy dumplings. You pour over the vinaigrette. You eat it all in a single orgy of consumption. If you use little frilly basil – micro greens, or maybe amaranth, or something else pretty – it will be completely spectacular. Sesame seeds on top too.

Buy Hetty's books. Make this salad. Put this vinaigrette on roasted broccoli, on all roasted vegetables, on plain rice, on mixed greens, on avocado toast, or rippled through mayo with cold chicken.

But mainly on these heirloom tomatoes, and crispy dumplings.

Tajín Salad

We were at the kind of birthday-treat taco restaurant where reservations are mandatory and it costs a thousand pounds a taco. I was not blown away by the tacos, per se – we are a big taco house, and you will be too by the next chapter – and the watermelon margaritas basically left me cold, but the *rim* of the watermelon margarita blew my mind. It was like a chilli-flavour Sherbet Dip Dab. I ate all the chilli Dip Dab off my margarita, then R's margarita. 'What is *that*?' I said, to the angular person behind the concrete bar. 'That?' they said. I nodded desperately. The angular person looked at me as if I was asking what a potato was. They held up a little bottle.

'It's just *tajín*,' they said. 'Have you never had it before?'

I had not. Shamed, but undaunted, I waited until the angular person had turned their back and googled it. It was available on Amazon. I had to have it.

If you have tajín, put it on a watermelon. If not: here. Here's the vibe. So very easy – the hardest part is cutting up the watermelon. And a cleaver through a watermelon is a cartoonishly joyful experience.

SERVES 4 AS A SIDE, 2 AS A MAIN, AND 1 AS A FEAST

400g watermelon
200g feta
small bunch mint
small bunch coriander
2 tablespoons extra-virgin olive oil
zest and juice of 2 limes

Dice the watermelon and feta into equal-size pieces. This weirdly matters? I'm not usually precise about chopping instructions, but if you can make these melon/feta pieces as neat and angular as you can, it will look extremely pretty and be very satisfying in the mouth. I do tend to dice them to the size of actual dice.

Shred the herbs as finely as you can manage, discarding any chunky stems.

Mix melon, feta, herbs together with the oil, lime juice and zest and salt; grind over plenty of black pepper; maybe sprinkle over some chilli flakes; serve immediately.

Notes and Queries

If – and only if – you happen to have it, citric acid – maybe 2 teaspoons of citric acid to replace the lime juice will give you an even punchier zing. Do not skip the lime zest, though, so this is an annoying note: it tastes incredible, but then you have two nude limes kicking around. And what can you do with two nude limes?

Margaritas, *claro*! Tequila, triple sec, the juice of your nude limes, 2:1:1. Salt the rims generously.

Herby Mango Salad

This is (very!) loosely inspired by my go-to Thai order: som tam, papaya salad. You can see just how loosely when I tell you that there is no papaya in this, at all.

This is basically because I find it hard to get hold of good papaya – but it is pretty easy to get hold of ok mango that could do with levelling up: bolshy fish sauce, sweet slippery little prawns, soft bold herbs, big handfuls of lightly pickled peppers and carrots and cucumbers and green beans. Apparently, one of the ways that fast food makes itself irresistible is to hit most of the base flavours at once: salty, umami, sweet. This does the same thing, except for an enormous bowl of mostly vegetables.

If I have a beautiful mango I like to eat it with my face, over the sink, in private; if I have ok mango, the kind that comes pre-sliced, this is the absolutely best thing to do with it. It never tastes more like itself – and never is more appreciated – as part of this wild orchestra of goodness. It is *peak* summer food: zero cooking, one hundred refreshing. This makes it my go-to grey winter lunch. I seek the opposite of outside: I seek to feel alive!

SERVES 4

1 tablespoon fish sauce
2 tablespoons rice wine vinegar
1 tablespoon caster sugar
1 red chilli
2 medium carrots
3 baby cucumbers (or ½ big cucumber)
50g green beans
1 long red pepper
300g chopped mango
10g mint
10g Thai basil
10g coriander
1 Romaine lettuce
150g cooked prawns or fried tofu; chopped chicken; crispy chicken thighs à la p. 39; whatever)
30g chopped roasted peanuts
1 lime
sriracha, if liked

In a much-too-big bowl (it will hold everything!), whisk together the fish sauce, vinegar, and caster sugar until the sugar dissolves. Thinly slice the red chilli and add it too. (Easy to omit if you're not a big spice house.)

Peel the carrots and use a julienne peeler to turn them into thin, pretty little strips. Toss the carrot strips into the bowl and let marinate for a minute. Halve and thinly slice the cucumbers: if you're using half a big boy, split it in half, and use a teaspoon to drag out the seeds. Discard the seeds, and thinly slice. Toss the cucumbers in with the carrots and stir.

Chop the raw green beans. If you can do this on the diagonal, so much the better. (Do not forget to take off and discard the stringy ends.) Add them to the bowl too. De-seed and finely slice the pepper, and stir the chopped pepper in as well.

(This is a good point to stop this part, if you're making in advance.)

Finely chop the mango into little dice.

☞

De-stem and finely shred the herbs then shred the lettuce (wash the leaves; stack the leaves; slightly roll the leaves in a bundle; slice the bundle across).

Mix the leaves, the mango, the prawns into the pickled vegetables.

Roughly chop the peanuts; quarter the lime. Divide salad into bowls; drizzle with sriracha, if liked; scatter with peanuts; set the lime quarter at a jaunty angle for individual jaunty squeezes.

Notes and Queries

Eat this by itself for lunch!

Eat it with a big handful of cooked vermicelli noodles (very Vietnamese)!

Eat it cold, over hot coconut rice: 200g jasmine rice, 1 tin of coconut milk, pinch of salt, steam until fully absorbed.

If you keep the components separately in the fridge – so pickled vegetables and vinaigrette in one Tupperware, chopped lettuce and leaves in another, prawns in their packet – it is a phenomenal make-ahead lunch for the week.

Feel free to leave out the prawns, which is a mad thing to say about a prawn salad, but is probably how I make it most of the time. Prawns are expensive!

Maple Pumpkin with Burrata

If someone were hoping to trap me in one of those trap nets that fall down to scoop up the unwary, or even (for a humbler villain) one of those boxes balanced on a stick – they would be wise to set the net – or indeed the balanced box – over a farmers' market.

I am, unfortunately, powerless to resist their siren song. A blackboard with an inept drawing of a carrot? Sign me up. I'm there. I'm there every week. I'm there whether or not we need anything. I'm certainly there whether or not we can afford it. I am there for the coffee in a little paper cup. I am there for the bread. I am there for beautiful meat. And I am there, above all, for the vegetables.

I am there, mostly, hoping for a Crown Prince squash. If the cartoon villain really wanted to be sure to get me, he could tie the net directly to the stem of the prettiest, daintiest Crown Prince squash on the stand. He could even go home early. It would be a perfect plan for him; it could not fail. Something about the Crown Prince squash is precisely calibrated to fill me with total delight and urgent desire: I must have it, I must own it! The deep orange flesh! The silvery sage-blue skin! The perfect pumpkin shape!

All this, in spite of the fact that I don't actually eat that much pumpkin. Or squash. I am not completely sure what the difference is, except that I love the word, 'pumpkin', and will use it at the slightest provocation. Something about the need for the big knife frightens me, maybe? I fear to drop either pumpkin or cleaver on my lovely feet. And yet…it's so worth it. It's so worth it for this, in particular – thick, smoky wedges of squash, scented with pine-y, peppery cardamom and spiky little fennel and sweet, caramel-y maple, and dolloped all over with burrata. When I first moved to London, I could only get burrata in one little cheese shop in Islington – nowhere near where I lived – and they flew it in from Italy, if you can imagine such decadence. Burrata is pretty much everywhere now, but it still feels genuinely special to me.

This meal feels special enough to call for it. Special enough, indeed, to brave both the fear of the big knife – and the potential villains waiting at the farmers' market. And incredibly easy.

☞

SERVES 4

400g squash (or pumpkin)
2 tablespoons olive oil
1 tablespoon whole cardamom pods
1 tablespoon fennel seeds
1 teaspoon extra-virgin olive oil
2 tablespoons maple syrup
2 burrata
1 tablespoon pomegranate molasses (optional)

Pre-heat the oven to 180°C.

With your sharpest knife and steadiest hand, cut your squash into thick wedges, about 3–4cm across, leaving the skin on.

Take a heavy cast-iron-type skillet, or other ovenproof pan, and set it over a high heat. If you have one with griddle lines, so much the better. Pour in half the olive oil, and sear the pumpkin wedges for 4–5 minutes. Flip them once they are a little blackened and repeat.

Lightly bash the cardamom pods and fennel seeds in a pestle and mortar, just enough to open the pods a bit.

Turn off the heat under the pumpkin/squash and shake the pods and seeds over the wedges. Drizzle with the good olive oil, and the maple syrup. Salt generously, and pepper even more generously.

Roast for 30 minutes – the wedges should be charred, smoky and completely soft.

Remove from the oven, put in a serving dish and tear the burrata across the top. Perhaps a drizzle more of really, really good olive oil and a drop of pomegranate molasses, if you happen to have some. It's one of those phenomenal ingredients that got so fashionable a few years ago that it's now very unfashionable, but listen: do not be a slave to fashion. It's existed for a thousand years. It's been great for a thousand years, and deserves to be great a thousand more. Serve with great bread – spreading the roasted pumpkin over the bread and topping with burrata – and a little sharp salad.

Probably do not eat the skins. (I do. I understand I am a freak. To me it is the best and crispiest bit.)

Notes and Queries

This pumpkin is a perfect fridge staple. Great cold; great diced up with feta and grains for a quick salad; great as is. Just don't add the burrata.

Crown Prince squash is the best one. Impossible to get hold of most of the time. Standard pumpkin, standard butternut squash, whatever you can get your hands on will benefit from the smoky maple treatment.

Kale Caesar! Salad Sandwiches

We used to have a local that changed hands approximately every 15 minutes, every new owner marked by a startling change in menu. The best roasts in town, swiftly followed by 'burgers only', with 'no food at all' hot on its heels. Then gastropub-adjacent small plates, then sandwiches and crisps, then every dish unhappily named after a musical act. Sometimes the actual menu would stay the same, but the food would be alarmingly different: different recipe, certainly, different cook, different everything down to the crockery and cutlery.

The vibe changed, too. Live music? All-day sport from three tellies at once, plus *The Best of Queen* at headache-volume through speakers presumably hijacked from an all-night rave? Quiet game of Scrabble or open-mic night every night? Nice staff? Mean staff? Flat beer or the best pint of your life? Impossible to know before you took the plunge. Sometimes it was the worst pub in town. Sometimes – rarely – the best.

Was there something dodgy going on? Was it haunted? I'll never know. What I do know, though, is that on the nights it was the best it was *the* best: a pub quiz just tough enough to crack, battered old armchairs by a roaring fire, whisky and ginger, and these sandwiches. These sandwiches only happened once, but by then we were wise enough to the pub's shifting sands to really appreciate them: thick toasted bread, drizzled with green olive oil, gold-striped griddled chicken, the *good* anchovies, fresh thick creamy Caesar dressing with a solid black pepper kick and the real Dijon, everything incredibly lemony and delicious.

Anyway, I assume the pub is long disintegrated into crime or ghosts – nothing with such high turnover could possibly stay golden for longer than, say, a single perfect sandwich – but the single perfect sandwich remains.

FOR 2:

1 lemon
100ml olive oil + 2 tablespoons
1 chicken breast
4 anchovies
2 teaspoons Dijon mustard
1 fat garlic clove, peeled
2 egg yolks
4 slices sourdough bread
2 handfuls (80g) cavolo nero, de-stemmed
Parmesan – if you have a block, great, most of it will go back in the fridge

If you start by putting the chicken in a speedy marinade, you can get some excellent flavour in the time it takes to do everything else. Zest your lemon directly into a Ziploc bag (other brands are available, and you can also use a Tupperware or just a bowl. I like Ziploc because I like to squish a marinade about with my hands). Cut the lemon in half and add the juice of one half to the bag, along with a tablespoon of olive oil, and generous quantities of salt and pepper.

Butterfly the chicken breast, by which I mean: slice it in half, lengthways, to give two thinner chicken breasts. Slip them into the bag, shut it and squish it all around with your hands to mix. Set aside for the duration of making the Caesar sauce.

Take the anchovies, mustard and garlic and put in a small bowl or the beaker of a stick blender. Blitz until (mostly) smooth. Add the egg yolks and the juice of the other lemon half and blitz again.

Slowly add the 100ml of oil, pouring it in a little bit at a time and continuing to blitz. Do not panic. It is correct. You are doing it right. Just keep adding it and keep blitzing and it will get thick. It will get thick!

Heat a pan (ideally with a lid) over a medium flame, and tip in the chicken and the marinade. Fry it for about 2–3 minutes a side, until golden brown. It's so thin that you will actually be able to see it cooking, the way you would with salmon, as the protein turns from shiny and liquid to cooked and firm (but still extremely juicy). Flip it.

Put the bread in the toaster. Do it slightly more toasted than usual, for the char.

Toss the cavolo nero into the pan for the last 2 minutes. Lid on.

Arrange the toasted bread on a board so that when you close the sandwiches up, they close perfectly, slice to facing slice.

Drizzle the toast with the last tablespoon of olive oil and spread thickly with the Caesar dressing – one side if you're normal, both sides if you're a fiend like me.

Thinly slice the chicken breast kind of...into diagonal slices, to get the maximum surface area. If you bring the knife through the chicken instead of straight down, that will help.

Arrange the chicken on the Caesar toast, arrange the kale on top of that, then thinly slice or grate some Parmesan over the top of that. Close the sandwich. Repeat for sandwich 2. Unreal.

Notes and Queries

Because I love greens – and love to make things more like a proper meal by including cruciferous vegetables – I have swapped out the lettuce for handfuls of black kale, wilted and crisped in the chicken pan, soaking up all the lemony juices. You can swap it back.

This makes much more dressing than you would need for two sandwiches because it's honestly not worth making less. Think of it as homemade anchovy aïoli (sorry, France) and use it on everything else: chips, dips, or even (dare we) just go back to a regular-degular Caesar salad. Good on the side of roast chicken. Great to idly dip most of a Little Gem lettuce into while you're standing by the open fridge thinking about what to eat next.

Tahini

My problem is that when I love something I am completely obsessed with it. It happens with everything. Sometimes, for instance, I will buy the same dress three times because I need to be wearing it absolutely 100% of the time and three is enough for there always to definitely be one ready to go. If the dress – *the* dress – is not available in the morning then the whole day will be off. Must I wear a different, worse dress? Must I wear the thing that is not the correct thing?

This is how I feel about tahini. Tahini for breakfast! Tahini for lunch! Tahini for an elegant little small-plate-based dinner!

Here's a humble two faves: tahini tomato toast and tahini dill cucumber salad.

Tahini Tomato Toast

A classic Ella brunch: thick slice of rye toast, Marmite, two roughly chopped tomatoes tossed with olive oil and sea salt, a blanket of fancy tahini, a scattering of sesame seeds.

Optional bonus: kimchi chopped with the tomatoes.

Optional, optional bonus: soft-boiled egg.

It is: amazing.

You can also fancy this up into a very serviceable little panzanella: take 1 small red onion, and cut into eighths. Pull apart into petals. Cover with 50/50 cold water and white wine vinegar, and a pinch of salt. Set aside for about an hour.

Take 6 very nice tomatoes, chop them up into nice irregular chunks and slices and tip them into a sieve over a bowl. Add a generous pinch of salt, and mix with your hands. Set aside for about 30 minutes.

Toast 4 slices of thick rye or rye-adjacent (seeded, sourdough, dense, dark, you know the drill) bread until crisp and a little charred in places. Rub with a garlic clove; drizzle with olive oil; spread with Marmite. Cut into chunks.

Toss salted tomatoes with drained onion petals (now bright pink) and 2 tablespoons extra-virgin olive oil.

A handful of basil, chiffonade-style: stack the leaves one on top of the other, roll up tight and cut into ribbons.

Toss together. Drizzle liberally with 2 tablespoons tahini.

If you happen to see them, amaranth micro-greens are super pretty here scattered on top.

If not: 1 tablespoon toasted sesame seeds.

Tahini Dill and Cucumber Salad

This has the feel, if I may say so, of a small plate at a fancy restaurant. I hope you love it as much as I love it. I hope you always get to wear your favourite dress.

SERVES 2

4–6 small cucumbers
zest and juice of 2 lemons
40g dill
4 tablespoons tahini
4 teaspoons Dijon mustard
2 teaspoons white miso
4 tablespoons boiling water
1 garlic clove
20g toasted sesame seeds, to garnish
1 tablespoon toasted sesame oil, to garnish

Optional extras: a soft-boiled egg, toast, Little Gem lettuce

Dice your small cucumbers into small chunks (skin is fine; the seeds should be pretty tiny too) and set them to one side in a bowl. Add the juice of both lemons, add a little salt. Shred the dill, add to the cucumbers and stir.

In another bowl, stir together the lemon zest, tahini, mustard, miso and boiling water, then grate in the garlic. It will go sort of clumpy, but don't worry! if you keep stirring patiently, then it goes very, very smooth. Maybe you add a little extra hot water, maybe not. Ideally, you would like a pourable consistency, like a good custard.

Divide the warmish dressing among little plates, one for each person. Spoon cucumbers onto the centre of the dressing. Add egg to one side, if using. Scatter with sesame seeds, drizzle over a bit of sesame oil, for flair. I sprinkled over some sea salt because I love salt.

Hot buttered toast, and a Little Gem lettuce on the side for dipping and scooping.

Notes and Queries

A soft-boiled egg on top makes this into a full-meal option. One egg per person: 1 minute of fast boiling, 6 minutes of lid-on off-heat sitting, into cold water and peel.

Caraway Beans on Toast

I suppose, more accurately, this is beans *with* toast, but that's not funny, is it? It is also about as far from classic and beloved beans on toast as you can get while still being entitled to the title of B-on-T, but it is, I hope, worth a similar place in your heart and repertoire: it is mega-cosy without being soggy or heavy! It is familiar without being boring! It is cheerful and impressive, which is the hardest of all combinations to successfully achieve! It has the kind of depth of flavour that makes people ask for the recipe! Plus, it is beans, and everyone seeks to eat more beans, no? It appears to be the universal resolution. Beans, and greens, and an incredibly beautiful fresh pesto sauce gently spiked with the gorgeous low-key funk of caraway seeds. A thick slice of lightly charred toast, drizzled with olive oil, and rubbed with garlic and salt and – get this – half a lemon. Lemon toast!

If you are not a caraway user, may I encourage you to abandon fear and go straight in? It is a lovely and underused bit of business: sort of like a cross between fennel and coriander seed, maybe? It is a fairly low-key investment, even if you turn out to hate it, and perhaps it will be a healthy experiment with the unknown. You won't hate it though! You will love it! And thus, you will learn to love the unknown.

SERVES 2

2 tablespoons caraway seeds
1 tablespoon pine nuts
2 garlic cloves, peeled
40g basil
20g Parmesan
3–4 tablespoons extra-virgin olive oil
2 big handfuls cavolo nero, kale, or other wiltable green
700g jar cannellini or other small white beans, drained
2 slices rye bread
½ lemon

Over a low heat, in a pan that's much too big and has a lid (it will hold beans!), toast the caraway seeds and pine nuts for a couple of minutes. Don't let them burn as they will take over everything. Remove from the pan, set to one side, and don't wash the pan.

While they are toasting, smash a garlic clove to a pulp in a pestle and mortar. Add the toasted pine nuts and caraway seeds and grind to a dun-coloured paste. As usual, it will smell amazing.

The good smell is one great reason to use a pestle and mortar for pesto; the other reason is that it is simply by far both the most delicious and the most satisfying way to make pesto. It just tastes so, so much better! And you will feel phenomenal about having done it. It is also not difficult at all.

☞

Wash the basil, without drying it, and toss a few leaves (no big stems) into the mortar with a teeny pinch of coarse salt. Grind to a paste. Repeat until all the leaves are nicely broken up into tiny pieces, and it smells even better. Grate in the Parmesan and slowly drizzle in almost all of the olive oil, stirring with the pestle. Stop when it looks like pesto.

Wash the greens, and strip out any particularly hoary stems. Put a spoonful of olive oil into the too-big pan, and set it over a medium heat. Toss the greens, still wet, into the hot oil, put the lid on and shake. Steam-fry for 5 minutes.

Push the greens to one side; warm the beans in the other half of the pan.

While the beans are warming, do your toast: toast it normally in the toaster until slightly more done than you'd normally do it (a little char is so nice), then rub vigorously with the other garlic clove and the cut surface of the lemon. Drizzle with olive oil, and sprinkle with salt.

Squeeze the lemon juice over the beans, and stir the greens through. Stir through the pesto, reserving a little spoonful for the top. Black pepper, lots of. Chilli flakes? Toast on the side. Done.

Notes and Queries

Fresh pesto from a nice shop; plus 2 tablespoons toasted caraway seeds, mixed through. It won't be as nice but it will still be mega-nice.

Pine nuts are a classic for a reason. Swap for walnuts, pistachios, pumpkin seeds, and be prepared to *grind.*

Green Chickpea Quesadillas

There was this place in the shopping centre, probably still is, that sold spinach flatbreads. They looked absolutely amazing – very thin, very crispy, full of cheese and bright green – and I was suckered in a thousand times. Never quite what I hoped for! Never enough. Never the dream.

This is, though.

Plus, chickpeas, for protein and health.

MAKES 2 QUESADILLAS

100g chickpeas
25g grated mozzarella
25g crumbled feta
big shake ground cumin (I guess a teaspoon, but really: just shake the ground cumin)
big shake dried oregano (see above)
1 big handful coriander
2 big handfuls spinach
1 tablespoon olive oil
4 tortillas

Tip the chickpeas into a bowl, and lightly mash. Mix with the cheeses, oregano and the spices, and season generously.

Finely chop the coriander and spinach and add to the bowl.

Oil; skillet; medium heat; tortilla. Press a generous handful of filling onto the warming tortilla, making sure to get some cheese around the edges, and top with a second tortilla. Cook for 4–5 minutes, then flip and repeat.

Slice into triangles and eat hot, melty, stringy and delicious. The dream.

Notes and Queries

My sister reports that this is an excellent vehicle for using up leftover chicken, if such a thing happens to be in your fridge.

My mother reports that tinned green lentils are an amazing substitute for the chickpeas. I never have any tinned green lentils, so I can't say, but all kinds of beans are pretty great. White beans especially.

Sorry to make you buy grated mozzarella: feel free to painstakingly chop up the expensive fresh kind if you prefer. It will not be quite as good.

Courgette and Brown Butter Tagliatelle

God, wouldn't it be nice to be elegant and simple and luxurious? I strive quite hard to be elegant and simple and luxurious, but mainly come to rest somewhere around cosy and/or tired. Luckily, this dinner does it all for us.

This is a Sunday supplement of a weeknight dinner, or a weekend lunch: one elegant rose trimmed from the garden in a sweet little bud vase, a linen tablecloth, a clean, thin glass of pale, cold wine, hand-shaped ceramic dishes, etc. You can whip it up in the kitchen while your companion tells you about art; you can put Satie on the record player and wear an elegant little shift dress and let the breeze kiss your bare arms as you shave fine slivers of courgette and tear great handfuls of basil and whisk egg yolks into velvety folds. The scent of brown butter will rise through the warm summer air; the fine white curls of sheep's cheese will tumble into the skillet; the music will lift, longing and decadent, through the long grass and full blossom blooms. *Oh, this*? you can say. *Oh, it's nothing!* You will be elegant; you will be simple; you will be luxurious.

Or, at least, this dinner will. Which is sort of remarkable when you think it's mostly just pasta with butter and cheese. What can I say? It's a combination that works. Ask any child you know. Happily, however, this is a version for grown-ups. I mean: I'm pretty sure most kids could find something to enjoy here, too. There's cheese, there's butter, there's pasta, there's eggs. What's not to love?

But with the tiniest of tweaks (and I mean tiny), it's possible to elevate that 10/10 no-notes banger of a cheesy pasta duo into something even the most refined of diners, and fussiest of adults, would order again and again and again. Also, it takes sub-twenty minutes and needs no knife. You use one vegetable peeler for the courgettes and the cheese, and squidge a bit of butter into a skillet to brown. You treat the basil sort of like spinach, and wilt it in the residual heat.

You do have to cook the pasta, for sure, but I have faith. You make a sauce with the brown butter and two egg yolks and a splash of pasta water, and it cooks like carbonara on the tagliatelle. It's like carbonara, but lighter because of the courgette, and brighter because of the handfuls of fresh basil, and deeper because of the brown butter, and sharper because of the sheep's cheese.

Are you in? Of course you're in.

☞

SERVES 2

150g tagliatelle
30g butter
200g courgettes (that's 2 normal supermarket guys)
35g strong, hard sheep's cheese
100g basil
2 egg yolks

The very first thing to do is to get your pasta on. Salted water, boil, 9 minutes maybe? You know how to make pasta. You will use about 1 tablespoon of hot, salty pasta water for the sauce, so don't drain it immediately.

Put your butter into a frying pan over a medium heat and leave to brown. You also know how to brown butter: after a bit it foams, you swirl the pan, it smells incredible, like hazelnuts, it goes a golden-brown colour and then you turn off the heat.

Using a potato peeler, shave your courgettes into long strips. You will wind up with a core of unshaveable seeds and bitty bits for each courgette, which you can either just put in the compost...or you can freeze to make a toy for a teething puppy. Your mileage may vary on this one.

Set the courgettes aside, and shave the cheese similarly. You will use almost all of this in the sauce, but save some – the most elegant curls – for the top.

Pick the basil leaves. You do not need the stems, and it doesn't matter if the leaves get a little torn. Think of it as super-charged spinach for this. Reserve the tiniest, prettiest leaves for the top.

Slide the egg yolks into a Pyrex jug, and beat until smooth. Slowly – no, slower than that! – add in your tablespoon of pasta water, stirring the whole time. (Think: like mayonnaise.) Then add your browned butter, also slowly, to make an emulsion and most of your cheese, stirring until it melts in the residual heat. You may need to add a drop more pasta water here, but go carefully.

Drain your pasta. Add your shaved courgettes, basil leaves and drained pasta back into the still-warm saucepan. Toss with the butter sauce to coat, and cook a little longer. Spoon into 4 bowls, and top with the last curls of sheep's cheese, the reserved basil leaves, and a mountain of black pepper.

Serve alongside some good bread, for mopping up, and a green salad with vinaigrette – something sharp and summery and fresh.

Notes and Queries

Feel free to add two big handfuls of baby spinach for extra health. Less elegant! But delicious.

Sheep's cheese can easily be swapped for any hard goat's cheese, or even a nice unpasteurised cow's cheese with lots of oomph. Ask a cheesemonger! You're that person now.

You could add crispy little pancetta bits. I'm just saying! You could.

Do not make this if you don't like basil or courgettes. (Looking at you, Dad.) Both courgette and basil are key flavours of this courgette and basil pasta.

The Toast Matrix

I was at a fancy party where I knew practically nobody. It was a work party for a fancy industry, in honour of a luminary, and everyone there – including the Luminary – was a fancy industry kind of person. Not me though! I hung around the buffet table and hoped someone would talk to me.

I reached for a little toast thing – salted cabbage, rich cheese, and was that? Oh, yep, that was honey. That was a real substantial drizzle of honey. Sea salt glittered under the tastefully soft lighting. It was delicious. I took another one. There were no napkins, but what did that matter? I knew nobody! I was merely a honey-eater at this party! I picked up a third in the spirit of free buffet and feasting.

At that moment a familiar face appeared from the throng.

'Hello!' she said. 'Come and meet [the Luminary]!'

My mouth was full of honey toast and so were my hands. The Luminary, just behind her, smiled genially and reached out a hand to shake mine.

'I'm so sorry,' I started to say, toast packing my cheeks like a bad hamster. 'I'm covered in honey—'

But it was too late. The Luminary withdrew his hand in horror.

'Do you know you're *incredibly sticky*?' demanded the Luminary.

Mutely, I gestured to the honey toast. 'I tried to warn you,' I said, limply, but the Luminary was lost to me forever. I hope he found a napkin.

It was worth it, though. It's almost always a good idea to drizzle toast with honey and sea salt. It's always a good idea to have fancy toast.

Toast is a baseline meal for me. A daily friend! A daily best friend who, unlike a Luminary, I'm always glad to see. And much like a best friend, it's always fun to see her get gussied up a little once in a while.

Think elegant; think dainty; think, as a general guideline: soft, sharp, frill.

Soft is self-explanatory. Even butter counts, if you keep it cool and thick. Avocado.

Sharp cuts through the soft. Jalapeño pickle. Lemon zest. Hot sauce.

Frill is something a little pretty. Microgreens are your best friend here. Any kind of sweet little sprouting business. A potato peeler is a great friend to you in creating little pretty bits: a thin sliver of radish! A rose of cucumber!

Some Toast Ideas	Soft	Sharp
Fancy New York!	...**full-fat cream cheese**...	...cut with **pickled jalapeño** and **dill**...
Fancy Tokyo!	...**soft single-egg omelette**, white and yolk not quite beaten together for a ripple effect, rolled to toast-size...	...**thin-sliced radish**...drizzle of **sriracha**...
Fancy London!	...**avocado**...	...**lemon zest**...
Fancy Breakfast!	...the good **peanut butter**...	...sweet **pickled jalapeño** relish...
Fancy Small Plate!	...**400g white beans**, blitzed with 3 tablespoons **olive oil** until smoothish...	...**salsa verde:** bunch of parsley, single green chilli, 1 teaspoon of Dijon mustard, a splash of white vinegar, a splash of olive oil, blitzed until smooth and drizzled...
Fancy Dessert!	...**fresh almond butter:** roast almonds for 20 minutes at 160°C... blitz with a little sea salt and a pinch of cardamom...	...**a sliced perfect peach**...
Surprising and Fancy Dessert!	...**soft goat's cheese**...	...**a sliced perfect nectarine, a sliced perfect tomato**, alternating...

Frill

...**smoked salmon**, rolled into roses...**pea shoots** curled between...

...**sesame seeds**...**nasturtiums** if you can get them...

...**microgreens**...

...chopped **roasted salted peanuts**...

...**4 best quality anchovies**...

...**honey**...good **granola**...

...**black pepper, honey** and **sea salt**...

Marzipan Apricots

Marzipan is in my top ten favourite words of all time. I also love to eat it.

If it were up to me, I would serve a block of marzipan after a meal: a dark slate, a slab of good marzipan, a little sharp ivory-handled knife. Thick black fragrant coffee. Cardamom pods tossed into the coffee pot.

A more sophisticated answer: dried apricots, slit along the top. A fat gold coin of marzipan tucked into each perfect pouch. A plate of these, and coffee, as always, as before.

Baklava

Buy baklava from good baklava shop. Serve in box. Napkins – or kitchen roll – necessary.

Frozen Grapes

If you take a bunch of grapes, leaving them all on the vine and stems, and freeze them, they become an extremely elegant dessert. They are somewhere between a very cold glass of wine, condensation on the outside of the glass, and a sorbet. Red? Black? White?

Choose the fattest and prettiest grapes you can. Big platter, plenty of space. Wide white china for pale green grapes; dark green or black, for black and bruisy purple. Sunshine through the window.

For a Gathering

Late-Afternoon, Early-Evening Party

Last Days of Summer Party

Grown-Up House Party

Baby Birthday

Big Birthday

Big platters, little bits, crowd-pleasers, play the hits. A crowd is what you make it.

We were arranging the flowers for the party. Tall purple allium in an empty cider bottle, scrubbed clean; nodding campanulas in some wonky ceramics; big bunches of tall grasses from the garden and some little sprays of peachy roses in a couple of jam jars. All different heights, which is, btw, the key to making your flowers look fancy: different heights, different shapes, not too many colours, candles all over the shop. We carried the table onto the lawn; put the good champagne in the freezer; hung fairy lights along the washing line; studded cocktail sticks with olives and anchovies and pickled chillies. When the doorbell rang we were ready for our guests: all two of them. Because party is a state of mind. And party is *also* what you make it.

I called this chapter *For a Gathering* because I didn't want you to see the word *party* and freak out. There's good stuff in here! Good stuff for everyday living! These are the things I tend to make for parties, organised into five potential kinds of party, but don't skip this chapter just because you're an indoors boy with none-to-four friends: there's solid dinner potential here. Onion farinata with caramelised onion and anchovies! The best pizza dough! A sour cream-type dip that works just as neatly with Wednesday broccoli as it does with Saturday night crispy potatoes. An entire array of tacos and taco-adjacent bits that can be cannibalised and repurposed for all manner of weeknight spectaculars. People love to have tacos at a party because making them is like a party game in itself: a fun craft activity! Interactive! I love to have tacos at a party because I love to have a week of taco leftovers hanging out in the fridge.

You will always find me in the kitchen at parties. This is because it's the best place to be, vibes-wise, but also because it gives you best access to the delicious things there. This is especially true if you are cooking. I am pleased with these recipes because they are pretty evenly divided between 'I like to be cooking at a party so I have something to do with my hands' and 'I wish to prepare everything in advance for more time to be at my own party'. You can be both. They are also good for small parties, of maybe six people, up to as many as you want, provided you are prepared to toil gently for a day beforehand.

Size up, size down. Double as necessary. So: party vibes below, of any size. I have divided them loosely into five parties, but don't feel constrained by this: I just like the idea of pulling a party menu down from the shelf and having it all there ready to go. A couple of easy cocktails. Paper napkins, paper plates, paper tablecloths. Crispy things, nibbly things, things with the DIY thrills if (ideally) not the flavour profile of a hotel buffet. Plus, a couple of sweet bits you can stick a candle in and sing happy birthday to – and meringues, because nothing says birthday like meringues. Exquisite, interesting, fun to make with people, fun to make in front of people, fun to make for people. And also delicious! Send out your invitations at once.

If you don't feel like sending out invitations, make these things anyway, and eat them all yourself. Light the candles! Buy the flowers yourself! Say it with me: *a party is what you make it.*

Late-Afternoon, Early-Evening Party

Frying-Pan Beer-Can Pizza

Smoky Rosemary Palomas

Small Jar, Large Salad

Frying-Pan Beer-Can Pizza

Here's the vibe of this one: a party where the true centre, as at all good parties, is the kitchen. An afternoon-to-evening party, a day-to-night kind of vibe. Saturday, late afternoon, maybe?

A bunch of people – maybe four? six? – will come over! You can eat pizza and listen to records! You can make a jug of rosemary palomas, the perfect pizza-day cocktail! You will dance in the kitchen with your best friends and eat unbelievable hot, crispy, complex-dough-simple-topping, oh-my-god-did-you-actually-make-this-yourself pizza with your hands! And instead of dessert you can get a block of the good chocolate, and break it up with your hands onto a nice wooden chopping board, and you can eat the good chocolate with the last people at the party – your *very* best friends – while you play Mario Kart!

(And listen: if Mario Kart has long ago left your wheelhouse, may I recommend getting back in the swing of it? It is, quite literally, fun for all the family.)

People will drift in and out; you will sling pizza about like a pizzaiolo, you will feed between four and, say, twelve people in this way. Maybe sixteen with sides, but I think that's your limit: more than that and you will start to feel like a drudge. If pizza ever starts to feel like a burden, you've gone wrong somewhere: pizza should only, and always, be a joy. Pizza party! Even the phrase sparks a kind of pre-teen pre-snark gladness. You can make some big salads in advance; you can make the rosemary palomas in advance; you can have a bunch of kitchen paper about. And this dough is very fun to make, and easy to play with.

People who like to talk about pizza dough will tell you that the best kind of pizza dough is slow-fermented, at least overnight, and often in the fridge. Some of these people even make a kind of pre-ferment – hideously known as the 'poolish' – to, like, double down on the flavour. The worst thing about this is not even the name: the worst part about this is that they are right. The slowness of the rise *does* give a better flavour. But come on. I am still not a slow-rise person! If I want to make pizza now, I want pizza now, not in three days. If I think I might want pizza in three days, and I have to serve my future self like a serf at this time, I will be annoyed; and in direct consequence of that annoyance I know I will not even *want* the beautiful slow-fermented pizza in three days. It will sit in the fridge for perhaps one week, becoming feral, and when it edges alarmingly close to sentience I will have to put it in the bin and be cloaked in shame.

So how to get the big fermenty flavours without three days? How to do it in three hours?

The answer, obviously, is beer. I am not a big beer drinker, so I'm probably not being fair when I say that this is the best possible thing to do with a can of beer. Even for beer fans, though, it's pretty great. I use a low-ABV, super-hoppy thing, and the flavour is never boozy: it just kickstarts everything, brings out all the dark maltiness you might expect in a slower-rise crust, balances the sugar and the rich good umami of proper sourdough bread. Just...quicker.

I borrowed the two-flours trick from the pizza chef Nicola Jackson-Jones and master baker Dan Lepard. It is hard to *innovate* in the *pizza space* (as the entrepreneurs say) without knowing that you are sitting in the palm of giants: people for whom pizza is their life. Pizza, for me, is a Saturday afternoon, and I am extremely grateful to the real pizza people for the groundwork they do for us, the merely extremely hungry. And I am hungry just writing about this. Make it! Make it now, for tonight, and call your friends.

NB I make my dough in a stand mixer, and I truly recommend you do the same. It makes it extremely painless.

MAKES 8 SMALL PIZZAS

400g strong white bread flour
150g plain flour, plus extra for rolling out
1 teaspoon instant yeast
330g room-temperature hoppy lager
20g olive oil
2 teaspoons fine salt
400g tin chopped tomatoes
200ml red wine
4 anchovies
2 garlic cloves
3 sprigs rosemary
2–3 balls mozzarella
20g basil, leaves picked
other toppings as desired: cured meat, roasted squash, blackberries, pesto, mushrooms, olives, extra olive oil to drizzle, etc.

Mix the flours and yeast together in the bowl of a stand mixer. With the motor running, and the dough hook on, slowly add the beer and oil. (I mix them together in a jug and weigh them for accuracy.) (On a wet day you may need 2–3 tablespoons more strong white bread flour.)

Sprinkle in the salt as the dough comes together. Don't be tempted to add it earlier, as it will kill the yeast. Knead on a medium setting for about 10 minutes. It should be supple and lovely: if you press a finger in, it should spring back.

Rest the dough for about an hour somewhere warm. I have inexplicably – get a life! – spent some time discovering that the perfect warming temperature is about 26°C. I do not need you to be this specific! Nobody needs to be this specific! Just normal warm is fine. On top of a radiator with a tea towel over; in the airing cupboard; on the back of an AGA (imagine); in the oven turned on low; in a sunny spot on a hot day.

After about an hour, the dough should have doubled in size. Pull the dough out of the bowl and punch it flat. Pick it up and fold it over itself: stretch it a little bit, then fold it in half. Turn the dough by 90 degrees, and stretch and fold again. Repeat until you have stretched and folded every side. Back to the warm place! Leave it for…1 hour? 4 hours? How long is really up to you.

After the second rest, cut the dough into 8 equal-sized balls. Using your hand like a claw-cage around each one (as if your hand is one of those claws in the grabber machines on a pier), roll the balls on the kitchen counter: this increases their surface tension and makes them tighter. Back to the warm place, this time as 12 balls of dough, for 1 hour.

In this hour, you can either make the palomas and the salads, or you can make the pizza sauce. I like to do half my pizzas with pesto from a fancy shop and half with tomato sauce.

Pre-heat the oven as hot as it will go: this is 240°C on mine, but your mileage may vary.

☞

Tear the mozzarella. I would recommend, also, cooking any toppings that might leak water: mushrooms, squash, courgettes, etc. I just roast them in the pre-heating oven with a bit of salt and oil.

Take a pizza ball, and make it into a pizza base. Roll it in flour, then play with it until it's round and the same size as your skillet base. You can do this with a rolling pin, but it's easiest in my opinion to simply stretch it out with your hands. To keep the shape and keep it really thin, I actually stretch the dough ball out over a Pyrex bowl. I sort of tug and pull it until it's circular, then use the bowl to help.

While you're stretching the dough, heat a splash of olive oil in an ovenproof skillet. High heat. Slip the dough into the hot oil, still over the heat. It will sizzle! This is good. This gets the crispy base that is so often missing from oven pizza. Quickly spoon on some of the tomato sauce and sprinkle over a light scattering of mozzarella. You will add more mozzarella when it comes out of the oven: this is simply the initial cheesing.

Into the oven with both the pan and the pizza. People will have come into the kitchen now, lured by the scent of frying things and cheese. They can have the first one. Ten minutes? (In this time, I stretch another base, so it's ready to go.)

When the cheese is melted and the edges crispy, take the pan out of the oven. Slip the pizza onto a serving board; add more mozzarella, which will melt in the heat, and a handful of fresh basil leaves.

Hand to someone immediately, tell them to slice it into quarters and hand it round, while you repeat for every ball of dough. Do not forget to save some quarters for yourself in the kitchen. Do not neglect to feel as amazed by your own pizza skill as everyone else.

Notes and Queries

I make the tomato sauce in a way so simple it almost seems stupid to write a recipe for it: I reduce a tin of tomatoes with half a tin of red wine, a few anchovies, a couple of garlic cloves, and some stems of rosemary. Simmer for about 45 minutes, until it's the right thickness for pizza sauce, and then season with lots of salt and pepper and olive oil.

Smoky Rosemary Palomas

The perfect accompaniment to pizza. Also, perfect because you can make it virgin just as easily and deliciously, which is vital for hosting once you're out of your twenties. There is always someone not drinking. Often that person is me!

For the rosemary syrup:
4 sprigs rosemary
150ml water
150g caster sugar

For each drink:
50ml smoky mezcal (or any tequila)
10ml rosemary syrup (above)
50ml grapefruit juice
ice
soda water, to taste

Stick the rosemary, water, and sugar together in a heavy-bottomed pan over a low heat. Stir until the sugar dissolves and simmer for a minute. Pull off the heat, and let sit for 15–30 minutes. Pluck out the rosemary sprigs – if they are pretty, save them for garnish, if not, throw them away – and let the syrup cool completely. (This is just a simple syrup, and we use it in place of agave nectar because I love smoky rosemary, and I never have agave.)

Shake the mezcal, the rosemary syrup and the grapefruit juice together in a shaker with ice until the shaker is very cold to the touch.

Strain into a tall glass over more ice; garnish with sugared rosemary if using.

Repeat these pretty pink drinks, until you run out of mezcal or everyone is asleep.

Virgin version: leave out the mezcal; add a splash of smoked water. You are welcome.

Small Jar, Large Salad

I am not giving a proper recipe for salad here. If you've already made pizza and palomas, that's enough, but people *will* be grateful for a green thing, even if they don't know they want it.

You need some bagged, pre-washed salad from the shops, ideally with a bit of flavour – rocket, watercress, something like that. One bag (and, indeed, one small jar of dressing) for every 4 people.

You need a small jar.

You need to put the following things into the jar:

2 tablespoons very, very nice olive oil
zest and juice of 1 supermarket-size lemon
1 shallot, very finely minced
1 garlic clove, peeled and crushed with the flat of a knife
1 teaspoon water
2 teaspoons Dijon mustard

Put the lid on and shake vigorously until combined. Pour over leaves and toss with your hands until completely coated.

Notes and Queries

No pizza? We're talking olive oil croutons (chunks of bread, drizzle with olive oil and sea salt, in the oven at 160°C for 30 minutes) and mozzarella, and fresh basil leaves. And really, this is all you need. Maybe some kalamata olives, torn? Maybe some fresh tomatoes, if it's summer? Maybe some fresh peaches, if it's summer? But you really only need the bag of salad.

Last Days of Summer Party

The Peppers Thing

Caramelised Onion and Anchovy Farinata

Tarragon and Tomato Olive Oil Tart

Bomb Lolly

ORTIZ
ANCHOVIES in olive oil
ANCHOAS en aceite de oliva

The Peppers Thing

I always know a recipe is a keeper when I have written it down for people so many times that I can search my phone for it with a single word, a single phrase. For this I search 'the peppers thing', and it never fails me: hit after hit. Off it goes to live its own life! Off we all go, making this delicious thing every summer!

Maybe you already know it, maybe not. One reason I love this one is *because* it feels like we all already know it: not old like, say, Ancient Rome, but old like a newspaper clipping, old like a Polaroid falling out of a second-hand book: *August, 1973* scrawled on the back, and let's say it's Tuscany, maybe? Let's say it's some kind of Italian terrace, some kind of summer holiday; everyone beautiful, everyone in stripy bikinis and big hats, and seeming not to know that the summer was almost over, although in a sense the summer for them will never be over, pressed between the pages of a tired paperback like a flower. Their faces, faded in the photograph but so bright in the being, the light on the hills, the jug of wine on the table. The loaf of bread. And in the centre of the table, still in the battered oven tray, rust tinging the edges – these peppers. These peppers! Roasted until charred, sharp with red wine vinegar, plump with cherry tomatoes falling apart, salty with anchovies. So simple; so complex. All the proper flavours; all the good classic old flavours. Play the hits! Play the old song again! Play the old summers again, the way it used to be, the way it could be again. Could we be like that? Will we be like that?

Open the doors; get the good olive oil, the anchovies; pour the wine; put the peppers in the oven, make some crispy farinata in place of good Italian bread. Call your friends. Take pictures. Write the recipes out for each other.

SERVES 4–6
4 red peppers
2 tablespoons olive oil
4 garlic cloves, peeled
16 cherry tomatoes
1 tin anchovies
2 tablespoons red wine vinegar
30g basil
focaccia, to serve

Pre-heat the oven to 180°C.

Slice the peppers in half, losing the seeds and pith, but keeping the stalks. Place cut-side upwards on a baking sheet. Generously drizzle with olive oil, and season with abandon.

Thinly slice your garlic and halve all your cherry tomatoes. Open the tin of anchovies.

The peppers are little boats! Fill the little boats with cherry tomato halves, slivers of garlic and 1–2 anchovies per boat. Drizzle over the oil from the anchovy tin, and the red wine vinegar. Roast for about 30 minutes, or until charred.

Tear the leaves from your basil, and toss into the hot oil of the baking tray. Serve as is, with bread, and a lot of good red wine.

Caramelised Onion and Anchovy Farinata

You know sometimes, not that often, how you look around and your life looks like how you wanted it to look? That's how I felt eating this. I was having brunch! With some new friends! And their friends! The house was beautiful! The coffee was strong and good! The farinata – which I had never had before – was still sizzling against the sides of the skillet! We cut thick slices and had it with a sun-dried tomato pesto and the sun was coming through the high, tall windows of the beautiful house and I thought, *I am in a Richard Curtis film.* The farinata had a crisp golden outside, and a creamy, almost custard-y inside, flecked with rosemary and black pepper. The sea salt on the top sparkled in the light. *This can't last*, I thought. *Nothing this good can last!* But it did, and now I make this farinata all the time.

I add a layer of caramelised onions, and sticky melty anchovies for extra oomph. It doesn't keep at all well, which is the downside, but it is simply perfect in the moment. And who could ask for more than a perfect moment?

SERVES 6

200g gram flour
60ml extra-virgin olive oil
2 teaspoons salt
2 sprigs rosemary, leaves picked and chopped, + 3 whole sprigs
8 big shallots
1 tin of anchovies

Whisk the gram flour, olive oil, 400ml warm water, salt and chopped rosemary together until it's as smooth as custard. It will be frothy on top. Set aside until the shallots are caramelised – so, about an hour?

Peel and finely slice the shallots. Tip the oil from the anchovy tin, or a tablespoon of normal olive oil, into the pan in which you want to make the farinata: you want this to be a cast-iron skillet or a large shallow enamel thing. Add the sliced shallots and, over a low heat, cook the shallots very, very slowly until they brown and the natural sugar begins to caramelise. Throw in the anchovies until they melt.

Pre-heat the oven to 220°C. Bring the heat under the shallot pan to very high, and get the pan extremely hot. Pour in the batter; hope it sizzles; place the three rosemary sprigs in the centre like a heraldic bit of foliage.

Slip into the oven, and bake until the top is very crispy – 10–15 minutes? Serve immediately and very hot, straight out of the pan.

My friend Katya once served this with red pepper pesto, like out of a jar, with sun-dried tomato in it, and it was absolutely unbelievable.

Tarragon and Tomato Olive Oil Tart

I truly do get so sad about cooking tomatoes in summer. This is one for the blazing days that start out slow and misty: bake the pastry early until crisp, then in the heat of the day spread with whipped and herby yoghurt, spoon over a truly beautiful, bright, ripe-tomato-salty-olive combo, and strew liberally with tarragon and basil. Tarragon is a lovely and underused herb: underused, at least, by me. I bought some on a quest to recreate a particular unavailable spice – didn't work, but I was smitten. A little aniseed-y, a little fennel-adjacent, but gentler than both: maybe even a little sweet. It's like liquorice for people who don't like liquorice.

Basil I can't ever get enough of. I have to resist buying it in big bunches to have around the house like flowers: I love the sweetness and strength of it; I love how it perfumes everything from a single bruise. Nobody needs telling that basil and tomato is a classic combination; basil, tomato and tarragon? A new trio is in town. Fat kalamata olives for a bass note, the olive brine and some red wine vinegar to sing the soprano? For sure. This is a real hymn to olives, actually: olive oil on everything, so it's worth getting the good stuff.

I give two options for the pastry: you can buy it, you can make it. If bought, you want the best puff you can get, and godspeed to your fantastic lunch.

If made, listen: it's a little faff. I won't lie! It needs chilling and re-chilling! But I think it's entirely worth it: this olive oil crust is so flaky, so tender, and, if you swap the egg for soy milk, vegan. And it makes the perfect backdrop for the tomatoes. Just do it once, and tell me I'm wrong.

SERVES 6

For the pastry:
60g really nice olive oil
160g plain flour
1 teaspoon salt
2 teaspoons white wine vinegar
1 egg
OR
1 sheet best puff pastry

Start with the pastry, if making it yourself. At least an hour before you want to start, put the oil and 50ml water in the fridge.

Stir together the oil, flour, salt and vinegar. Slowly add the ice-cold water to make a supple and not-too-sticky pastry. Shape into a block and roll out to about the thickness of a pound coin: I do this between two sheets of greaseproof paper. Lift onto a baking sheet and freeze flat.

Brush the frozen pastry with beaten egg, and – once frozen, and ready to prepare the tart – bake at 180°C for 20 minutes. Let cool completely on the baking sheet.

☞

MAX
UNIT
ON
TARE
DURONIC

For the strained yoghurt:
1 garlic clove
10g chives
400g goat's yoghurt (or plain Greek yoghurt)
zest of 1 lemon (save the juice, squeeze over green salad to serve alongside)
2 teaspoons salt
2 tablespoons really good olive oil

For the topping:
200g tomatoes
2 tablespoons really nice olive oil
100g kalamata olives (to blitz) + 50g kalamata olives (keep whole)
2 tablespoons olive brine from the jar
2 big garlic cloves
2 tablespoons red wine vinegar
20g tarragon
20g basil

While the pastry is chilling (either time), make the strained yoghurt. Crush the garlic, finely chop the chives and mix through the yoghurt, along with the lemon zest and salt. Set a fine-mesh sieve over a bowl. If you have it, line the sieve with muslin. If not, it's ok! Either way, spoon the yoghurt into the sieve, and let strain for as long as possible. Ripple through the olive oil just before serving – don't stir it in completely.

Also while the pastry is chilling, blitz together the tomatoes, olive oil, olive brine, olives, garlic and red wine vinegar to make a chunky and delicious sauce.

De-stem and lightly tear the soft herbs; tear the reserved olives into pieces.

Assemble the tart, on baking sheet: spread soft dollops of olive-oil rippled goat's yoghurt across the pastry. Tomato topping. Herbs everywhere. Olives everywhere.

Serve with green salad, dressed only with the leftover juice of the lemon. Maybe – maybe – a little more olive oil.

Bomb Lolly

Bomb, and her little cousin the Bomb Lolly, were such a fundamental part of my childhood summers I am always surprised they don't form a more solid cornerstone for summer culture as a whole. I actually have never met anyone, outside of my immediate family and the families we grew up spending summers with, who understands properly about Bomb and Bomb Lolly.

When I talk about it people like to tell me I mean *bombe*, and listen, I suppose I sort of do: *bombe* is the fancy Italian semi-spherical gelato-type number that did big business in the eighties, and Bomb Lolly is like if that fancy Italian left, like, Milan to run a commune in the mountains. No ice cream, just whipped crème fraîche mixed with berries; water, a little sugar, a little lemon juice depending on the tartness of your fruit; and handfuls of crumbled meringue swirled through. It's most like, I suppose, a kind of frozen pavlova, either in a bowl or in lolly moulds (depending on if it's B or B.L.). Any berries you want. The sound of the summer.

MAKES 12 LOLLIES, SOME FOR NOW, SOME FOR LATER

500g frozen berries
400ml crème fraîche
100g sugar
250g meringue (shop-bought is fine; recipe on p. 146)
100g white choc chips

Blitz the frozen berries with 100ml water until smooth. Whip the crème fraîche with the sugar. Crumble the meringue into the crème fraîche.

Layer the berries and crème fraîche meringue either in lolly moulds (perfect) or swirl together in a Pyrex bowl (also perfect, less of a lolly). Freeze until set.

Melt white choc chips by putting the bag, unopened, into a mug of hot water. Snip off one corner when completely soft, and drizzle liberally over frozen lollies. It will set immediately.

Grown-Up House Party

Roast Potatoes

Sheet-pan Leek Latkes

Toffee Apple DIY Pavlovas

BOMBAY
SAPPHIRE
LLY PRAT

Roast Potatoes

The single best house-party snack in the world is several trays of very hot roast potatoes. They suit everyone; are vegan, gluten-free; extremely easy; are crispy, which is crucial to a party snack; are salty, ditto; can be eaten with your hands, double ditto; soak up excess booze like nothing on earth; and every single person in the world loves them.

I learned this from my friend N., who has very good parties, at least in part because of their commitment to the roast potato. People are *delighted* when you whack out a tray of roast potatoes at a party! People are beside themselves to see the humble roast potato elevated beyond the confines of a roast dinner. Drunk people, particularly, go nuts for a potato. For something to be both drunk snack and hangover cure truly elevates it to the ranks of the elite. Weddings? Funerals? 4am dance-off recovery station? We were at the pub once in very early January and the barman brought us a bowl of very hot, very salty, very crispy roast potatoes. 'We need someone to eat all these potatoes,' he said. 'Can you help?' We were having quite a depressing time, and it isn't making too much of it to tell you that the bowl of roast potatoes really turned things around for us. Bring out your trays of roast potatoes, and ideally something to dip them in, and people will lose their minds.

You almost certainly know how to roast a potato. It will be something like: plenty of hot neutral oil or goose fat, depending on your vegetarians; Maris Pipers or other fluffy variety; par-boil first; drain; shake the saucepan; then into the hot fat to roast for 40 minutes, shaking twice, at 200°C. I like to par-boil them until they are almost actually boiled: I love lots of little fragments sizzling in the hot fat. I love to put sprigs of thyme and whole garlic cloves in the hot fat too! But you don't need telling. I'm just telling you: make a tray of roast potatoes, and one batch of dip, per, say, 4 people at your party, and everyone will be so happy.

For dips, then, may I recommend this one? Some homemade mayo, p. 232. It's tangy! It's salty! It's completely irresistible! It tastes kind of like a Pringle!

Incidentally, we eat this most often drizzled over broccoli as a regular dinner side. This is because we eat dinner a lot more often than we have parties.

4 tablespoons goat's yoghurt
juice of ½ lemon
2 teaspoons salt
2 teaspoons onion powder
2 teaspoons garlic powder
20g chives, finely chopped
20g dill, finely chopped

Stir together. Serve hot potatoes on baking trays; serve dip in whatever bowl you made it in. Minimal fuss. Maximum joy.

Sheet-pan Leek Latkes

But say, for example, you want to feel fancy at your house party.

Ultimately, the same rule still applies: crispy, delicious, eat with your hands. Ultimately, potato is a perfect starting place. But you must level up sometimes, no? And a levelled-up potato is, of course, a latke.

If you finely chop a leek, and add it to your standard potato latke, something amazing happens: the leek sort of caramelises and burns a bit, and it adds this extremely nice, slightly unexpected texture to the whole thing.

If you then top your leek latkes with a dollop of sour cream, and a teeny tiny spoonful of crab meat? Unreal.

A few beautiful, tiny beads of salmon roe? Good grief – I see we're at the embassy, madam! Pour me a perfect vodka soda, and let's change the world!

If you make these in the oven, heresy though it is to genuine latke-makers, you buy yourself the freedom to mingle at the embassy party, and your silk slip will not smell like hot fat.

This is a bonus to people who love to mingle attractively at expensive parties, especially if those people also want a reputation for being the greatest hostess the embassy has ever seen. You've not met the ambassador's wife? Darling, you must – she makes the most delicious little potato things I've ever seen. She's just over here in conversation with the Duchess of Sto Helit and the ghost of Noel Coward, and her hair doesn't smell like cooking fat *at all.*

1 leek
500g peeled potatoes
70g flour
1 teaspoon baking powder
1 teaspoon salt
1 large egg
2 tablespoons oil
1 tablespoon flaky sea salt

To serve:
sour cream
crab meat
salmon roe
dill

Pre-heat the oven to 210°C.

Finely shred the leek. I slice mine down the middle, rinse them thoroughly under the tap (always with the grime!) and then slice the thinnest tiny half-moons I can. Kind of roughly crumple them into a bowl, so the half-moons fall apart into ribbons.

Grate the potatoes. You can use a Magimix if you can be bothered to wash it up, but I actually never can: I just use the normal side of a box grater. It is not that fun to grate potatoes but it's over fast.

Mix the potatoes with the leek, and tip into a clean tea towel. Wring out over the sink, getting as much starchy potato water gone as you possibly can.

☞

NB: *This makes about 24 small ones, so I usually double the recipe for a party and buy one pot each of cream/crab/roe*

Return to the leek bowl, and mix with the flour, baking powder, and salt. Lots of black pepper. When incorporated, add the egg, and stir together with your hands.

Drizzle a baking sheet, possibly two, with oil and shake to coat. Using a spoon, dollop the potato mix onto the baking sheets – about 12 per sheet – and flatten out nice and thin. Sprinkle with the flaky sea salt. Bake for 20 minutes or until golden and obviously very, very crispy. Flip upside down on to a platter – this gives you a perfect flat surface for additional delight.

Serve with a teaspoon of sour cream, a half teaspoon of crab meat, a couple of dots of beautiful golden-orange salmon roe, and a little sprig of dill. And, perhaps, some very cold vodka.

Toffee Apple DIY Pavlovas

We're all familiar with the grown-up house-party snack rules now: crispy, delicious, eat with your hands. There is no reason these rules don't apply to desserts.

Consider please: a bowl of glossy, chewy, crispy-outside marshmallow-inside, brown-sugar meringues; a bowl of thick-sliced roasted apples, dusted with a glittering shake of cinnamon and cardamom demerara; a bowl of gently whipped cream, made more complex with mascarpone, spiked with golden whisky and speckled with black vanilla.

A hollow in each meringue to fill with soft whipped cream; a spoon of sharp-sweet spiced caramel apple to settle into the cream. A meringue in each hand. A perfect party mood, no? Maybe a glass of whisky on the side to end the night right.

People think meringues are much harder than they are; I, myself, love these meringues so much I actually can't make them unless people are coming over. I am not a fan of those meringues that are just hollow, puffed-up sugar: I love texture in a meringue; I love textural contrasts. I love the shatteringly crisp outside and the chewy, sticky, fluffy inside. I love the way it melts like candyfloss in the mouth. I love brown sugar for its depth of flavour, and the way it can do all these things at once. They are also, hooray, very easy.

SERVES 12-ISH

For the meringues:
1 teaspoon apple cider vinegar
4 egg whites
200g light brown soft sugar
30g golden caster sugar
1 tablespoon flaky sea salt

For the apples:
2 tablespoons demerara sugar
1 tablespoon ground cinnamon
1 teaspoon ground cardamom
6 Bramley or other sharp apples
60g butter

Make the meringues the night before, or at least, the morning of. Meringues are about a million times easier than people think, if you don't fuss about them. Wipe down the bowl and whisk of a stand mixer with apple cider vinegar. (You can do this with any vinegar, but doesn't apple cider feel thematically correct?). Separate the eggs, setting the yolks aside for something else. (Little cheesy biscuits (p. 154)! Mayonnaise (p. 232)! Caesar dressing!)

Pre-heat the oven to 120°C, and line two baking trays with baking parchment.

Tip the whites into the mixer, and whisk on a medium speed for maybe 6–10 minutes, until they form stiff peaks. Stiff peaks means that if you put a spoon in, and lift up a bit, the bit you lift will stand upright and not droop over. People say that you should be able to turn the mixer bowl upside down and none of it should fall. (These people have more faith in themselves than I have ever had.)

☞

For the cream:
500ml double cream
50g mascarpone cheese
¼ teaspoon fine salt
50ml whisky
1 tablespoon vanilla extract
seeds of 1 scraped vanilla pod

When you have achieved stiff peaks, begin to add your sugars. Do this a tablespoon at a time, beating well after each addition, and keeping the whisk running. This took me about 7 minutes to add it all.

Spoon tablespoon-sized dollops onto the prepared baking trays. Sprinkle lightly with flaky sea salt, and bake for 1 hour. After 1 hour, turn off the oven, and leave them in there, for at least 2 hours, but ideally overnight. You are basically just drying them out, that's all!

(The next day, remember to remove the meringues from the oven.)

Mix the sugar, cinnamon and cardamom together in a bowl. Peel and core the apples, and cut each into eighths. (You can always cut them into eight, then remove the seeds and core from each one, if you don't have a corer.) Toss the apples in the spiced sugar, arrange on a baking sheet and dot with the butter. Bake for 25–35 minutes at 180°C, or until soft, collapsing, and chewy-sticky in places.

Whip together the cream, mascarpone, salt, whisky and vanillas. You want it to be soft, not fluffy; to lie in beautiful seductive folds across the spoon rather than stand up cheerfully like an Aero bar. If you're unsure, stop. It will be amazing.

Platter of salted brown-sugar meringues.

Platter of soft, cinnamon-scented apple wedges.

Big bowl of whipped cream.

Plenty of spoons, plenty of napkins.

Baby Birthday

Heart-shaped Sandwiches

Little Cheesy Biscuits in the Shape of Every Fruit the Very Hungry Caterpillar Ate in the Course of a Working Week

Brown Butter Cornflake Cakes

Miso Vanilla Krispie Treats

Brandy and Champagne

Heart-shaped Sandwiches

Here's a controversial opinion: I truly believe that one of the number-one most chic occasions, hosting or attending, is a baby birthday party. I mean it! If you have a baby, invite me to the birthday party. Actually, ask me to help plan your baby birthday party.

If a children's birthday party is chic, something has gone wrong somewhere. But a baby birthday party? The kind of baby birthday party at which the baby itself has, like, minimal say in the planning? The kind of baby birthday party at which the baby is, in fact, the centrepiece – the star of the show, of course – but not, per se, the host?

A baby birthday party is chic because it is usually a daytime affair, the guest list is usually fairly exclusive, and the vibes are always sort of gentle. There is usually a range of ages – baby to grandparent, for example – and nothing is getting too messy, except in a very literal sense. Also, you can do charming bunting that – for all other occasions – would be painfully twee. You can, in fact, give in gracefully to all your most whimsical desires. Nothing is too much; no darling little wish too silly. Crudités spelling out the baby's initials? Little cheesy biscuits in the shape of every single fruit the Very Hungry Caterpillar ever laid eyes on? Exquisite sandwiches stamped out with pretty little cookie-cutters?

Champagne cocktail, and a salted burnt-butter cornflake cake?

It really is all to play for.

unsalted butter
soft white bread
cucumber
white wine vinegar
white pepper
smoked salmon

snowflake cutter

The trick to really extraordinary sandwiches is the butter. You simply have to regard the butter as a key ingredient of the sandwich – not a condiment, but an ingredient as vital as the bread. I know someone who has made sandwiches for the crowned heads of Europe, and this is how she makes sandwiches. Does your baby deserve a sandwich fit for a queen? Of course your baby does.

This is why, for both of these sandwiches, you will cut the cold butter with a potato peeler. No spreading: just the thinnest, most beautiful curls of butter, laid across the bread.

For cucumber: cut the cucumber in half, scoop out the seeds, and slice very thin. Lay two layers of thin, thin cucumber across the layer of thin, thin butter. Sprinkle with white wine vinegar, and season generously with salt and white pepper. The white pepper is the touch of genius here: it's the thing that elevates this beyond 'cucumber sandwich' and turns it into 'holy God, a cucumber sandwich'.

For salmon: smoked salmon on the butter; plenty of black pepper; no need for salt.

Another layer of thin, thin butter; top part of sandwich.

And then – the fun comes in, by which I mean: cookie cutters.

Depending on cutter, there is a real chance that you're going to eat the larger part of these sandwiches as a … look, let's call it a kind of starter. We refer to the bowl with the offcuts as 'the trough'. This is for the adults hosting the baby birthday, as opposed to the adults attending the baby birthday. This is because food waste is bad, cute tiny sandwiches are cute, and also because preparing for a baby birthday party is one of the nicest bits of the party, and what could be nicer than nibbling a negative-space smoked salmon snowflake while you lay the table with little pretty things?

I think this actually might be true of all parties: the joy is in the creating (and also in the debrief afterwards).

Anyway: using an appropriately-themed cutter, stamp out your sandwiches. Snowflakes. Stars. Hearts and flowers, with all our love.

Little triangles with the crusts cut off would be very refined for adults, but I don't know: why not lean in to the magic?

Little Cheesy Biscuits in the Shape of Every Fruit the Very Hungry Caterpillar Ate in the Course of a Working Week

Of course you can make these little crisp, glossy, flaky cheesy biscuits into normal circle biscuits, or even small precise squares, and bash them out in 15 minutes, but in my heart they will always be the shape of every fruit that the Very Hungry Caterpillar ate in the course of a working week.

This is because: I am a sucker for all forms of whimsy.

I cut the templates out of an old box with a scalpel. Then I lay the cardboard down on the rolled-out sheet of cheesy pastry, and scalpel around the templates. Then I peel away everything – all the pastry – that *isn't* every fruit the Very Hungry Caterpillar ate in the course of a working week, poke a hole in the middle with a straw or sriracha lid, and slide what remains straight into a hot oven to crisp and bubble and flake.

Is it hassle? Oh, of course. Is it worth it? For me, every time. It is also very nice, I think, to make something silly once in a while; to do something creative and pointless, something that has no possible endpoint except increasing the sum total of human joy in the world.

200g plain flour
100g cold butter
150g grated cold Cheddar
50g Parmesan
1 teaspoon mustard powder
½ teaspoon cayenne powder

Thank God, for a recipe that starts by asking you to make templates out of an Amazon box, the cooking part itself is simple: blitz everything together in a food processor.

When it comes together as a dough, tip out, form into a ball with your hands, and wrap in cling film to chill for at least an hour.

Pre-heat the oven to 190°C.

Roll out between two sheets of baking parchment to about a 5mm thickness. Stencil out your biscuits. Peel away any pastry that isn't a Hungry Caterpillar (or a square or a circle) and slide the baking parchment onto a baking sheet. Bake for 6–8 minutes, and let cool completely.

Repeat until pastry is all gone.

look familiar?

Brown Butter Cornflake Cakes

Ludicrous!

I really am so sorry to do this to you, but I'm going to have to ask you to go along with it, at least partly for the bit. The two recipes that follow really crack me up, but also: fantastic stuff, everyone is thrilled to see them, you I hope will also be thrilled to see them. PTA bake sale gone grown up! Brown butter, burnt butter, miso, sea salt!

Cornflake cakes! Krispie cakes! Oh yes.

The first is this: a golden syrup, brown butter, sea salt cornflake cake.

I am a sucker for the chocolate classic, but I wanted something more refined here: if by refined you mean a vehicle for golden syrup. Which I always do. I'll eat vegetables for every meal; take vitamins; get plenty of fresh air and exercise, but you can pry my beautiful Tate & Lyle green-gold Bible-adorned tin out of my cold, dead-from-too-much-refined-sugar hands. I don't even care about sweet things necessarily. I just really, really care about golden syrup.

50g butter
100g walnuts
3 tablespoons golden syrup
vanilla extract (optional)
100g cornflakes
1 tablespoon flaky sea salt

You will need a small, square tin 20 x 20cm

Brown the butter as slowly as you can be bothered to brown it: heavy saucepan, low heat. It will melt; then foam up; then foam up more; then, after a bit, turn golden brown; and then very brown. This is the step you want.

While the butter is foaming, roughly crush the walnuts – leave some whole, reduce others to dust. You want it all. Line a small square tin (20cm x 20cm) with baking parchment.

Dip a tablespoon in the butter (a mere dip, tipping any melted butter back into the pan). This is very helpful in stopping the syrup from sticking to the spoon.

Syrup into butter; stir. A splash of vanilla extract if you like, but don't be heavy-handed. Stir.

Stir in the walnuts and the cornflakes, crushing a few as you go. Spoon into the prepared tin, and press down hard with the spoon. Sprinkle with flaky sea salt, and chill completely for at least 2 hours.

Slice into very thin, elegant bars. Serve sparingly.

Miso Vanilla Krispie Treats

Same theme; vanilla-freckled miso-scented variation. Plus, the texture that comes only from marshmallows. Make these if you need the treats to be extremely sturdy, for example if the baby birthday is outside, or a picnic. They are fantastic picnic birthday food. Also, they take a candle very well.

Eric Kim in the *NYT* puts toasted sesame seeds on and through these. I recommend. (The pink sesame seeds are umeboshi flavoured, sour plum, and I love them both for their beauty and their Tangfastic-esque edge.)

300g marshmallows
100g butter
2 teaspoons white miso
2 vanilla pods, scraped (or 2 tsp good extract)
150g Rice Krispies or similar, unbranded puffed rice cereal
2 teaspoons flaky sea salt

You will need a 28 x 22cm roasting tin

Pre-heat the oven to 180°C.

Line your roasting tin well with baking parchment. Make sure there's enough extra over the edge that you could fold it back over the top, like a lid. Tip in your marshmallows. Stick them in the oven while you do everything else.

Butter in a saucepan and melt over a medium heat. It will melt; then foam up; then foam up more; then, after a bit, turn golden brown; and then very brown. This is the step you want. (If you take it any further than that, it will be blackened butter, which I love but is divisive.)

Turn off the heat (on pan and on oven). Stir in the miso and the vanilla. It will spit! Be careful! Stir in thoroughly then incorporate the marshmallows. The marshmallows will melt; you just have to keep stirring.

(Similarly, later: the sugar will come off the pan and the spoon; you just have to keep scrubbing.)

Fold in the Rice Krispies. Stir to combine completely.

Tip the mixture into the pre-lined tin, slightly sticky still with marshmallow, and use the folded-over edge of the parchment (or a silicone spatula) to pat it all down. Sprinkle lavishly with flaky, pretty sea salt, and leave to cool completely in the tin.

Serve in thin slices, or, if you're feeling decadent, cut it out in little shapes with the cutter. Grown-ups can have the offcuts.

Brandy and Champagne

Brandy and champagne at a baby birthday party? But of course. What demands champagne more than a sustained and successful attempt at living? Especially if the living in question is being done by someone very small and reasonably hapless, who requires an awful lot of help to keep at it. Bitters on a sugar cube for obvious metaphorical reasons; brandy to bolster you up; champagne to celebrate. (The baby can have milk.)

Per person:
single sugar cube
6 drops of bitters
25ml brandy
champagne

A sugar cube in each martini-type coupe glass.

Six drops of bitters on each sugar cube.

Brandy over each sugar cube, to melt in the base of the glass.

Champagne poured over, to top up.

Santé, friends! Santé, baby! Happy birthday to you!

Big Birthday

Chipotle Yoghurt Crema

Cascabel and Black Garlic Dip

Charred Pineapple and Sesame Salsa

Purple Tortillas

Caramel Cumin Cauliflower

Pig Cheek and Queen Bean Burritos

Bay and Cumin Carlin Peas

Sticky Lemon Cake

Chipotle Yoghurt Crema

There is never a bad time for tacos. Tuesday taco night? For sure.

If you would like to feed a lot of people – say, for a big birthday bash (that's big birthday in both the sense of a big number of years and a big number of guests) – this is about as good as it gets: a table full of tacos, followed by an extremely beautiful, lively lemon cake with a candle in it.

A Mexican-inspired feast, of which you can make as much or as little as you want. You can buy in guacamole, you can buy in salsa, you can buy in tortilla chips. You can buy as many fancy extras as you like, as long as you make a couple of perfect bits from here.

Non-negotiable: a beautiful stack of fresh tortillas, wrapped in foil until torn open in a plume of steam. If you can be bothered, I beg you to give making them a go: not complicated, though they take a minute to get right, and once you get it right, it's a game changer.

Within the tortillas: something dark plus something bright. On the dark side: refried-bean-style carlin peas, earthy with bay leaves and black pepper; or crispy brown-sugar caramelised cauliflower. On the bright side: a vivid, smoky pineapple and avocado number.

Plus: this chipotle yoghurt mayo, which – quite frankly – you need in your life. Crudités! Tortilla chips! Spooned over every single taco in the bunch!

---

3 tablespoons yoghurt
1 tablespoon mayo
1 tablespoon chipotle paste
½ teaspoon salt
zest and juice of ½ lime

Mix. Good for dipping vegetables in, also.

Cascabel and Black Garlic Dip

You know when you open your diary and you've written, for example, *CANCEL SUBSCRIPTION* in all caps with no indication of which subscription needs cancelling? That's me and this recipe: it's a title, the word 'delicious', and the cryptic message 'back of chilli packet'. I've Googled; I've been through the spice drawer; I've got no idea what I meant, but, listen it's delicious. Here's your opening salvo, ideally alongside the chipotle yoghurt opposite, served with tortilla chips and perhaps a margarita.

Cascabel is a beautiful cherry-coloured ball of a pepper that rattles with seeds and smells like tobacco. The best thing to do with a cascabel, should you be able to bear to cut it up, is to soak it in the juice of 2 little limes until soft.

Blacken 3 big tomatoes in a dry skillet over a medium heat then toss them, the softened chilli, the lime juice, and 6 cloves of black garlic into the blender and blitz until smooth. Heaven.

Charred Pineapple and Sesame Salsa

Whenever I think about pineapples, I think about the fact Christopher Wren loved pineapples so much he put them all over the top of St Paul's. It's true! I once had a meeting on the top floor of a building right by St Paul's and the person I was meeting was so happy about the pineapples that she stopped the meeting to take me outside to show me them. And there they were! Golden and imposing and obviously, completely, pineapples.

I both love and hate thinking about this, because I love how much people in the past loved pineapple: how exciting it must have been to see a pineapple for the first time; how absolutely unbelievable it must have tasted. I hate thinking about this because then I want to eat pineapple, but pineapple the way Christopher Wren ate pineapple: the food of kings, a symbol worthy of God. I want to eat the pineapple people in Victorian novels ate: extraordinary and startling and precious and rare. And then I go to Tesco and buy a pineapple, and it's never the pineapple of my heart.

Pineapple, in England anyway, is often a poor relation of itself. You expect this, maybe, from the pre-sliced stuff you get in the meal-deal aisle, but it's very disheartening to buy a big proper pineapple and find that it tastes more like pineapple squash than the real deal. Sometimes it's even bitter, just plain old unripe, spiny and mean-tasting.

Happily, however, there is a cure for this. As with all hard, unripe fruit, if you blast it in a hot pan until it blisters, you will create – tease out, maybe? – some of those beautiful flavours that Christopher Wren knew and the novelists remembered. The sugar will caramelise, become deeper and darker; the sharpness will be tempered; the bitterness fade to a deep, resonant bass note. Mix that with, for example, the brightness of yellow pepper, sweet soft avocado, a dusting of lime zest and a big handful of toasted, nutty, smoky-warm black sesame, and – listen – there's a non-zero chance you, too, will wish to put a big gold pineapple on top of your house. It's really, really good. It's somewhere between a salad and a salsa, depending on how finely you cut everything up, and I put it on tacos and burritos and plain rice and, it must be said, just eat it with a spoon.

If peeling your own pineapple, be ruthless: those little eye bits are spiky and will never be nice. The smaller you dice it, the more surface area you'll have for lovely char.

SERVES 8 WITH OTHER THINGS

3 tablespoons black sesame seeds
1 teaspoon neutral oil
200g pineapple, peeled and cut into small dice
1 avocado
2 yellow peppers
zest and juice of 1 lime
small handful coriander leaves, finely chopped (optional)

Toast your black sesame seeds in a nice dry skillet, over a medium flame. Just give them 2 or 3 minutes: just enough to bring out the flavour properly.

Tip the sesame seeds into a bowl and add the oil to the pan. Let it sizzle; tip in the pineapple. Stir once, and then – sorry – you will have to leave it alone for a bit. Every time you're tempted to stir, you stop it catching on the bottom of the pan, and (counterintuitively for most cooks) that's exactly what we want it to do. After about 10 minutes, turn the dice so that another side blackens. Give it a bit of a stir 5 minutes after that.

Finely dice the avocado and the yellow peppers. Probably even finer than that. Tip into a bowl with the zest and juice of the lime. Do not worry if your lime yields very little juice. That's limes for you!

Burnt pineapple and toasted black sesame into the bowl. Big stir. You can add very finely chopped coriander here, if you want to! Salt and pepper to taste, but be generous. Try not to eat it all before you serve.

Purple Tortillas

Tortillas are both easier and harder to make than you think, but the really key thing is that they are also ten thousand times better than anything you can buy in a shop. Once you get good at making tortillas – and I will not lie to you, it will probably take a couple of goes – you will be able to make tortillas at home that are as good, and perhaps better, than those at literally any taco joint you care to name. And you will be able to do it *any day you like*. The power of any night being taco night is basically irresistible to me: there is almost nothing I won't taco. Not now we can make the tortillas in half an hour. Also, it's fun! It's fun to make tacos! And it is fun to make tortillas and impress your friends and neighbours!

It is worth buying the special flour, which comes in ordinary white/yellow, or exciting blue/purple. It is worth buying the taco press, or at least asking for it for your birthday. I hope you know that I would never, ever, tell you to make something if it wasn't worth it – if you could buy anything even half as good in a supermarket – so please believe me. Making a huge stack of these for a party will take you an hour, but it will be worth it. And I think you will love it, too.

Tortillas can be sensitive and all hobs and kitchens aren't the same, so you'll need to play about with this. You'll need to learn to feel. But you will! You will learn, and when you've learned, they will be perfect every time.

MAKES 12 TACOS

Start with your masa. You'll smell what it's meant to taste like already – deep, earthy, almost leathery. 150g masa harina (blue or white) and a pinch of salt into a big mixing bowl; stir in the salt, then add 150ml warm-not-boiling water.

Mix the corn and water into a kind of shaggy paste. It will take a little while to come together. Try to use your hands for this: it's a sticky business but it's easier to judge the consistency by hand than with a spoon. When the dough starts sticking (and it will!) pick it up and knead it. Unlike bread, there's no real technique needed here; you just need to keep working it. If bits fall off or there's corn left in the bowl, press it into the main ball and keep going.

If you've made pasta, don't expect it to be the same: it won't stretch out or change consistency in the same way, but you'll know when it's done because the deep cracks that keep appearing will stop appearing as much and you'll end up with a dough that feels

☞

smooth, pliable and cohesive and not entirely unlike Play-Doh. It smells, it must be said, exactly like the kind of high-end Play-Doh I craved so much as a kid. I wanted to eat it then; I want to eat it now.

If the dough feels heavy and wet, add a little extra masa harina; if it just won't stop cracking, add some more water. Once your dough stops cracking when you press it, let it rest in the bowl for about 30 minutes.

Take out a small lump from your dough. Roll it between your palms into a smooth ball about the size of an avocado stone. Then you'll want to either roll it out with a rolling pin into a rough circular shape or, and I *strongly* recommend this, use a taco press. In fact, please, *please* use a taco press – life is simply too short to hand-roll tortillas.

Either way, set the ball between two sheets of baking parchment. If you don't do this, it will stick. It just will. Roll with the pin, or press the press down firmly. Hold it for a few seconds. If you like, adjust it and press again – the aim of the game is to get the dough as thin as you can.

Repeat this until you have a small army of raw tacos, and heat a dry frying pan to about medium-high. Now gently (they're prone to breaking) put your tacos into the hot pan. Maybe four at a time, tops? Don't be tempted to overcrowd the pan. After about a minute or two, flip them over with a spatula – they should have a nice blistery cratered look, like the surface of the moon. Another quick blast on the other side and they're done. A plate – or bamboo steamer, like for dumplings – in the oven on very low will keep them warm. This makes us 12 small tacos; so serving about 4. Double up as appropriate.

Caramel Cumin Cauliflower

The problem with vegan options at a party is that if the vegan option is actually delicious, everyone will eat the vegan option, leaving the actual vegans with nothing. And this *is* delicious. The only option is to make an absolute ton of this. Double? Triple? I don't know how many people are coming to your party, but I can eat half this by myself. (Eep.)

So make a ton of it, and your best case – your absolute best case – is that tomorrow's dinner is fantastic. Tacos today; rice bowl tomorrow; salad the day after that. Big flavour, minimal effort. So easy! So delicious!

SERVES 4

1 cauliflower
2 tablespoons soft dark brown sugar
1 tablespoon flaky sea salt
½ tablespoon ground cumin
2 teaspoons pul biber
sesame oil

Chop the cauliflower into florets: some small, some medium-small, some little bits of rubble, some long and stalky. Just chop, and then rinse in a sieve (this is so you don't lose the rubble). Do not dry. Tip still wet into a mixing bowl. (This remaining water plus the sugar rub makes the caramel.)

Combine all the rub ingredients, and rub together: cumin sugar smells amazing, and kind of smoky. Tip onto the damp cauliflower and massage in. This takes, like, 2 minutes and is actually quite a pleasant nubbly-type feeling on the hands.

Big frying pan/sauteuse, with lid. The lid is vital. Heat it over a medium flame and add a splash of sesame oil. Drop in a little piece of cauliflower to see if it sizzles. If it does: all the cauliflower in, lid on, shake the pan so that the cauliflower lies in a single layer across the base of the pan. It is vital that each piece touches the hot pan or it will not sear and get nice and burnt. Potentially, you may need to do this in batches: I do. It cooks down, so I just add the second batch in once the first has shrunk a bit.

Now leave it alone – a nice round 20–25 minutes – until caramelised and smoky and delicious.

Pig Cheek and Queen Bean Burritos

Great meals are made up of skill, ingredients and time, and you really only need two out of three to knock it out of the park. A fabulous cook with no good ingredients and an empty day can whip up something out of nothing, for sure; and if you've only got ten minutes and a fridge full of beautiful treats wrapped in wax paper, congratulations, you are Nigel Slater and this is *Real Fast Food*.

But even a wonky cook, given the right shopping list and plenty of time to let things simmer, can make something outrageously nice. *This* is outrageously nice. If you're even a little uncertain about cooking for a crowd, and want to do something spectacular: here.

A child could make this recipe but you could also pay £18 a portion for it in Central London and not feel ripped off; and that, to me, is the sweet spot. Stick this on the table at the party; a big dish of rice; some salsa on the side. A stack of tortillas for people to make their own mini-burritos or little fold-y tacos. Perfect.

SERVES 8

1 tablespoon ground black pepper
1 tablespoon coriander seeds
1 tablespoon cumin seeds
1 dried ancho chilli
1 dried chipotle chilli
3 tablespoons pork fat, cut into chunks, or neutral oil
2 red onions
2 peppers
8 garlic cloves
2 tablespoons plain flour
1 tablespoon smoked paprika
1kg pig cheeks
440ml Guinness
1 tablespoon Mexican oregano
1 teaspoon dried thyme
1 cinnamon stick
1 dried black lime

You will need a very big pot, like a Le Creuset-type casserole with a lid.

So: take your black pepper, coriander and cumin seeds and toss them into your pot. Don't add any oil, and set the pot over a medium heat. Toast for 2–3 minutes, until the smell rises up and meets you, and the cumin seeds darken. Toast the dried chillies, too, just a bit. Set the chillies aside, but tip the spices into the mortar and grind.

Toss the pork fat chunks into the pot, and turn the heat back up to medium.

Let it cook down, maybe 10 minutes, probably while you finely chop the onions and peppers and mince the garlic. Stir the pot every so often.

Mix the flour with the paprika in a bowl and lightly coat the pig cheeks with the mixture.

Toss the floured pig cheeks into the hot fat and brown all over. Five minutes? Yank them out again, and deglaze the pan with a big splash

3 x 400g tins chopped tomatoes
2 x beef stock pots or cubes
50g 80% dark chocolate
700g queen black beans
corn tortillas, to serve

of Guinness, using a wooden spoon to scrape up all the delicious bits. When the Guinness is no longer bubbling, add your finely chopped vegetables and garlic, and cook for 10 minutes more, until soft. You could cook them for longer. Lid on your pepper grinder; grind all your lovely spices directly into the softened vegetables, and stir well. Add the oregano and the thyme and any remaining flour/paprika mix. Stir again.

Pork cheeks back in; also the toasted chillies; the cinnamon stick; the black lime. Add the tinned tomatoes and wash out the tins with the Guinness. Add that too. Add all the Guinness. Chuck in the beef stock pots and the chocolate. Stir until the stock dissolves and the chocolate seems to be melting; stick the lid on, and let simmer for 4 hours, stirring occasionally. After about the third hour, take off the lid and let it reduce. That's it! It's just a question of putting stuff in a pot!

Finally, stir the black beans into the chilli. Don't do it sooner than this: the beans will disintegrate completely. We want some to fall apart and thicken the broth, but some to stay intact for texture. Serve in the cooking pot. No need to borrow trouble for the washing up.

Notes and Queries

Almost everything about this recipe can be made to work for you. Pork cheeks can be swapped out, if you can't get hold of them, for 50% (so 500g) ox cheeks, or short ribs, or brisket and 50% (500g) pork mince. It truly is best with pig cheeks, but don't let this stop you making it if you can't get hold of them.

Mexican oregano is *not like* Italian oregano! It's a completely different plant with the same name!

As a rule of thumb, with chillies: ancho (dried poblano pepper!) is kind of fruity, chocolatey, almost raisin-y; chipotle (dried jalapeño!) is smoky and spicy. Anyway, do your best here. Ancho and chipotle are both available in many supermarkets and online, and they really do add something amazing to the vibe. Do not add regular fresh chillies as it will not be the same.

Black beans can be any beans, really, but the queen black beans you buy in big jars are absolutely unbelievable here.

Corn tortillas: you know where to get tortillas. Also, any flatbread will do, and also if you just skip the tortillas everything works great as a 'burrito bowl', which is a lot like saying a 'sandwich bowl' but does convey the necessary information.

Bay and Cumin Carlin Peas

The carlin pea is to England what the black bean is to Mexico: a staple food, a working food, a party food. Something celebrated, and something special; something salty and zingy and cosy all at once. If you've never eaten them, listen: imagine the best chickpea you ever had, with a hint of Puy lentil and an ancestral chestnut somewhere in the DNA. They soak up flavour in seconds, and are the sort of comfort food that make you feel better just for eating them: physically, emotionally, culturally. They have been basically widely forgotten, in terms of 'daily meals', which is kind of monstrous when you discover how delicious they are. You can do basically anything you would do with a chickpea, anything you would do with a lentil, anything you would do with a bean.

So it seemed, then, a natural swap from refried beans to refried peas. Garlic, toasted cumin, and a few bay leaves: earthy, deep, a little smoky.

You can buy them dried and soak and parch them yourself; or, as here, buy them cooked for mega ease. If you buy them jarred, as I hope you do, this recipe takes mere minutes. Minutes! And they will keep well until the party is in full, taco-seeking swing.

SERVES 2 (FOR DINNER) OR 6 AS PART OF A SPREAD

1 tablespoon cumin seeds
2 tablespoons olive oil
4 garlic cloves
1 tablespoon tomato purée
6 big bay leaves
1 tablespoon ground black pepper
700g cooked queen carlin peas

In a heavy-bottomed saucepan, toast the cumin seeds over a medium heat. Tip into a pestle and mortar and grind finely. (My favourite smell, maybe?)

Add the olive oil to the saucepan. Crush in the garlic and cook gently until golden. Add the tomato purée, the crushed toasted cumin seeds, the bay leaves, a pinch of salt and the black pepper. Add the beans and stir. Add 50ml boiling water and stir.

Cook for 10-15 minutes, stirring occasionally and crushing lightly against the side of the pan for true beany joy.

Notes and Queries

This is actually pretty good with any jarred bean. I would say I eat some variant on these beans most weeks?

Garlic paste makes this quicker for a weeknight.

I'm both sorry and happy to tell you that if you have, for instance, a box fajita kit (known in our house as 'going to Mexico'), these beans make a fantastic and very fast protein-boosting addition. This is their main job in my life and I bring them out at parties to equal joy.

Sticky Lemon Cake

Bring this out with a gold candle in, top lightly dusted with icing sugar, and you're laughing. Glowy pools of caramel-y lemon curd? Chewy crispy edges, like the best kind of cookie? A tender, pale yellow crumb, gently flecked with lemon zest and fine-ground coriander seed, and smelling of sunshine? Like a kind of lemon Battenberg, but without any food colouring? Not too sweet, sharp with zest and juice? It is spectacular.

The coriander seed, while subtle enough to get round coriander-haters, adds a beautiful depth to the citrus. The almond makes everything smell like marzipan.

I had been playing with the lemon curd + almond cake equation for a while before I landed on this one. It's a bit inspired by Nigel Slater, the king of curd, and a bit inspired (or, I suppose, sense-checked, as I had been making something like it for a long time before I got round to Googling it) by a 2002 recipe by Jody Adams from *The New York Times*. I really love that baking is always a conversation, like a little party in itself.

It is the kind of cake you want to make (and eat) all the time, but that works perfectly for a party because it can be made in a single tin with minimal hassle, and served from the tin it's made in. I used to do icing with this; now I don't bother. It needs nothing but itself! It can come out into a lightly darkened room, garlanded with flame, and be the star.

Notes and Queries

You don't have to make the lemon curd yourself, but I really encourage you to do it: the nice thing about the curd, here, is that the whites you don't use in the curd give the cake that chewy delicious macaroon-y edge; and the yolks you don't use in the cake give the curd extra richness and thickness to allow it to almost but not quite set when swirled into the batter. And the lemon curd here is about twice as sharp as a shop-bought curd, which is such a good foil for the dense fudge sweetness of the actual cake. Also, it's not difficult, at all. This makes enough for the cake, plus a jar for eating and spreading on toast. There is no point making less lemon curd.

Things to do with extra lemon curd: toast, obviously. Greek yoghurt. Impromptu cheesecake on a digestive biscuit. Lemon tarts: basic shop shortcrust, rolled out, stamped out to fit a 12-hole tart tin, a teaspoon of curd in each one. I usually put a little pastry heart on the top. Bake 15 minutes at 200°C. Dust with icing sugar.

The real answer: sit on the kitchen counter, eat with spoon for dessert. Take two teaspoons a night, and call me in the morning.

☞

SERVES 8–12

For the lemon curd:
4 lemons
50g butter
50g caster sugar
2 eggs + 2 yolks

For the cake:
120g butter, ideally softened, but I am so bad at remembering, plus extra for the tin
zest of 2 lemons
120g caster sugar
1 teaspoon baking powder
1 tablespoon coriander seeds, finely crushed
½ teaspoon fine sea salt
120g flour
2 eggs + 2 whites
80g ground almonds
flaky sea salt

Lemon curd is much easier than people think. Heatproof bowl – like Pyrex – set over a saucepan of simmering water so that the bowl doesn't touch the water directly. Zest of 2 lemons (you'll use the rest for the cake) and juice of 4, butter and sugar into the bowl, and stirred with a whisk until the butter melts.

Then the whole eggs and yolks, lightly beaten and poured in slowly and whisked even slower over the same low simmering heat. It will seem like it will never get thick! It will, though! It will. Which is the whole satisfying point of curd. It will make a beautiful frothy swirl on top, and you will think it won't work, and you will keep stirring, and you will think it's beautiful but not working, and you will keep stirring, and you will start thinking that maybe you went wrong somewhere, and then! And then it will work. You will notice it is thickening and think maybe you are imagining it improving, but you aren't! It really is working out all right.

Let it cool while you make the cake itself.

Pre-heat the oven to 180°C.

Cream together the butter, lemon zest and caster sugar until light and fluffy, then beat in the baking powder, crushed coriander seeds, salt and flour. Add the eggs and whites and beat again until smooth. Fold through the ground almonds.

Line a baking tin (I use a 20cm x 20cm square heatproof dish) with butter and baking parchment, pressing it down firmly into the edges.

Dollop the batter into the dish and smooth out. Spoon the lemon curd on top of the batter in about 12 equal teaspoon-sized dollops and use a skewer to draw a line between the dollops, pulling them into a kind of a teardrop pattern. Don't be afraid to use plenty of curd, and don't forget the edges.

Sprinkle with flaky sea salt and bake for 30 minutes. Golden-brown on top, with a slight puckering-caramelising of the curd. A skewer will come out clean from the cake, but not from the curd.

Gold candle on top.

With a Tablecloth

Martini for Two

Gildas

Attractive Tins

➣•➢

Spring
Asparagus Fritters and Lazy Béarnaise
Marinated Bavette Steak with Green Salad
Rhubarb and Custard

➣•➢

Summer
Manhattans
Prawn Pasta Paella
Supermarket Cherry Pie

➣•➢

Autumn
Sesame Cheese Straws
Six-Hour Lamb with Za'atar and Anchovy
White Chocolate and Tahini Snickerdoodles

➣•➢

Winter
Squash-Hazelnut Romesco
Miso Mushroom Ragù
Smoky Tea Chocolate Pots
Damson Vodka for All

Napkins. Candles. Exquisite.

Sometimes you want to impress people. Here is how you do it. Absolutely foolproof and no room for error: make yourself a martini, pick your season, get ready for praise. You are the Domestic Goddess. You are F. Scott Fitzgerald on the Riviera. You are Circe the sexy witch. Roll out Grandmother's dinner service; roll out the French linen; roll out the little rose-coloured glasses with the stars etched in. Light three dozen candles and cut the big lights. Curtain up. Let's go.

A note on hosting: the chic thing to do, per Nora Ephron, is to plan four things: protein, vegetable, carb, and a surprise. Three ordinary things, and a bowl of something delightful and unexpected, like little roasted crab apples. Delightful!

My advice is almost the same, but not: you should certainly *plan* to make around four dishes, and *know in advance that you are going to ditch one.* This is because when you are making food for a fancy dinner party inevitably one thing takes longer than you think and then the kitchen is a foul mess and then you realise your hair smells of onions and you still need to make the béarnaise and now the compost bin needs to go out for the egg shells and they will be here in *oh Jesus, thirty-five minutes – where has the day gone.*

Giving yourself the secure knowledge that you can do without one of your elements is buying yourself a bonus, like, hour in the day. Plan to make flatbreads and know you have back-up parathas in the freezer. Plan gildas for a starter, and swap them both for an open tin of expensive anchovies. Plan to make soufflés, and swap them out last minute for a supermarket cherry pie. A perfect piece of cheese and a glass of sweet wine? Beyond chic to skip pudding for *that*, and both you can keep in the fridge until needed.

Have back-ups; be unafraid to run to the shops; be unafraid to ask your guests to bring things. The most elegant way to host is breezily. The worst way to host is high-maintenance. I think these four menus will be nice and manageable, with plenty of places for skipping things and shortcuts, so listen: skip away.

Beautiful stuff, bare feet, lots of candles. Flowers all over the shop. Cold martinis all the way to hot coffee and the washing-up.

Martini for Two

I am a specific and picky martini drinker: very cold and very dry, with a generous glug of olive brine, in a deep pink coupe glass with little stars engraved on the rim. I like three olives, and to have the jar of olives nearby so that there's never less than three. I like the olives to be green. I like the martini to be very strong and very large. Much like dear old D.P., I like to have exactly one martini – two at the very most – and I like to drink it quite slowly, ideally in firelight. Ideally, someone else is making them for me.

A martini alone; a martini in love; a martini before the party starts.

If you're hosting, do this first. Do this before anyone arrives. Do this while you're laying the table; while you're in the bath; while you're getting dressed and spraying perfume and shaking flowers looser in their vases. Martini first. All else will follow. All else will follow.

MAKES ONE LARGE; TWO NORMAL

20ml vermouth
ice
100ml dry gin
olives
olive brine

Shake the vermouth vigorously in a shaker filled with ice. Pour down sink (through the strainer, so keeping the ice and residual vermouth).

Add the gin, and shake again. Pour into a martini glass (ideally chilled or frozen). Add three perfect green olives, the green all green things aspire to be.

A splash of brine. (Four teaspoons of brine, if you have a problem.)

Drink with closed eyes; let the week slip away.

Gildas

Cocktail stick. Big fat green olive. Anchovy, removed from tin, and loosely rolled. Slippery yellow pickled chilli. Repeat.

Attractive Tins

Open a beautiful tin. Open many beautiful tins.

Ideally, you pull the lid back, like, seven-eighths of the way, so it retains that, like, essential *tinned food* quality? *Do not decant*. Trust me on this: no person worth inviting to your dinner party will not get a kick out of how big the big tin of Perelló olives is. It doesn't go out of style! It will never go out of style!

Toothpicks in a little silver shot glass, ideally, right next to the tins.

With a Tablecloth

BERTHE
FILETS DE THON
à l'huile d'olive
PEPUS
BERBERECHOS AL NATURAL
FÆRØSK LAKS No. 1
Faroe Islands salmon
FLASH GRILLED.
PAPA ANZÓIS
ARTESANAL
SARDINHAS
COM AZEITE
Cornish Sardines
FILLETS IN OLIVE OIL
BONITO DEL NORTE
WHITE TUNA
en escabeche - pickled sauce
BERMEO
1926
ZALLO
MESTRE SAÚL
FILETE DE ATUM
Alalunga
COCOCHAS
MERLUZA EUROPEA EN ACEITE DE OLIVA
REGNBUE ØRRED
Danish freshwater trout
Scottish MACKEREL
SARDINAS A LA ANTIGUA
LOS PEPERETES
Octopus with garlic and chilli
OLASAGASTI
VENTRESCA DE ATUN CLARO
CANNY MUSHROOMS
CHESTNUT MUSHROOMS
GARLIC, SAGE & THYME
PAPA ANZÓIS
ARTESANAL
CAVALAS
COM AZEITE
Nº 11
CHIPIRONES RELLENOS EN TINTA
BONITO DEL NORTE
WHITE TUNA
en aceite de oliva - in olive oil
ZALLO
SARDINHAS EM MOLHO DE TOMATE
Pinhais
ORTIZ
ANCHOVIES in olive oil
PEPUS
ALMEJAS AL NATURAL
CANNY MUSHROOMS
MAITAKE MUSHROOMS
TARRAGON & BALSAMIC VINEGAR
Nuri
SARDINHAS EM TOMATE
LOS PEPERETES
Boneless Sardines in Olive Oil
PAPA ANZÓIS
ARTESANAL
SARDINHAS
COM MALAGUETA E AZEITE
MINERVA
DESDE 1942
MACKEREL FILLETS
IN OLIVE OIL
MINERVA
SARDINES IN OLIVE OIL
120g
PITER
SILD No. 1
Norwegian Sea herring

BERTHE
FILETS DE THON
à l'huile d'olive
PEPUS
BERBERECHOS AL NATURAL
COCKLES IN BRINE
CHILLI & SOY SAUCE
MUSHROOMS
Sardines in Olive Oil
LOS PEPERETES
FÆRØSK LAKS No. 1
Faroe Islands salmon
FLASH GRILLED.
Cornish Sardines
FILLETS IN OLIVE OIL
BONITO DEL NORTE
WHITE TUNA
en escabeche - pickled sauce
BERMEO
1926
Thunnus alalunga
ZALLO
BONITO DEL NORTE
WHITE TUNA
en salsa catalana - in red sauce
ZALLO
FILETE DE ATUM
MESTRE SAÚL
Nuri
LEMON SPECIAL EDITION
PESCADO FRESCO Y SALVAJE
Alalunga
COCOCHAS
MERLUZA EUROPEA EN ACEITE DE OLIVA
Scottish MACKEREL
IN OLIVE OIL
El Velero
SARDINAS
A LA ANTIGUA
en aceite de oliva
PAPA ANZÓIS
ARTESANAL
CAVALAS
COM AZEITE
MACKEREL
MAKRELE
Nº 11
MAQUEREAUX
MAKREEL
OLASAGASTI
VENTRESCA DE ATUN CLARO
EN ACEITE DE OLIVA
ELABORADO A MANO
CANNY MUSHROOMS
CHESTNUT MUSHROOMS
GARLIC, SAGE & THYME
CHIPIRONES RELLENOS EN TINTA
PEPUS
BONITO DEL NORTE
WHITE TUNA
en aceite de oliva - in olive oil
BERMEO
1926
Thunnus alalunga
ZALLO
SARDINHAS
EM MOLHO DE TOMATE
Pinhais
PEPUS
ALMEJAS AL NATURAL
CLAMS IN BRINE
PEQUEÑAS SMALL
PEPUS
SARDINHAS EM TOMATE
Nuri
LOS PEPERETES
Boneless Sardines in Olive Oil
PAPA ANZÓIS
ARTESANAL
SARDINHAS
COM MALAGUETA E AZEITE
DESDE 1942
MINERVA
MACKEREL FILLETS
IN OLIVE OIL
DESDE 1942
MINERVA
SARDINES
IN OLIVE OIL
120g
PÍTER
SILD No. 1
Norwegian Sea herring

Spring

Asparagus Fritters and Lazy Béarnaise

The vision: late March, early April, a chill in the air but still sunlight through clean windows. You know that part where you truly believe for the first time in months that winter will fade? The kind of day where you understand why spring cleaning is a thing; the kind of day where you want to shake out all the rugs and wash the windows and change the sheets. Green shoots coming up through the earth; blue sky; cold and clear and how you move to the sun like a cat. You want to be alive again! You should ask people to be alive again with you! A dinner party for the first days of spring: green leaves and yellow lemons, still with the leaves on; goldy-yellow béarnaise speckled with green tarragon; bavette steak seared hard and sliced thinly across the grain; the new asparagus as elegant as a pencil shrouded in shatteringly crisp, almost translucent, snow-white batter and flecked all over with little crystals of sea salt.

I had this vision for these for a long time and was too afraid to enact it, at least as far as the asparagus was concerned. I'm not superbly confident with frying – proper frying, I mean, the kind where you can slosh the oil about – but this was about three hundred times easier than my fears. A thin tempura batter; a spatter-guard bigger than my pan (so cheap; such a game changer); a pair of tongs. Bold movements! A bold plan! And, in true narrative tradition, the boldness rewards itself: the asparagus-ness of the asparagus thrived and the batter was perfect.

These are less fritters than *fritti*: in Venice they serve hot little fried things stacked up on greaseproof in all the bars by the canals. You sit looking at the sun setting on the water; you drink your Campari; you eat your crispy little delicious things with your fingers. Seafood; vegetables; all kinds of things dipped in the lightest of batters. These are called *fritti*, and it is maybe from this hazy image of Venetian excellence that I pulled this notion of a first course. Or, no, not really a first course: more just a first part of an ongoing nice time. I love to do dinner parties as if I am running a small Venetian bar: I love to bring out beautiful things as they occur to me, when they are at their best. If this isn't what Venice is like, *don't tell me.* It's what it's like in the cookbooks. Let me live like in the cookbooks!

☞

SERVES 4

For the asparagus fritters:
70g cornflour
70g plain flour
1 teaspoon salt
100ml very cold sparkling water
230g asparagus, the thinner the better
enough neutral oil to fill your pan to a depth of about 1–2cm

For the lazy béarnaise:
2 tablespoons good mayo (if homemade, see p. 232 and skip the extra yolk below)
1 very good quality egg yolk
15g tarragon
the really good olive oil

Using chopsticks, whisk together the cornflour, plain flour, salt and sparkling water. You're looking for a double-cream consistency: thick, but not clumpy. Set aside to rest while you make the béarnaise.

Listen: it's not béarnaise. It might as well be. Take the very best shop mayo you can get your hands on; whisk in a raw egg yolk until completely combined. Finely chop the tarragon and stir through with a pinch of salt, and plenty of black pepper. Set aside. (Before serving, drizzle in a swirl with the really good olive oil, for fanciness.)

Brutally chop the tough ends off your asparagus. Baby asparagus should be fine as is; hoary old asparagus will need a heavier hand. Drop the asparagus into the tempura batter.

Fold 3–4 layers of kitchen paper over a baking sheet. Crumple up a sheet of baking parchment and line your serving platter with that. (Two-stage system for avoiding greasiness.)

In a heavy-bottomed, steady-feeling pan, over a medium heat, gently bring the oil up to a shimmer. Be extremely careful, and please use a spatter-guard if you can.

You may need to do this in batches. Using tongs, lift the asparagus into the hot oil, and shallow-fry until crispy – the edges should be turning golden. This will take between 2–4 minutes, depending on your asparagus. Lift out, and onto the kitchen paper. Repeat for all the asparagus.

Stack on the greaseproof paper serving plate and sprinkle liberally with flaky salt.

Serve immediately, with lazy béarnaise for dipping.

Notes and Queries

Alternative, low-key suggestion: the radishes on p. 80 and good butter.

Marinated Bavette Steak with Green Salad

Bavette, or skirt steak, is one of those cuts that used to be cheap and is now not at all. Still, it's *cheaper* than buying almost a kilo of any other kind of steak; it's more of a prospect, I think, for feeding a dinner party in hefty elegance. The marinade breaks it down just a little, to keep it on the tender side – it's not as tender as fillet, and never will be, but the flavour is so, so worth it. Especially marinated: shallot, garlic, beautiful bright lemon. And big deep iron from the meat itself.

It does not feel fashionable to love steak at this time. My God, darling, think of the environmental impact! And yet for me it is *the* meal; it's the one, and the heart wants what the heart wants, something that transcends my moral quandary and transforms it into pure animal hunger, thinly disguised as dinner for a businessman in the eighties.

My feeling about steak is something so far beyond sophistication that it almost comes full circle: a certain purity of desire, like sex or going outside on the first bright cold day of spring. I just want it! Like the heart, the soft animal of the body famously (ish) wants what it wants, and the condition of almost all soft animals is hibernation, followed by hunger.

And they will persist, these inconvenient desires, until the people in the high tower figure out how to replace our weak and feeble flesh with robo-suits synced with the perfected routines of the San Francisco tech-kings.

But I, for one, will miss my human longings. So perhaps I will enjoy them while I can. The caramel crust, the emperor-purple inside, the splash of ruby blood, real and true, at the centre! Slice it across the grain. Serve in thin, diagonal strips. A green salad, dressed with some siphoned-off pre-marinade.

SERVES 4

1 tablespoon black peppercorns
6 garlic cloves
1 echalion shallot
1 large unwaxed lemon
4 tablespoons extra-virgin olive oil
800g bavette steak
400g mixed salad (rocket, watercress, herbs)

Big pestle and mortar. Grind the peppercorns – a nice satisfying job – and then bash the garlic cloves lightly to shake off their papery peel. Tip the peeled garlic cloves into the mortar, and keep bashing until crushed into a rough paste.

Peel the shallot and chop roughly. Add to the mortar with 1 tablespoon flaky sea salt, to help grind it down, and bash to release lovely aromatic shallot-y oils. Zest in the lemon, and stir in the olive oil.

(Set aside 1 tablespoon of the marinade, and mix with the juice of the lemon and 1 tablespoon water. This will be salad dressing.)

Lay the bavette out on the chopping board. Cover it with cling film and bash it hard all over with the end of a rolling pin. (Maybe you have a meat tenderiser! Use that!) Remove cling film.

Set the bashed bavette into a wide, shallow dish (or Tupperware) and pour over half the marinade. Turn the bavette; pour over the other half. Cover tightly and set aside for at least an hour.

Get a skillet very hot, as hot as you can go without setting the house on fire. Sear the bavette for 4 minutes; flip; repeat. Lift out onto a carving board – ideally one of those wooden ones with the gully around the edge for juices – and let rest for 10–15 minutes. This resting is so key with bavette; if you cut into it too soon, it will feel tough and you will feel disheartened.

Slice into thin diagonal strips, across the grain.

Salad onto a platter, drizzled with the set-aside lemon-y dressing.

Serve the steak on the carving board with two forks for helping yourself. Good bread; the bottle of olive oil.

Notes and Queries

'Against the grain' is something you hear a lot in culinary circles and it's both important and simpler than it sounds. Meat has a grain like wood – lines of fibre running through it – and you need to slice across those lines. You want to break up the natural structure of the muscle to make it softer and nice to eat, basically. Lines go one way; knife goes the other way. Warp and weft!

This is enough for about 4 people, with bread and asparagus. The marinade will stretch to anything up to about 1.2kg, so probably two 600g steaks, and serving 6.

Rhubarb and Custard

I simply can't imagine anything nicer than rhubarb and custard. Thick, golden custard, almost the texture of a just-set pannacotta; beautiful little parquet floorboards of sharp-sweet, vibrant pink forced rhubarb; gentle warmth of cardamom and true spice of real vanilla. A classic for a reason. There is something very charming about taking a school-dinner classic and making it something beautiful and sophisticated.

Cooking rhubarb in a pan is always a tricky thing: it goes stringy and wet about ten times quicker than you think, and falls apart the second you take your eye off it. It seems like it should be easy, and this way, it is: roasted quickly in cardamom sugar, and arranged like perfect parquet, it stays whole and fork-tender without falling apart.

If rhubarb is harder than it seems, custard is easier. You can obviously just buy a tub of very, very fancy custard. I must confess that I probably would, almost always, buy it. I buy much too much, and I don't really have any shame about it. I love to have a nice time! I love to feel good in the kitchen! I absolutely hate to feel under pressure at all!

But sometimes, if you're doing something simple, it's nice to do it perfectly, no? And I think you can. This one is especially good because where you might otherwise use cornflour, you use *custard powder*. I can't remember where I learned how to do this, but what a good joke that doubles as a truly excellent hack. It thickens in the same way as cornflour, but with just a hint of classic custard. I love it. I absolutely love it. All of this reheats like a dream, but also, serve hot or cold. Easy, easy, easy.

SERVES 4

For the rhubarb:
400g rhubarb, ideally forced for pinkness but don't let that stop you
50g golden caster sugar
2 teaspoons ground cardamom

For the custard:
400ml double cream
1 vanilla pod or 1 tablespoon vanilla extract
6 egg yolks
2 tablespoons Bird's custard powder
60g golden caster sugar

Cut rhubarb into 4cm lengths, ideally on the diagonal, like the boards in a parquet floor. I am sorry to tell you that I do actually use a ruler for this, but it is worth it as it looks so lovely.

Stir the 50g sugar and the cardamom together in a big bowl, then toss the rhubarb in the big bowl too. (I find it impossible not to steal a bit here. It's so nice! So sharp and sweet! Like being a kid in a candy shop – or, in my case as a kid, the local post office.)

Pre-heat the oven to 180°C.

You will need two baking trays of similar size. Line the bottom tray with baking parchment and arrange the rhubarb neatly across it. Again: think parquet. Sprinkle with any remaining sugar.

Sit the top tray over the bottom tray, like a lid, and roast for 12–15 minutes.

☞

Tip the cream into a saucepan, scrape in the seeds from the vanilla pod, and bring to a very gentle simmer over a very low heat. (Stick the vanilla pod itself into a jar, and fill with caster sugar and leave alone for a month or so for gorgeous vanilla sugar.)

While the cream comes to a simmer, take a big bowl and whisk together the yolks, the custard powder and the 60g caster sugar until the sugar dissolves.

Pour the hot cream slowly, bit by bit, over the pale yellow yolks, whisking the whole time with the other hand. Once you've got all the cream incorporated, tip everything back into the saucepan over the same low heat.

Stir gently and constantly for about 4–5 minutes, until it thickens and comes together. It will! Don't worry! You're looking for something the texture of melted ice cream; and then to take it just a step thicker, something that folds in beautiful ribbons into the bowl.

For serving hot: take the dish of rhubarb to the table, and a beautiful bowl full of your beautiful custard.

For serving cold: spoon custard into individual bowls and top with rhubarb. Cover tightly with cling film and keep in the fridge until needed.

Summer

HEIRLOOM TOMATO FRENCH
£6.98
SAN MARLANO TOMATO
£5.50
KG
SPAIN
PRINCE de BRETAGNE
LES MARAÎCHERS
PRINCE de BRETAGNE
LES MARAÎCHERS

Manhattans

When I was 18 I moved to Paris, which is such an annoying thing to have done, isn't it? It was, of course, transformative in every possible way.

One transformative moment, among many: dinner with friends of friends of my parents.

Fruman and Marian were from Chicago, and they lived in one of those Parisian apartments I have otherwise never been inside of; I think possibly it was in the 6th, somewhere expensive, all along one side of a courtyard in a sort of beautiful 18th-century building. It was one of those summer evenings where the air smells like smoke, the air a little hazy. I rang the bell and changed my life – at least my hosting life – forever. It was like walking into a different kind of movie: it was like walking into a Henry James novel.

Americans in Paris! Candelabras, old mirrors with dark spots on the glass, a long table with no tablecloth and a drawer full of jangling heavy silver cutlery. Big strange paintings, books in other languages, everything with a weight to it like a Clara Peeters picture, salt cellars, bowls of oranges, candlelight. Miles Davis, *The New York Times* crossword, and Manhattans in heavy glasses. I had never had a Manhattan before. I was in love.

I was in love with all of it. I don't remember what we ate, or what we talked about. I think they gave my parents a favourable report; at least, that I was alive, and doing my best.

Our paths never crossed again. Every time I make a Manhattan – every time I do *The New York Times* crossword – every time I lay the table with heavy cutlery, heavy glasses, arrange fruit and flowers in a bowl like a picture – every time it looks the way I want it to look, like a Dutch still life – I think of them. Sometimes things take years to shape you, but sometimes it's a sip. Cherry; whisky; bitters. Smoky summer air. A heavy glass. This is what you wanted your life to be, and here it is.

FOR 1 MANHATTAN

50ml rye whisky
2 dashes Angostura bitters
25ml sweet vermouth
25ml dry vermouth
ice
the best maraschino cherry you can find
splash cherry liqueur

A Manhattan can be sweet, dry, or – and this is really the name, with a capital P – Perfect. A Perfect Manhattan is half dry vermouth, half sweet vermouth: adjust according to your own taste, but know this one is Perfect. Capital P.

Freeze your glasses first, always. Shake whisky, bitters and vermouth with ice. Spoon cherry and a little, little splash of cherry liqueur into a heavy, chilled glass. Pour the Manhattan over the cherry.

Serve with the crossword, strange jazz, and a door opening onto the future.

Prawn Pasta Paella

A balcony, somewhere in Spain, maybe? Doors open to the kitchen. Terracotta everywhere. Sun setting over a gold-stone city, rose-coloured light. Music drifting up from the street below, also cigarette smoke, laughter, the scent of oranges, probably, from an orange tree in the street. Oranges in the street! That's where we are. Sundown, somewhere in summer, table laid for too many people for the table. Blankets over the backs of the chairs for when the dark settles, not yet, but soon. Candles in lanterns. A heavy cast-iron pan with handles on both sides: sunset-coloured enamel on the outside; sunset-coloured, sea-scented, prawn-sweet, somehow smoky, pasta paella on the inside. Lid off to release the steam; pasta cooked in beautiful, comforting, complex prawn-head broth; mussels opening to reveal plump orange bellies; all the good rich golden colours, flecked green with parsley and black with pepper. A jug of white wine; a jug of cool water. Linen napkins. This is what it feels like to make this! This is what it feels like to bring this to the table, wherever you are! I want this for you and also for me.

This is basically a Valencian dish called *fideuà*, except more so: fideuà is like a paella, except with fine angel-hair pasta in place of the rice. This is like that, except we make a prawn-head bisque – genuinely achievable, I promise – and cook the pasta paella in that until everything is soft, and there is a golden tahdig-style crust on the bottom of the pan. This is the best part and you can scrape it up with your spoons once everything else is gone. And everything else *will* be gone.

It is one of those dishes that is maybe a *little* ambitious, for sure, but is also a joy. Do you need to buy expensive seafood? Yes. Do you need to shell half a kilo of raw prawns? You do. Do you need to blitz and strain and bring to a simmer? Oh, certainly. Certainly! I hope I have given you enough reason to trust me if I tell you that I think you will enjoy, if not every single element of this, then the experience as a whole. A lovely faff!

Consider this a Saturday project: morning ambling along to the fishmonger, coffee in hand; sunshine walk home; afternoon at the kitchen counter, music on, glass of something cold and delicious. An early evening bath; a little black dress. Open the doors, Manhattan in your hand, candles dancing in their lanterns. Smoke and the sea. Sunset dinner.

☞

SERVES 4–6, DEPENDING ON HUNGER

500g shell-on, head-on, king prawns
40ml olive oil
8 garlic cloves
4 shallots
4 big tomatoes on the vine
3 teaspoons sweet smoked paprika
1 teaspoon saffron strands
2 bay leaves
500ml fish stock
2 celery stalks
250g monkfish tail, chopped into chunks
50–100ml white vermouth, in splashes
150g mussels (or clams!), scrubbed and de-bearded if necessary
250g vermicelli or angel-hair pasta, broken into short lengths

Peel the prawns. (*See note on following page.*)

Warm 20ml of the oil in a big pan over a medium heat. Fry the prawn shells and heads and tails for 5 minutes. The shells will go from slate grey to neon-vibrant orange.

Smash 4 of the garlic cloves with the flat of your knife; peel off the papery skin and toss the garlic into the prawn-y oil. Turn down the heat. Fry gently while you're doing everything else.

Peel and roughly chop two of the shallots and toss them in. Stir. Using the coarse side of the box grater, shred the tomatoes into a big bowl; set the bowl aside for later and toss the tomato skins into the shallot-prawn-garlic pan. You can also add the stalk from your tomatoes: it acts kind of like a bay leaf, but more tomato-y.

Add the sweet smoked paprika. Bloom the saffron in an egg cup – a tablespoon of warm water, plus the strands (stamens?), swirled until it's golden yellow – and tip that in too. Also, two bay leaves.

Add 500ml fish stock to the prawn pan. Stir, and bring up to a simmer for 30 minutes. (If you were given the monkfish bone with your monkfish, add this too.)

(This is a good time to clean the kitchen, and do some chopping: finely chop the remaining 2 shallots, the remaining 4 garlic cloves and the celery stalks. Now chop them even finer. While the chopping board is out, finely chop the parsley and set that to one side for garnish.)

Remove the tomato stalk, if used, and decant the prawn stock – what an extraordinary colour* – with everything in it, including shells and heads, into the blender. I use the Nutribullet here: if you do too, be careful to let it cool before blitzing. Blend prawn broth until very smooth – then blend again. Pour through a fine-mesh sieve, letting it drip slowly down while leaving the shells behind. (If you need to be speedy, push it through with a silicone spatula, but it won't have the clarity.) It should come to about 700ml, so add water to thin if necessary. Set aside.

Wipe out the pan with kitchen paper, and return to the heat.

Add in the remaining olive oil, and when gently shimmering, fry the prawns and the monkfish for about 3 minutes, until golden and a little crispy. Lift out, and set aside.

Scrape any nice bits off the bottom, deglaze with a splash of vermouth, and toss in the shallots, garlic, and celery stalks. Add the tomato insides. Cook for 15 minutes. Deglaze again with a big splash of vermouth.

Check the mussels here: I just scrub mine under the tap, and discard any that won't close when I tap them on the side. (Then I put them in a bowl with a wet paper towel on top, and stick them back in the fridge.) This is a great place to stop, if you want to get ready. The house will smell fantastic, and from here it's kind of just an assembly job.

Pasta goes into the pan. Stir. Broth goes over pasta. Stir. Another big splash of vermouth. Bring up to a simmer. Season generously with salt and pepper.

Cook for 15 minutes without stirring, to let it form a crispy golden bottom. Add in the cooked prawns; the cooked monkfish; and stir. Heat up. All the rest of the vermouth; all the mussels.

Lid on. Five minutes, or until the mussels open up completely. Plenty of black pepper. Serve from the cooking dish. Maybe you don't even need plates?

Notes and Queries

How to Peel a Prawn: peeling prawns is a knack, and don't think about it too much. Two bowls, one for outsides, one for insides. I like to have a little knife, but you can also use scissors; I also like to have a few sheets of kitchen paper because I am not fantastic about having sensations on my fingers and need to be able to dry them whenever I get weirded out by the whole business. I try not to get weirded out. A good way to engage with life, death, etc! Prawn heads and shells are, genuinely, the secret weapon to all big prawn flavour: they have this rich, sweet, almost-bitterness to them, and they taste almost *more* like prawns than prawn insides taste like prawns. I love them. Crick-crack the head from side to side; then squeeze and twist to pull away. Crick-crack the tail from side to side, then pinch it so it cracks in your fingers, and you can pull the hard chitinous bit away from the lovely frilly tail meat inside. You can either just wiggle off the shell, or you cut through the shell in a straight line along the back and pull it off that way. Score a straight line along the back of the peeled prawn and use the point of the knife to hoik out the black thin digestive tract bit just under the surface. Discard the digestive tract, obviously. Repeat for every prawn.

Supermarket Cherry Pie

My most served dinner-party dessert? Supermarket cherry pie. Guaranteed win.

If you're making a 5-stage pasta paella with £50 of seafood, there is absolutely no need to make anything else. If you want to lightly whip some cream, ideally spiked with whisky (see p. 149) then knock yourself out. If you want to buy some thick cream, decant it into a nice little jug, and bring that to that table, even better. If you want to buy the ivory, almost-clotted, cultured crème fraîche that comes in the little glass jar from Normandy... you don't even need to decant it. What am I saying? There is never a need to decant anything.

Autumn

Sesame Cheese Straws

Starters are overrated. In a restaurant, sure: go with God. In your own domestic kitchen, though? Come on. You do not want to be up and down like a jack in the box. You want to have a nice time, with nice people, and eat the delicious things you have made.

What is good, though, is to give people something to consider while you're finishing off the actual dinner, especially if the actual dinner has lots going on – such as, to pick an example completely at random, a slow-cooked lamb with yoghurt and pickles and flatbreads. If you were, for example, going to make a slow-cooked lamb with yoghurt and pickles and flatbreads, you might want something to occupy your guests before you call them to the tablecloth-ed table to marvel at your creation.

Which is, of course, why God invented the cheese straw.

There is so little need to fuck with tradition on a cheese straw, a confection so simple and so delicious that it is possible to eat roughly one hundred at a sitting. And yet, here we are. I wanted to make something that would chime pleasingly with said lamb: something that would feel harmonious, something that would set the tone for the main event, like the opening act at a gig or the shop at a theatre. Sometimes I pick up on a certain disdain, in some circles, for the matchy-matchy menu. Too cute!

But I *love* when things are cute. I especially love when they are both cute and full of toasted sesame, melted cheese, and black olives.

MAKES ABOUT 24. LEFTOVERS WILL BE SO WELCOME HERE

150g miscellaneous old cheese, including some Parmesan if possible
250g cold salted butter
2 tablespoons tahini
1 teaspoon salt
350g plain flour
50g sesame seeds
2 tablespoons chilli flakes
1 egg white

Blitz the cheese into fine crumbs in the food processor. Set aside all but about 2 tablespoons; leave those 2 tablespoons in the bowl of the processor. Cube the butter (just roughly is fine) and add to the processor along with the tahini, salt and the flour. Blitz again until it comes together to form a dough. If you need, feel free to add a tablespoon of cold water to help it come together. Tip into a bowl, cover with cling film and chill.

Toast the sesame seeds over a low heat (big dry skillet; no oil) until they turn gold, and even a few turn brown. Let them cool, then tip into the remaining crumbled cheese along with the chilli flakes. Stir.

Pre-heat the oven to 200°C.

☞

Split the dough in half. Form each block into a rough rectangle, then roll each out into a neat sheet between two sheets of baking parchment. Sprinkle half the sesame-cheese topping over each sheet, cover again with baking parchment, and roll out again.

Leave the parchment in place. Roll with your rolling pin, pressing the two layers – one of pastry, one of topping – into each other. Gently remove the top parchment and slide onto a baking sheet. Cut into strips, and wiggle each strip slightly apart from its fellows with the blade of the knife.

Brush with egg white, and grind liberally with pepper. Bake for 30–40 minutes, or until crispy and golden.

Notes and Queries

Something about the way the butter solidifies makes these especially delicious the next day. A perfect texture.

An egg yolk makes an excellent 'day after hosting' dinner of 'rice and egg yolk' carbonara (see p. 304).

Six-Hour Lamb with Za'atar and Anchovy

We tend to think of lamb as a spring thing – Easter, etc. – possibly because that is when the lambs are hopping and leaping about. It is obvious with even a tiny bit of thought that this makes no sense: the lambs, in spring, are very small. They are hopping and leaping about. They are not the large hefty boys one needs for a *leg of lamb*. The leg of an actual little lamb is very small, and probably not nearly as nice to eat.

Also, while it is possible to feel bad about eating little-lamb-qua-little-lamb because of the small hopping and leaping of it all, I have no real feelings about eating a big hefty autumn boy. This is because when I was a child we had a lot of these autumn boys and they were extremely violent: large mean lads who guarded the garden gate with all the indiscriminate vigour of a drunk bouncer. They were also then, as they are now, extremely delicious.

They are especially delicious when you cook them like this: lots of spices, lots of garlic, and anchovies for classic flavour, blitzed into a paste and rubbed into the whole leg, cooked slowly in stock and onions until the whole thing falls apart. It's based sort of faintly on what I think might have been a recipe by a Palestinian chef in a Sunday supplement about a decade ago: the allspice-fenugreek-cardamom combo feels quite Palestinian, no? Then I put anchovy in it, for classic lamb reasons, and also all that garlic, for deliciousness reasons. Serve it with a big herby salad to remind you that summer was here once; and salted yoghurt with olive oil rippled through it; and flatbreads, to make a kind of ineffably elegant kebab-adjacent treat. It's platters; it's everyone helping themselves; it's cosy without being heavy; it's comforting without being boring; it's familiar enough to be your friend while being unexpected enough to charm. I love this. I really, really love this.

☞

SERVES ABOUT A BILLION. NO, REALLY, SERVES 8, WITH LEFTOVERS

4 big red onions
2kg leg of lamb
3 tablespoons cumin seeds
3 tablespoons coriander seeds
2 tablespoons allspice berries
2 tablespoons cardamom seeds
2 tablespoons fenugreek seeds
2 tablespoons za'atar
1 bulb of garlic, cloves peeled
4 anchovies
2 tablespoons red wine vinegar
500ml lamb stock
50g coriander
50g mint
50g flat-leaf parsley
125g rocket
juice of 1 lemon
pinch of sumac (optional)
400g Greek yoghurt
2 teaspoons cumin seeds
flatbreads, to serve (optional)
1 tablespoon pomegranate molasses or honey
extra-virgin olive oil, applied liberally throughout

Oven on to 150°C.

First thing: four big red onions, sliced thin in half-moons and laid out on a big, deep baking tray to make a bed for the lamb. Drizzle with plenty of olive oil and a big pinch of sea salt.

The baking tray will contain liquid so it needs sides. Take your lamb from the fridge and the packaging; set it in the big roasting dish on top of the onions, and score the top of the meat through the fat.

Blitz or bash together the marinade – everything from cumin down to vinegar. If you're using a pestle and mortar, you will want to bash the seeds up first; then bash in the garlic and anchovies, then fold in the za'atar, and slowly add in 4 tablespoons of oil and the vinegar so that it makes a paste and you're not just splashing around. If using the Magimix or Magimix contender: just chuck it all in and blitz until you make a rough paste.

(Don't be tempted to add anything sweet here, like honey or pomegranate molasses: we will drizzle those over at the end and if you add it now it will burn.)

Rub this paste lavishly into the meat. Get it into all the little cuts and bits. Tip the stock directly into the tray, on top of the onions. Sprinkle the whole with a big pinch of sea salt, wrap in foil, stick it in the oven and walk away for 6 hours.

Actually, no: check it at the 3 hour mark to see if it needs more liquid. If so, feel free to tip in some boiling water. (Just a bit.)

Your jobs are: wash and pick the leaves from your huge bunch of coriander, your huge bunch of mint, and your huge bunch of parsley. Mix with a bag of rocket. This is a herb salad and it is perfect. Squeeze over some lemon; toss in a pinch of sumac if you have it and can be bothered. Find a nice bowl, arrange, and you're done with the salad.

Your other job is to put some thick Greek yoghurt artfully on a plate or platter, and drizzle with olive oil. If you would like to be fancy you can sprinkle some cumin seeds over the top.

At the 5½ mark, remove the foil, and turn the heat up to 200°C. This is how we get the crispy and delicious edges.

Warm through some flatbreads, or whatever.

At the 6 hour mark, take out the meat, and it will literally...fall apart. It will fall apart and you can shred with two forks, and stir the meat through the caramelised sticky onions beneath. Drizzle with pomegranate molasses.

This is it! This is all!

Set your yoghurt platter, your herb salad, maybe a few pink pickles and your stack of warm breads out on the table. Serve the lamb in the roasting dish with two forks for taking generous handfuls. Assemble plates; feast; feel so, so lucky you don't know what to do with yourself.

Notes and Queries

How to score lamb: 'scoring it' here means shallow cuts in a diamond pattern, so, first diagonal one way, then diagonal the other. This is to let the spice rub get into the meat. To me, the first time, this felt bizarrely intimidating, but it is easier than you think and you will be fine. It is also very worth doing.

Chicken stock will do in a pinch. Don't be making lamb stock from scratch.

Frozen parathas; soft pitta; yoghurt-pot naan? All good.

Pink pickled onions, p. 243.

You will have leftovers here, almost certainly, and you will want them. Fantastic sandwiches. Fantastic pie. (Rake through some chopped spinach, crumble over some feta, brush some filo with olive oil and scrunch it up on top. Sesame seeds. Black pepper. Bake 15-ish minutes at 180°C, or until lamb is piping hot and pastry crisp and delicious.)

White Chocolate and Tahini Snickerdoodles

Sometimes dessert is dessert, and sometimes dessert is a stack of still-warm cookies, sugar gently crackling, butter still a little molten. Sometimes dessert is a little cup of black coffee and a snickerdoodle.

What a perfect word! So perfect, in fact, that though these are perhaps closer to Arabic ma'amoul in texture, I can't help but call them *snickerdoodle* just for niceness. I think they count as snickerdoodle because you roll them in sugar, like a snickerdoodle.

So snickerdoodles, for grown-ups: snickerdoodles browned, toasted, and with some of the butter in the batter swapped for pure thick tahini. Snickerdoodles studded with slivers of white chocolate, and rolled in toasted and cinnamon-scented sesame seeds and brown sugar. Snickerdoodles you can make in advance, and then bake from frozen, like a magic trick.

MAKES 24

150g salted butter
80g tahini
150g light brown soft sugar
1 teaspoon vanilla extract
1 egg + 1 egg yolk
210g flour
½ teaspoon baking powder
100g white chocolate
3 tablespoons toasted sesame seeds
1 teaspoon ground cinnamon
1 tablespoon brown sugar
1 teaspoon flaky sea salt

You take your salted butter and you brown it down (saucepan, low heat, watch it until it foams and then subsides). You get about 110g brown butter, then, and you build it back up again with the tahini, poured straight into the bowl you're using.

Beat in the 150g sugar; add the vanilla, egg and yolk. Beat until smooth. Add the flour and baking powder; beat until smooth again.

Chop the white chocolate into uneven chunks and slivers. (I go diagonally across the bar.) Add this too, and stir to combine.

And then you either bake right away, or you set up the magic trick: roll the mixture into 24 tablespoon-sized balls, and stick them in the fridge in a Ziploc bag or Tupperware.

Either way, when you want to bake, you mix toasted sesame seeds, cinnamon, sugar and salt in a bowl.

Take each ball, and roll it in the sesame mixture. Line a baking sheet with baking parchment; six balls to a lined baking sheet. Ten minutes at 180°C. Squidgy, crackling, delightful. Serve warm, with coffee. Save yourself two, unbaked, in the freezer for tomorrow.

(Maybe 11 minutes for frozen.)

Winter

Squash-Hazelnut Romesco

Twist: it's not a romesco!

No, listen, I am sorry I lied to you, but it's the easiest way of telling you what this dip is actually like: creamy, complex, nutty, sweet, salty, a perfect mellow thing to sit gently and pass around until the ragù comes to the table. It's basically kind of *like* a romesco, but made for a British winter instead of a Catalonian summer: garlic, olive oil, red wine vinegar, hazelnuts, squash roasted – unpeeled and easy – until soft and scoopable. A quick blitz in a food processor. Taste for seasoning: add a splash more vinegar, a pinch more salt. Chilli, if you want. Wildly easy. Super nice.

This is, incidentally, also extremely good to have leftovers of, for the week, if your house runs on snacks the way ours does. This is a perfect 4pm boost, spread on rye toast or as a dip for seedy crackers, because it is mostly good fat, protein from the nuts, and an actual vegetable.

SERVES 6, WITH BREAD

wedge of squash, about 500g
1+ 2 garlic cloves, peeled
80g hazelnuts
3 tablespoons extra-virgin olive oil + 1 tablespoon extra
2 tablespoons red wine vinegar

Pre-heat the oven to 200°C.

Take your wedge of squash. I assume it's a wedge, at 500g: I buy mine in pieces from a local 'international supermarket', so it's always a little more or a little less. Scoop out the seeds, but leave the peel intact. Set in a little baking dish, drizzle with oil, and season generously. Tuck 2 little cloves of garlic under the curve of the squash. Roast for 45 minutes.

In a dry frying pan, over a medium heat, toast the hazelnuts until fragrant.

Tip the hazelnuts into the food processor and blitz fine. Squeeze in the roasted garlic; add the raw clove, along with the oil and vinegar and blitz again. When the mixture forms a paste, scoop the squash from the skin, and tip in. Blitz once more. You may need to add a splash of water here to loosen, but go easy: you want it to be smooth enough that your crackers won't break when you dip them, but not so smooth it's soup.

Taste: add salt, pepper, maybe a splash more vinegar. You could even add chilli flakes if you like, but it doesn't need it. Serve with crackers, bought or made; flatbreads, bought or made; or crisps (always bought, sorry). The soda bread on p. 224.

Miso Mushroom Ragù

Rich, wintry, wholesome: don't stint on the mushrooms, the miso, or the olive oil. Also, don't stint on the roasted garlic. In fact, don't stint on anything. The secret to really excellent dinner-party cooking is to do it with a generous hand. This is how restaurants do it, after all, and once in a while it won't kill you to go wild with the beautiful glossy rich fat and lovely layers of salt. In this we layer bouillon with miso; dark chocolate with roasted garlic purée (Belazu make a fantastic one in a jar); and mushrooms upon mushrooms upon mushrooms.

It's this layering of mushrooms that is the real secret here: we cook them both in multiple batches and multiple fashions. Some get minced down, and fried with the aromatics and onions; some are soaked, rehydrated with stock and vermouth, and added whole; and some are squeezed, torn, and fried in rosemary oil to be thrown in almost at the end. This gives you textures that feel satisfying in the way meat can feel satisfying; it also gives you a real satisfying depth of flavour, from the dried porcini broth to the slippery morsels of oyster mushrooms.

This is, happily, vegan. It is also pulse-free, dairy-free, and – if you check your labels carefully – gluten-free. It is a perfect all-purpose dinner if you don't know what dietary requirements are required, but also if you do, and every single guest seems to have a different thing going on. (If they are allergic to mushrooms, then I'm sorry, I cannot help you.) I love when a dinner is vegan by accident. This one truly was an accident, born out of a failure to buy anchovies, and the happy realisation that miso was doing an even better job at the anchovy trick: depth, punch, resonance.

If you are not vegan, or anything-free, rejoice! I didn't make this for vegans. I made this for you, and I think you will love it.

I am, however, sorry to say that you will probably need two big pans. I use a big casserole (referred to below as Pan B), and a smaller, shallower casserole (Pan A). Ideally, both should have lids, but I know that's asking quite a lot. You will figure it out.

SERVES 6, GENEROUSLY, PROBABLY WITH LEFTOVERS

450g chestnut mushrooms
4 sprigs thyme
3 tablespoons red miso
3 tablespoons roasted garlic purée
3 celery stalks
3 big shallots
1 leek
75ml white vermouth
70g mixed dried mushrooms (ideally including porcini)
1 tablespoon bouillon powder
250g shiitake mushrooms
125g oyster mushrooms
25g dark chocolate
4 sprigs rosemary
pasta, to serve
hard cheese, to serve (optional)
olive oil

Wash your chestnut mushrooms under a running tap. This is not advised for mushrooms in most cases, because they are little sponges, but in this case, it works for us: once washed, squeeze and wring them out over the sink to get rid of as much water as possible. They will fall apart in your hands, which is what we like. Keep wringing and squeezing while you heat 1 teaspoon of olive oil in your shallow pan. Pan A! Throw in the thyme, and then the chestnut mushrooms. Cook for 15 minutes over a medium heat, stirring occasionally, then stir in 2 tablespoons of the red miso and the roasted garlic purée and leave alone on the medium heat for about 15 minutes further, to form a kind of golden-brown crust on the bottom. Think of this, if you're a meat-eater, as you would with mince: letting it caramelise, letting it get good.

While this is going, finely chop the celery, shallots, and leek. Set them frying in the bigger pan (Pan B) with a teaspoon of olive oil.

Tip the crispy, disintegrating mushrooms from Pan A into said Pan B with the sofrito.

Turn off Pan B once the sofrito is where you want it. (Soft.)

Deglaze Pan A with a generous splash of vermouth, and scrape up all the lovely bits. Then tip your dried mushrooms into Pan A, with the rest of the vermouth, the remaining red miso, bouillon powder, and 500ml water. Bring up to a simmer, stir until the miso and bouillon dissolve, turn the heat down low, and cook, covered, for 30 minutes.

While this is happening, finely slice your shiitake mushrooms (so nice to slice!) and tear your oysters. Do not wash these if you can help it; just brush them clean of any dirt.

Tip everything from Pan A – so mushrooms rehydrated, miso-bouillon broth – into Pan B. Turn the heat back on. Stir; grate in the dark chocolate.

Stick Pan A back on the heat. Let it dry for a few seconds; then deglaze with a splash of vermouth. Scrape. Add in 1 teaspoon of oil, and 1 sprig of rosemary. Add in a handful of shiitake mushrooms, few enough that you can still see the base of the pan, and cook for 4–5 minutes, until golden. Tip into Pan B. Repeat – including oil and rosemary – until all your shiitake are done, then the oysters. Deglaze if necessary, and tip that into Pan B too.

☞

Make some pasta here; I do tagliatelle, and I am happy to tell you that I simply cook it in Pan A. Salted water, bring to a simmer (also, helpfully, removing any stuck-on bits), drop in dried flat pasta. Cook, following packet instructions, to al dente.

Add a splash of pasta water (Pan A) to the sauce (Pan B), maybe up to a couple of splashes. Season with salt and pepper.

Drain the pasta; return to Pan A; dress with butter, and maybe some very finely chopped dill. Bring Pans A and B to the table. Hard cheese, if you like.

Notes and Queries

Make this work with whatever mushrooms you can get. A variety is delightful! I like to use a lot of weird mushrooms – not weird mushrooms, behave – but these you can get at most big supermarkets and I hate to send people off to scavenge for weird mushrooms if they could get great results in the regular shop. If you love to go to stalls at farmers' markets, feel free to swap in any delightful mushrooms you think might be fun.

Red miso has a real depth that the caramel-y white can't quite match here. Try to get it! But white will be fine too.

Roasted garlic purée can be made at home (see p. 242) but, equally, you can buy it in very nice little jars. Both are fully fine here. No difference detected.

Smoky Tea Chocolate Pots

I once ran into an old schoolfriend sitting on a log in my local park, drinking lapsang souchong. It was surprising because I had last seen her ten years and 5000 miles away, and here she was sipping delicately from a small enamel mug. Her enormous dog lay placidly in the long grass. She didn't seem surprised to see me. 'Tea?' She took a second little mug from her backpack. We had a cup of lapsang souchong – smoky, bitter, mysterious – and I tried to pry her for information on people I used to know. She shrugged. 'Everyone's the same,' she said. 'Everyone's just the same!' We finished our tea and she shook the mugs out onto the ground. 'It was nice to see you!' I said. 'We should meet up again some time!' She smiled at me, completely unguarded and entirely as I remembered. 'We probably won't,' she said. I was nonplussed. Then she laughed. 'You're just the same as well,' she said. 'It was lovely to see you! Have a lovely day! Have a lovely rest of your life!' She hugged me briefly and called to her dog, and they went off together. She was right; we never met up again.

But I do think of her every time I make lapsang souchong: warm, mysterious, a little bitter.

Fun fact: if you whisk boiling water and dark dark chocolate together, however you do it, you will get something like chocolate mousse.

If you whisk boiling lapsang souchong and dark dark chocolate together, with a generous helping of olive oil and a pinch of salt, you will get incredibly grown-up chocolate mousse.

Actually, it's more like a chocolate crémeux: smooth, rich, luxurious. You want to share this with your favourite people and an espresso. This serves at least four, but plated correctly – i.e. barely plated, a generous dollop smudged across a plate, drizzled with olive oil and scattered with sea salt – you could stretch it to six.

SERVES 6

4 lapsang souchong (or 'Distinctively Smoky') teabags
180g 70% chocolate
2 tsp smoked water
30ml + 30ml + extra to serve (so 60–70ml total) extra-virgin olive oil, the really nice kind that smells sort of green
1 tablespoon flaky sea salt

Bring 150ml water to a boil in a saucepan, and drop in the teabags. Steep for at least 15 minutes, then bring back up to a simmer. You will probably have about 120ml remaining, allowing for some steam.

Roughly chop the chocolate, and tip into the bowl of a stand mixer or large bowl. Pour over 3 tablespoons (30ml) extra virgin olive oil, then pour over the 120ml of hot strong tea and the smoked water.

Let sit for a couple of minutes, then stir to make sure all the chocolate is fully melted. Whisk on high (I use the top setting of the KitchenAid or beaters) for 10 minutes, beating really well to make sure it's aerated. Look for a smooth, swirly consistency, kind of like buttercream.

This is a great place to pause, if you are hosting: it will sit quite happily in the fridge for 2 hours or even 2 days.

At pudding time: bring back up to room temperature, add the last 30ml olive oil, and whisk for a further 5 minutes. Either divide into ramekins/mismatched glasses (classic!) or, to imitate an elegant small-plates type restaurant, spoon a lazy quenelle onto a white plate. (Two spoons, shaping, make one quenelle.) However you serve: drizzle with extra virgin olive oil; scatter with flaky sea salt.

Notes and Queries

Without the extra whisk, and plus the fridge time, you'll get something closer to the ganache-y inside of a chocolate truffle. Roll into balls, coat with cocoa powder. Voilà! Truffles. A friend of mine once announced many years ago that she would be inaugurating her Famous Truffles for a New Year's Eve dinner party. We looked admiringly at the ingredients on the countertop. Twelve hours later, via a significant change of plan, we wandered home through the dawn, me carrying my shoes, her missing her shorts, hair matted with gold toffee vodka. The truffles have remained a beautiful dream ever since. Maybe these could be your Famous Truffles?

Add extra olive oil to rewhip until perfect. You can add more than that. More than that, even.

Damson Vodka for All

Damson: one of my all-time favourite words, up there with *samphire* and *marble* and *wrangle*. (A weakness for a short A may be deduced.)

There is something sort of fairy tale about it, as a word, but there's also something a little fairy tale about damsons in general: a dusty, bruisy-looking little sharp-sweet mouthful of a plum. You can buy them at markets, and not generally supermarkets, which adds to their magic.

As a little girl I used to play in a damson orchard, if you can believe such a thing (of course you can), and I ate probably thousands of them raw: tart as rhubarb, sharp as sherbet. Cooked, they taste like the best plums you ever had; bottled in booze, they taste like heaven. It's like a sloe gin, but plummier. If sloes are what you have – and sloe-picking is one of life's true uncomplicated delights – this recipe, such as it is, will also work for beautiful black-button-eye sloes. If gin is what you have, use gin.

But there's something about damson vodka instead of sloe gin, fond as I am of the latter, that just feels right to me for right now. It feels fun and classic and nostalgic and new, and it tastes like a dream.

When my mum makes this, she never strains out the fruit, which means that by the time you've drunk a full jar of vodka, you've still got the sweetest, richest, booziest plums you've ever seen. You can use them, if you don't plan to get drunk on snacks, to spice up an apple crumble; with rich roast meats; maybe just solo, dolloped over thick cream.

(The stones are a problem, for sure. You can strain to remove the stones if you're so inclined. You can attempt to pit the damsons, absolutely. Mostly we just spit them out.)

500g damsons
300g golden caster sugar
700ml vodka

Wash the damsons. Wash a big jar. Put the damsons in a freezer bag in the freezer until solid; put the big jar in the dishwasher on the hottest cycle.

Bash the frozen damsons with a rolling pin (satisfying!) until the skins crack. Go hard. Bashed-up damsons and sugar in the perfectly clean jar. Pour over the vodka, seal the jar, and shake. Leave for at least 2 months.

Strain and serve in the prettiest small glasses you own.

To Asia, With Love
Hetty McKinnon
PRESTEL
NIGELLA LAWSON

For the Week Ahead

Bread and Butter

Champagne Tomatoes

Sunset-Cured Trout

Dad’s Mayo

Lars's Remoulade

Kimchi Remoulade

Tuna Mayo

Egg Mayo

That Scallion Sauce

Toasted Sesame Seeds

Crispy Shallots

Caramelised Garlic

The Pink Onions

The Green Sauce

The Bright Green Sauce

The Black Dal

Cure-All One-Pan Beans

The Chicken Matrix

Coconut Breakfast Bars

Tony’s Treacle Anzacs

Cendrine’s Cannelés

Velvet Ribbon Peach Cake

Bread. Roasted Garlic. Snacking Cakes, etc.

IMO, simultaneously the most overambitious and underrated kind of cooking is the 'cooking in advance' kind of cooking. You've been here before. So have I. We've all thought about being the kind of people who meal prep, no? We've all failed to become the kind of people who meal prep? We've all run up against our grand ideas about what we'll want to eat five days from now, and our total lack of matching Tupperware? Sure. We are among friends.

This, however, is the kind of cooking in advance that I really fucking love: bread, butter, little delicious bits to psych you through the week. Consider: little bits to add to whatever you do feel like cooking later on! A very nice mayo to jazz up your sandwiches! Biscuits for lunchboxes! Scallion oil and crispy onions to put on, in my opinion, literally anything, including a bowl of plain rice for the night when you truly have nothing left! I'm not going to pretend that you're going to do all of this every Sunday, but please: permit yourself to imagine a life when you do maybe one bit of it, one Sunday, and don't you feel great about life? Perfectly ambitious. Perfectly rated. You're going to love this. What I love most about this chapter, reading through it, is that everything in it is something I make so regularly that I don't even need to open my notebooks to type it up. It's all just...in there, top of the dome, ready to go. I think – hope! – these things will fill this place in your life: recipes you make so much you no longer need this book at all.

Bread and Butter

Take one tub of cream, ideally on a Sunday-night supermarket discount; a couple of pinches of salt; plus some odds and ends of flour (rye, oatmeal, plain, spelt, whatever you've got) and a dollop of treacle. Result? Fresh soda bread, and, incredibly, *fresh home-churned butter.*

It is genuinely absurdly easy to make your own butter at home, and you should. You should do it at least once, just for the bizarro sense of accomplishment: butter! A thing from a shop! Made by you! You can wrap it in baking parchment and tie the ends with string and imagine you paid £7 for it in the kind of grocery store where there is no visible plastic and the labels are either handwritten or in Spanish.

If you can get the cream on a good deal, it is significantly cheaper than any butter you will buy in this kind of grocery store, and also *you made it.* You can use double cream or for a fancier, more cultured-butter taste, do half cream and half crème fraîche. You just beat it until it becomes whipped cream (good kind); then beat it more until it becomes too-whipped cream (bad kind); then beat it more until it becomes something that looks a lot like butter – and buttermilk. You wash the butter until it's clean; you siphon off the buttermilk and make a loaf of soda bread. Butter for the week ahead, but soda bread for Sunday night.

This is because for the week you need a different kind of bread – sliced for sandwiches, easy to grab out of the toaster – which I am sorry to say I have never got into the routine of making. I have a very nice routine of going to the bakery! I love the bakery! They have coffee there! I keep meaning to make bread on the regular – get a sourdough starter, learn what it is, etc. – and yet somehow it never sticks. Some day! Some other day, some other book. For now, though, I can offer you this: home-churned butter, and a single simple loaf of soda bread, warm with rye and treacle and caraway seeds. I suggest you put a chicken in the oven, and use the bread to mop up the beautiful glossy pan-juices. Sunday night sorted, and butter every day for the week ahead. Also, you will feel like an innkeeper in a fantasy novel. You are Hulda of The Bannered Mare, and the weary traveller will find rest at your door.

For the butter:

600ml double cream, or 300ml crème fraîche + 300ml double cream

1 tablespoon flaky sea salt

Tip the cream(s) into the bowl of a stand mixer fitted with the whisk attachment. You can do this with a hand mixer, certainly, but it will be a lot of…standing, so try to acquire a stand mixer if you can. If your stand mixer has a lid, so much the better. Lid on if possible.

Beat the cream(s) on a medium setting then keep beating. It will pass through the stage of perfectly spoonable soft thick whipped cream, heaven for putting on puddings; and into 'whipped cream from a can'; then into 'gone-wrong whipped cream from a can'; and then into a bad hinterland for a minute or two. You will think it

For the bread:
125g rye flour
75g plain flour + 2 tablespoons extra
75g whole oats
1 tablespoon caraway seeds
1 teaspoon bicarbonate of soda
1 teaspoon fine salt
buttermilk
1 tablespoon treacle

has gone wrong. Leave it beating; turn your back for half a second; suddenly you will hear a completely unexpected sound. The sloshing will alert you to the fact that it is no longer cream! It is two things: butter and buttermilk! The vital thing now is to *completely* separate the two: any buttermilk left in the butter makes the butter go bad, and also, we want as much buttermilk for the bread as possible.

Set a sieve over a bowl. Scrape the butter clinging to the whisk back into the bowl, and tip the whole thing, butter and buttermilk both, into the sieve. Buttermilk drains into bowl; butter remains in sieve. Leave it there for a minute while you wash up the bowl and whisk of the stand mixer.

Butter back into stand-mixer bowl, and re-whip for a minute. Tip it back into the sieve, scraping down the sides to drain any final scraps of buttermilk. Fill the stand-mixer bowl with very cold water, and plunge the butter into it, using your hands to knead it. (Cold water stops it melting.)

The water will go cloudy; drain it, refill, and repeat. Repeat, in fact, 3 times: kneading and washing the butter in the water.

Tip onto some baking parchment, and knead in the salt. Wrap in said baking parchment, and set aside.

Pre-heat the oven to 180°C. (If I were doing this? I would have put the oven on at 200°C, right at the beginning, put a chicken in for the duration of the butter-making and now be turning it down to 180°C.)

Weigh out your flours and oats, caraway seeds, bicarb and fine salt. Stir. Mix in the buttermilk you just made (it should be about 220ml), and also the treacle. It makes a very wet-looking dough, but don't worry, it's correct. Use the reserved flour to coat your hands so that you can form it into a roundish, flattish patty. Set this on top of baking paper.

Score the top with a cross – I just use a normal sharp kitchen knife – and use the baking paper to lift into a casserole dish with a lid. Lid on. Bake for 40 minutes.

(Check it's done by rapping the bottom: if it sounds hollow, you're golden.)

Serve warm, with the butter. Plenty of the butter. (Maybe also a chicken.)

Champagne Tomatoes

I must speak my truth: I am deeply afraid of fermenting anything. I am afraid of fermenting things because I hate explosions and dying of botulism.

The problem is that I absolutely love fermented things. I love to eat fermented things and I love to look at fermented things and I would love to have a row of jars shining, like an old-timey innkeeper (see recipes passim) or Constance in *We Have Always Lived in the Castle*, with all the colours beautiful and bright.

So I had to get over the fear somehow, and this was how. I was seduced both by the easiness of the recipe – least terrifying of all fermentations – and by the fact that I found out that Olia Hercules calls these 'champagne tomatoes'. How could I resist? Two things I love!

Plus, I think they work best with the worst kind of cherry tomatoes, which is such a win. I read a million recipes and took the plunge: cherry tomatoes; salt brine; basil; bay; dill; done. Obviously, one must sterilise the jar. Hot dishwasher; hot oven. Also, I don't keep these very long, due to my fears, although I know objectively you *could*. They are fizzy and bright and sour and only explosive in the way of a taste sensation. Salads! Pastas! On toast! Through grains! Little snacklet!

Also, fermented things are so good for you in every possible way. My zaniest and most hippie belief is that daily kimchi cured my anxiety disorder, although there can be no possible basis for this fact except maybe the glorious and harnessable power of placebo. All I know is, when I eat fizzy fermented things every day, I stop getting stomachaches and start being brave.

So let's do it: let's be double brave, and make our own. It will be worth it, and probably we won't even die. We may even live forever, powered by fizz and champagne tomatoes.

40g sea salt
400g cherry tomatoes
20g (small handful) basil
2 bay leaves
2 sprigs dill
1-litre very clean Kilner jar

Bring a litre of water to the boil, add the salt and let it dissolve. Let the brine cool completely.

Pack the cherry tomatoes tightly into the clean jar, and tuck the herbs around the sides. Pour the brine over the cherry tomatoes, leaving about a 3cm gap at the top between the lid and the waterline but making sure every tomato is fully submerged. If you need to, you can use a weight to keep them from bobbing up cheerfully. Ed Smith suggests filling a clean Ziploc bag with water and sitting it on top, which is in my view the idea of a genius.

Flip the lid closed without sealing, and set aside somewhere dark for a few days. You can cover with a towel and leave on the kitchen counter. This is why it's nice, unscary, low-key fermenting: four days? Five? I would eat a tomato that had been out for five days, wouldn't you?

Stir when you get up; stir when you go to bed. Taste after 4 days. If fizzy enough – champagne-like! – seal shut, and stick in the fridge. If not, repeat the next day. Easy, easy, easy.

Sunset-Cured Trout

Like all cured fish, this has just enough old-explorer cold-North edge to give a little heft to the canapé platters, sits pleasingly in a bagel, can top off a rice bowl or lend a silky depth to a pasta sauce. It can be sliced for sandwiches; it can be ribboned through salads. What a fantastic week. Bonus chic, also, because it looks like a sunset: beautiful pinks and oranges from the citrus-beetroot salt tinge all the way through the pretty flesh. Also, you made it yourself. It takes maybe 15 minutes, and smells like citrus.

1 medium citrus fruit of your choosing
100g salt
75g sugar
1 cooked beetroot
2 trout fillets, about 500g

The hardest part is getting hold of the trout, so feel free to use salmon if that's easier for you. I love trout, though, and it tends to be slightly better environmentally.

The second hardest part is zesting the citrus. If you can get it, blood orange is pretty and on theme; if not, a beautiful lemon? Zest the citrus, and mix with the salt and sugar in the bowl of a processor. Roughly chop the beetroot, and blitz to a grainy paste.

Rinse the trout under a cold running tap, and pat dry with kitchen paper. Settle it into a Tupperware, and pack all around with the beetroot salt mixture. Put in the fridge, and don't look until 48 hours have passed.

Remove from the cure. Rinse again; pat dry; and thinly slice, across the grain, as needed.

Dad's Mayo

My dad was on the anti-ultra-processed-foods train before anyone else I know, but happily for us, his loving family, it mainly manifested as a profound commitment to making homemade mayonnaise every single week. What a win.

Homemade mayonnaise is a fully different beast to the supermarket kind. Without wanting to fall too far down the processed foods rabbit hole, it's impossible to deny that the flavour of even the nicest supermarket mayonnaise could mostly be summed up as 'substance, creamy (?)': home-made mayo is rich, golden, spiked with lemon and Dijon. You can mix in roasted garlic! You can mix in tarragon! You can mix in finely chopped kimchi, if you are a kimchi-head, like me!

There are, of course, one billion tricks and tips to making mayonnaise – a stick blender in a jug is the obvious, but my dad's method – unorthodox and powerful – is to use one single whisk of a two-pronged electric hand whisk. Two is too many! None is too few! He also would like you to know that it's crucial that everything is at room temperature, not fridge-cold, and this is the best mayo I know so I recommend you believe him. I always do, anyway.

He is the kind of cook who never does anything on instinct without first consulting several variants of the kind of cookbook he trusts above all: large manuals, preferably in French, describing every possible permutation of every kind of sauce. These are the kind of cookbooks I will never write, and I regret to disappoint him in this manner. I hope by honouring his immaculate mayo skills here, I can make it up to him. Also, I hope that you love this mayo as much as we do.

MAKES 1 JAR

2 egg yolks
2 teaspoons Dijon mustard
1 teaspoon white wine vinegar
1 teaspoon fine salt
1 teaspoon crushed white pepper
200ml sunflower oil
2 teaspoons lemon juice

Dampen a piece of kitchen paper, and fold it in half. Set it on the kitchen side, and put a mixing bowl on top of the paper. This is to stop it moving when you whisk! Isn't that clever?

Yolks, mustard, vinegar, salt, pepper in the mixing bowl. Add a drop of oil and whisk until incorporated. Another drop, ditto. And another drop. Same as before. Drip in the oil very slowly, whisking with your single electric whisk the whole time. Do not stop whisking!

When it is recognisably mayonnaise, stop adding oil and stop whisking: lemon juice, maybe a pinch more salt, maybe a pinch more pepper. Voilà! Mayonnaise!

cookworks

Lars's Remoulade

My friend has a friend – maybe he is also now my friend? – who is Danish, fastidious, and lives on a roundabout. He has no postcode and everything in his tiny pre-fab house is thoughtfully fashioned, like an unusual man in a children's book: a copper pipe with blue and red switches for water, a Pegasus pulley system for drying and storing clothes that sits flat against the ceiling, a kitchen tucked into a corner. The whole kitchen is about the size of a normal kitchen table. He is extremely mysterious to me.

I have never known him arrive at any kind of party empty-handed: cocktails for a birthday party, cocktails for New Year, and – most relevantly – remoulade for a barbecue. A barbecue is not a barbecue without Lars's Danish remoulade.

We planned one year to make hot dogs on New Year's Eve at midnight; forgot. The next morning we crept downstairs in our hangovers to find that Lars had gone, leaving only a jar of homemade remoulade in his wake. We cooked all the sausages we had intended to feed twenty, and ate them with remoulade and crispy onions, and the year crystallised into gorgeous clarity: a year that started this way would have to be both a year of surprises and a year of treats.

This remoulade is apparently very traditional in Denmark: a hot dog, plus remoulade, plus crispy onions. It is also, now, traditional for us. I hope Lars's remoulade becomes tradition for you too.

The mirin is Lars's twist. I recommend it.

10g parsley
½ shallot
2 dill pickles
1 tablespoon capers
120g mayonnaise
2 tablespoons Greek yoghurt
1 teaspoon Dijon mustard
1 teaspoon curry powder
1 teaspoon turmeric
1 teaspoon white wine vinegar
1 teaspoon mirin, if you have it

Finely mince the parsley, shallot, pickles and capers. Combine everything else; let sit for a couple of hours. Spoon onto hot dogs; dollop over salad; serve with soft-boiled eggs and Ryvita for the easiest lunch.

Kimchi Remoulade

This kimchi remoulade I stole from a small-plates-and-wine place named Fourth and Church (on the corner of Church Street and Fourth Avenue, in Hove). I assumed it must be impossibly difficult to make at home. Not so! I asked them; they told me; I'm telling you: basically just mild kimchi and great mayo.

100g sweetheart or white cabbage
1 teaspoon fine sea salt
4 tablespoons mild kimchi
2 tablespoons great mayo
1 tablespoon toasted sesame seeds

Finely shred the cabbage into a bowl and massage with the sea salt until damp and yielding. This is mostly just a question of squeezing.

Fold through the kimchi; fold through the mayo. Scatter with sesame seeds.

Tuna Mayo

I understand that you understand how to make tuna mayonnaise, or 'tuna salad' as our American friends call it. Nonetheless, I do really believe mine is superior. Or, no, not superior, as I have ultimate respect for your own personal vibe: perhaps merely an exciting change in pace.

1 celery stalk
½ red onion
1 teaspoon caster sugar
1 teaspoon rice wine vinegar
1 tablespoon sesame oil
2 x 150g tins tuna, drained
2 tablespoons mayo
1 teaspoon Dijon mustard
1 tablespoon light soy sauce
4 tablespoons peas

Finely mince the celery and the onion, and tip into a bowl with the sugar, salt, vinegar, sesame oil. Stir, and set aside for 15 minutes.

Add everything else, and stir to combine.

Egg Mayo

My supermarket meal deal varies as to snack and drink, but the central tenet is always the egg sandwich. Orange juice? Fizzy water? Cherry Coke, if the day is going very slowly? Could be a flapjack or a packet of salt and vinegar crisps (Walkers? Discos? Hula Hoops?). It's all to play for! But the egg sandwich never changes.

I make a batch of this, put it in a Tupperware, and it's a real transformer for lunches. Sorry to the supermarket meal deal, but this is the *real* deal. Good in the fridge for three days, so this makes enough for three sandwiches: go classic with cress and soft white bread, or – personal favourite – spooned into a pitta bread, plus watercress, plus cucumber, thinly sliced, drizzled with white wine vinegar and sprinkled with sea salt?

6 eggs
1 tablespoon chopped capers
2 tablespoons finely chopped flat-leaf parsley
2 tablespoons mayo
2 teaspoons Dijon mustard
black pepper

Bring a saucepan of water up to a rolling boil. Slip in the eggs, and turn the heat down to a simmer. Cook for 6 minutes and 30 seconds: this sets the whites hard, and mostly cooks the yolks, with just enough jammy inside.

In this six and a half minutes, finely chop the capers and parsley. You can also add chives! You can also add– sorry about this– finely chopped olives. If you were American, it would be very normal to add celery, but that is not for me.

Fill a bowl with cold water; immediately plunge the eggs into the cold water and peel underwater. Drain off the water; throw away the shell; and return the eggs to the bowl. Dollop in the mayo and mustard and mash together with a fork. Fold in the capers and parsley and season generously with black pepper.

That Scallion Sauce

About a hundred years ago, in Chapter One, there was a truly great takeaway, somewhere Vietnamese-adjacent, I guess, although they sprawled cheerfully into neighbouring countries too. One of their best sprawls was this, or something like it, which came in little plastic clippy pots tucked into the rice.

It was a spring onion shredded so far down and simmered (?) maybe (?) in some kind of (?) oil (?). It definitely had ginger in. It was salty and slick and pretty and delicious. It was barely cooked, but certainly not raw. It was the perfect contrast to all roasted meats – the sticky chicken thighs, the tender pork belly – and the next day, if there was any left, on avocado toast or crispy aubergine or plain rice. Peanut butter toast, also. Alongside chilli crisp on all stir-fries, noodles, baked sweet potato. There was never any left. It was big flavours in an elegant little pot; it was deceptively simple, clearly impossible to make at home.

The only way to save ourselves? Order two more little pots on the side. Two *at least*.

Anyway, it turns out to be unbelievably easy to make at home. The trick is that you cook it *off* the hob; you chop everything very fine, and then heat the oil to shimmering before pouring it over the finely chopped spring onions and ginger. This keeps the texture beautiful: slippery with onion, glossy with golden oil. Plus, as a bonus, if you make it at home you get to keep the oil too: a ginger and spring onion oil in which you can cook anything even remotely Asian-inspired and give it a huge lift.

1 bunch (about 120g) spring onions
100g fresh ginger
120ml neutral oil
1 teaspoon toasted sesame oil

Trim the spring onions: take off the root ends, and any grimy bits of tattered peel or shabby green ends. Mince very finely. Peel the ginger (either carefully with a teaspoon, or quickly with a knife) and mince just as small. I tend to go over the ginger-spring onion heap with the knife again once it's all minced.

Scrape into a heavy heatproof bowl.

In a high-sided saucepan, to avoid splatters, heat the neutral oil until sizzling. (Test: drop one tiny flake of ginger into the oil. If it starts to deep-fry, you're good to go.) Pour a quarter of the boiling oil very, very carefully over the ginger and spring onion. Stir. Repeat. Stir. Repeat. Stir. Repeat. The boiling oil cooks the ginger and spring onion instantly, while keeping their texture and colour.

Stir in the sesame oil, and a pinch of salt. Let cool and taste again. Spoon over greens, roasted aubergine, crispy chicken, sweet potatoes, whatever needs a bright, fresh boost.

Toasted Sesame Seeds

This isn't a recipe, but if your sesame seeds are the ordinary, untoasted kind, you are missing out on a world of niceness by not toasting them. The flavour is several hundred times better, more complex, and more satisfying: toasted, it's able to hold its own in marinades, crusts, salad dressings, bread rolls, on roasted aubergine or roast chicken or a falling-apart leg of lamb. If you've ever wondered why your sesame seeds don't taste that sesame-y – it's because you need to toast them. Happily, you can! You can do it right now!

Just toss a couple of tablespoons of sesame seeds into a dry frying pan over a low-medium heat, and cook, stirring occasionally, until they start to darken into a lovely golden colour. Turn off the heat – they will keep darkening for a couple of minutes – and decant into an airtight jar. I do this about once a week.

Crispy Shallots

We use these for everything. They can go on a salad, on a soup in place of croutons, on a dip or a dal or a tuna mayo sandwich, on roast meat, roast pumpkin and all roast vegetables, on any kind of noodle or rice or pasta dish to add texture and vibe. We are fairly liberal with their application. There are so few things in this book that you couldn't add some extra dimension to with a handful of crispy shallots.

The thing is that they are pure allium and pure salt, so they go with everything. Everything! Make some!

You can buy them in little plastic tubs from an international supermarket, or online, but if you do, please put them on a dry baking sheet in a 180°C oven for 10 minutes before you use them. Those tubs are not properly airtight! They will not be as shatteringly crisp as they should be! The baking helps, but it's not as good as making them yourself.

I hate to fry, honestly – I'm anxious and dyspraxic; it's not a fantastic combination with a pan of boiling oil – but I love crispy shallots so much I make an exception for these.

The trick is to use a mandoline slicer on your shallots to keep them all at an even thickness, so they cook at the same rate. The other trick is to have the sieve (over a bowl) set up before you start, ditto some kitchen paper to hand.

400g shallots, the big ones, not the tiny ones (unless you love slicing)
500ml neutral oil
kitchen paper: so important I put it in the ingredients list
2 teaspoons fine sea salt

Using a mandoline on the narrowest setting, thinly slice the shallots. Tip into a large, heavy, high-sided saucepan and cover with oil. (The shallots should not be touching the bottom, so feel free to add a splash more if so.) Cold shallots; cold oil. Stir the shallots so that they fall apart. I use chopsticks.

Put your sieve in a big heatproof bowl. Arrange some kitchen paper on the side. (Helpful: do this on a carving board with a gravy runnel, or a baking tray with a lip.)

Flick on the heat to high, and bring up to a simmer. Cook for about 10 minutes, stirring as much as you can be bothered: they will bubble, go pale gold, and then real, rich, proper gold. The worry here is overdoing them: they will keep cooking in the sieve.

10 minutes, then? Maybe 11. Whisk them off, and tip them into the sieve, shaking gently to remove the oil. Shake onto the kitchen paper, in a single layer, and salt generously while still hot.

Let cool, and store in an airtight jar. Apply to everything.

Caramelised Garlic

There is nothing special about this roasted garlic, except that I truly do make it about once a week and it's a real, radical game changer.

If you don't already roast garlic, may I recommend you do it right now, just to have in? Things you can do with it: make many of the recipes in this book; make anything with regular garlic in twice as nice and with ten times the depth; soup up a shop-bought sauce to make it taste like it took you hours in the kitchen; ditto shop-bought soups; rub it on toast; drop it into the blender for hummus; whisk it into mayo for roasted garlic aïoli *even if the mayo came from a shop*; mix it with butter for garlic bread gone classy; stir it through a ragù; whisk it into tahini; beat it into a marinade; beat it into mashed potatoes; beat it into mac and cheese; beat it into a standard vinaigrette for a salad dressing of kings. It goes into everything. (Roasted garlic cookies? Roasted garlic ice cream with vanilla and olive oil? Listen, no. But maybe? I feel like I can see it, but I don't feel like I can sell it, if you know what I mean. I might try it though.)

You can leave it whole in the fridge, and just squeeze out cloves as needed, or you can get the whole thing sorted in one go, and blitz it to a fine purée for ease of spooning into things. Either way!

3 bulbs garlic
2 sprigs rosemary
3 tablespoons olive oil
1 teaspoon white wine vinegar

Pre-heat the oven to 160°C. Get rid of any extra papery bits on the garlic bulbs, but don't split them up and don't actually peel them – just lose any flappy bits.

Slice the top off the garlic, like a little lid, and set in a little enamel-type dish: big enough to fit three garlics, if you have such a thing. Tuck in the rosemary, season generously, and drizzle over all the olive oil. Cover tightly with foil, and roast for an hour.

Allow to cool. Squeeze each little tender clove out of the skins and into the jug or bowl of a blender. Tip in the olive oil, removing the rosemary, and add the vinegar. Blitz smooth. Store in a clean jar for up to 5 days.

The Pink Onions

How many times can I give this recipe? *At least once more, Miss Risbridger.*

When I look back through the many, many pink pickled onion recipes I have written, it is startling to me how different they all are, and how basically similar the onions always turn out. A weirdly jarring experience! I had actually forgotten that I didn't always do my pink pickled onions the way I do now. My past selves and I are at odds, and yet, the feeling and function of the pink pickled onion remains the same.

The pink pickle is a constant in a world in which change is the only other. This should be very comforting to you, because basically, it's impossible to go wrong here. Change the vinegars! Change the sugars! Skip the boiling water bit altogether! Add soy sauce or fish sauce or rhubarb and ginger! Put in less, put in more: it doesn't actually seem to make much difference. Only make them, because pink onions are the perfect thing for making an effort, without needing any effort at all from you.

2 red onions, peeled and sliced on the thinnest blade of a mandoline, or as evenly as you can manage
50g fine salt
50g caster sugar
150ml rice wine vinegar

Sliced onions in a Tupperware.

Whisk the salt and sugar with 50ml boiling water until both dissolve. Stir in the vinegar. Pour over the onions, and leave to sit for at least an hour, but up to 24.

That's it. Use anywhere you'd use a pickle, especially a pretty one. Legs of lamb. Crispy chicken. Rolls. Wraps. Sandwiches. Soups. Salads.

The Green Sauce

This green sauce is probably 50% Laurie Colwin, 50% this Italian trick called broccoli ripassati, which vanquished my hatred of boiled broccoli forever. If you boil broccoli (or, in this case, steam it), then drag it round a frying pan with olive oil, it falls apart into a very ugly but very delicious sauce. Garlic is a must, obviously, as is lemon. So what happens if you add even more goodness? Courgette, because it melts down so nicely; cavolo nero for extra green; pecorino cheese for saltiness and depth. Perhaps you have eaten some variant of this before, but I feel boldly confident in my version. I think this one is really solid.

It is perfect in winter with linguine or risotto; it is perfect in a big sandwich or as a dip in high summer. A versatile, lovely, zingy business! It freezes like a dream, can be made in big or small quantities, can be used for so many purposes. It is also, of course, absurdly easy: you sauté a few green vegetables, and blitz them until perfectly smooth. That's it.

Please don't be concerned by the quantity of beautiful olive oil in this recipe. You can use less! It won't be as silky and decadent, but you can. Anyway, use it like a condiment; use it with discretion; assume the Mediterranean diet and live forever. (Feel free, also, to add more. Pour more over to store, at least, but add more if you want it to be even silkier.) This does one good main meal for 4 with pasta, and then a bit leftover for toast and sandwiches and dips.

MAKES ABOUT 8 PORTIONS

100ml + 100ml very good green olive oil
6 garlic cloves
1 lemon
2 courgettes
1 head broccoli
100g pecorino cheese
10 big stems of cavolo nero (up to about 200g)

Take your biggest skillet or shallow casserole. It needs to fit a lot in it – two courgettes, two heads of broccoli – so go as large as you can.

Over a medium flame, warm 50ml of the olive oil. Bash the garlic cloves with the end of a rolling pin, or similar, and take off the skins. Chuck the garlic into the oil whole (bashed, but basically whole) and let them sizzle a little. This is such a good way to get a lot of garlic oomph without it catching and blackening. (I'm not averse to burnt garlic, but it's often the *only* flavour in whatever it's in – which is, ideally, not what we're after here.)

Zest in the lemon. Grate in the courgette (I turn the box grater 90 degrees, for the bigger holes) and stir. It will instantly smell unreal. Let it simmer for a bit while you finely chop the broccoli. Toss that in too, and stir again.

Keep cooking. If it starts sticking (it shouldn't; it's full of lovely golden olive oil), stir it. Cook for about 35 minutes: in this time, shred the cavolo nero and grate the pecorino. You can also juice the lemon.

☞

GREEN SAUCE

When the broccoli is perfectly soft – much softer than al dente, practically falling apart – taste. You will probably want to season: go wild with black pepper, but go easy on salt for now. Throw in the cavolo nero, and cook for 5 minutes more.

Decant into the food processor. Add the lemon juice, and the pecorino. Drizzle in the remaining olive oil. You may need to add some cold water, too, if it looks like it isn't smoothing enough. Blend until perfectly smooth.

Toss through pasta, and top with more pecorino and black pepper. Spread on pizza, and top with mozzarella. Dollop into slices of toasted sourdough, along with fresh tomatoes, soft sheep's cheese, and prosciutto. Dip crudités into it.

Notes and Queries

I think this is probably the best combo of green things, but you know what: knock yourself out. If you've got one courgette and two heads of elderly broccoli! If you've got a mega-bag of kale! If you've got a variety of cruciferous stuff going gently grim in the bottom of the fridge!

The Bright Green Sauce

If you don't have a recipe for salsa verde, may I offer you this extremely ramshackle version? I blitz together whatever herbs are in the fridge with anchovies, Dijon mustard, garlic, oil and salt until it tastes right. Then I use it on everything: soft egg pittas, strips of tender steak, white fish, toast, rice, pasta...

All quantities are relative. All ingredients are relative. Taste, taste, taste. It should be luminously zingy and fresh and bright. You will not taste the anchovies.

ABOUT 4, GENEROUSLY

50ml olive oil
1–2 garlic cloves, peeled
50g parsley
10g basil
10g coriander
1 green chilli
2–4 anchovies
2 teaspoons Dijon mustard
1 tablespoon white wine vinegar

Blitz smooth, really smooth. Taste. Salt. More oil? More vinegar? A splash of water to loosen it?

The Black Dal

About a thousand years ago, when the world was new, I was talking at an event about how much I loved the black dal at Dishoom.[†] The black dal at Dishoom is properly called *dal makhani*: buttery, rich, intense, a complete and perfect meal by itself. Give me black dal and a roti and I could be happy forever. I would never get bored with the black dal.

This was, I must make clear, so long ago that this was still an opinion worth saying out loud: now, I think, it's become such received wisdom that it's like saying you love kittens or sunshine. To love the Dishoom black dal is to be human; to eat the Dishoom black dal, divine.

Anyway, I said all this. And then, after the event, a person came up to me and asked me if I wanted to know her auntie's secret to perfect black dal.

The best advice I can give anyone interested in food is to always say yes to questions like this. I always love to be told a secret, but the secrets of an auntie? In culinary matters? A blessing from the heavens.

I told the person yes, please. And the person said to me: *the secret to perfect black dal is Heinz tomato soup.*

I mean, my God. This is the kind of secret I live for, and now I give it to you. It not only works, but it is transformative. It shaves at least a couple of hours off the cooking time, although it is still the slowest possible business, but it also adds something indefinably delicious that I can't quite explain. I made five batches of black dal in one day, using four different recipes and one secret Heinz tomato, and the Heinz tomato won in every taste test hands down. The texture was better! The flavour was better! It was outrageous.

Black dal is never going to be a quick dinner, but it is, at least, an easy one, and the most delicious thing you will ever eat. There is no getting around the fact it will take you fully all day, which is why it's in here: for the week ahead, for the months ahead. You're cooking not just for tonight (and you should eat it tonight) but for the future: make an enormous batch and freeze it in portions, and you will be grateful every day going forwards that you did it. Even if it's not even a day you're planning to eat it, you'll know it's there. And you'll feel better for it.

This is not the Dishoom black dal, in that it has different timings, different quantities of most ingredients (if not the lentils themselves) and also several different ingredients, including tinned

[†]*Dishoom is a small chain of Indian restaurants which have also become a kind of cultural phenomenon. This is because their food is very, very nice; and also because their branding is* unreal. *To go to a Dishoom is to have a classy time! They will give you a great allergen menu! They will keep the lights at a good level, play good music, and the food will be delicious! Dishoom: a reliably good time. This could be their new slogan, should they need it. I have never had a bad time in a Dishoom. Everyone loves Dishoom, and I am no exception*

☞

soup, but it is *like* the Dishoom black dal in that it is the best one, and also I cribbed extremely careful notes from their cookbook on *how* they get it so good. It is not the Dishoom black dal, but it is the Dishoom knowledge.

The second most useful thing anyone has ever told me about making black dal – after 'the tomato-soup trick' – is the bit in the Dishoom cookbook which explains that it's less about timing, and more about noticing. I love an instruction like this because I always worry, when I'm cooking to a recipe, that things aren't going exactly as written: things take longer! Things go faster! It's a minefield! So I love to be told to just give in. Keep your eyes open; keep stirring and tasting; you'll be fine. This goes for all recipes, not just this one. This makes a vast quantity. It does about 4 meals of 4 with rice and bread, but I'm most often eating it solo.

MAKES ABOUT 12 PORTIONS

300g whole urad dal
2 black cardamom pods
1 cinnamon stick
2 teaspoons cumin seeds
¼ teaspoon cloves
4 teaspoons coriander seeds
2 teaspoons garam masala
1 teaspoon chilli powder
50g garlic purée
50g ginger purée
50g tomato purée
400g tin Heinz tomato soup
100g butter
2 tablespoons double cream (coconut yoghurt is a great substitute)

Wash the dal really, really well. I do this in three changes of water: dal into your biggest saucepan full of cold water, stirring it with my hand so it all floats about, letting it settle down again; and then repeating. Then I rinse it in a sieve until the water runs clear.

Back into the saucepan; cover with a lot of cold water (to the top of the pan, pretty much). There is something very peaceful about looking at black lentils under very clear cold water. Set pan over a medium heat to bring to the boil. Back down to a simmer. Skim off any grotty scummy bits if they arise and add more boiling water if it looks a bit dry.

Cook for a good long time, until the dal is very soft. 3 hours. Maybe even 4. This is a big time difference, for sure! The thing here is to know when the dal is done: if you squeeze a single lentil, it should be creamy, not crumbly and hard.

Tip the cardamom pods, cinnamon stick (snapped), cumin seeds, cloves and coriander seeds into a spice grinder or a pestle and mortar. Grind fine, and mix with the garam masala, chilli powder, garlic, ginger and tomato purées.

Drain the dal and return to the pan. Add the tomato soup, the spice purées, and the butter. Top up with 200ml cold water. Turn the heat up, and cook for 30 minutes, stirring the whole time.

Turn the heat down, and keep cooking. Keep stirring. This is the commitment bit. You will need to be stirring pretty regularly to stop it sticking for, oh, about 2½ hours. You can do other things too! And it's totally worth it! But you need to have an eye on the hob, and be ready to stir with vigilance. If you can see the lentils above the surface, top it up with boiling water.

The creaminess must come from within the lentils, not just because the water has all boiled off. Keep stirring; keep tasting. You'll know when it's nearly there because it will taste almost like a perfect black dal. The individual lentil bits will break down and start to thicken, and you will just know. You will!

Dollop in the cream, and stir. 10 minutes, lowish heat. Serve with rice, flatbreads, a spoon straight into the saucepan. The rest – about the same again, twice – goes into Ziploc bags, laid flat, in the freezer. Your future self has never loved you more.

Cure-All One-Pan Beans

I used to call these 'smoky brothy herby beans', mostly because that was what I kept typing into Google. I had a yen for something! I had to know if it existed!

What I was hoping for was, like, something very green-feeling: something bright *and* smoky at the same time, if such a thing were possible, like a fire made of new wood. Like the first cold days of spring: lively and outside-ish and fully wholesome.

There are approximately ten billion recipes for things called 'smoky beans' or 'brothy beans' or 'herby beans', in various combinations, but none of them were my thing. Imagine my joy, then, when a nice person named Farzaneh told me about a Persian soup called *aash-e-jow*.

It was, basically, everything I had dreamed of. It had a bizarrely curative effect, thanks, I think, to all the beans and lentils and barley: it made everything feel better.

I cannot promise this is an authentic aash-e-jow. In fact I can promise you, probably, that it is not. I am not Persian. I have never been to Iran. It's just that I think these smoky brothy herby beans are the beans of my dreams,.

I make this in quantity – probably 4 1-litre ziplock bags, so 4 big meals – and freeze it. It is literally always welcome.

4 echalion shallots
6 garlic cloves
4 tablespoons extra-virgin olive oil
1 teaspoon ground turmeric
2 teaspoons ground cumin
400g kidney beans, jarred or tinned
400g chickpeas, jarred or tinned
150g pearl barley
75g basmati rice
75g green lentils
1.5 litres stock
50g dill
50g parsley
50g coriander
20g mint, plus a few extra leaves for garnish
200g baby spinach
2 tablespoons yoghurt
20g crispy onions (p. 241)

Finely chop your shallots and mince your garlic. Heat 2 tablespoons of oil in a large shallow pot, ideally with a lid, over a medium flame. Add the chopped shallots and cook for 5 minutes. Turn the heat down and add the garlic, turmeric and cumin.

Stirring gently, cook for another 5 minutes. Add the beans, the chickpeas, the barley, rice and lentils. Stir to combine, and pour over the stock. Bring up to a simmer.

Lid on; cook for 45 minutes on a low heat. If it needs more liquid – if it looks solid and not brothy – feel free to splash in some more water.

At some point, strip your herb leaves from their stems, and finely mince the leaves along with the spinach. Fold all through the broth. Cook for another 15 minutes.

Serve in the big pot, drizzled with good olive oil, dolloped with yoghurt, scattered with a little more mint and crispy onions.

You need literally nothing else. Just spoons.

Notes and Queries

If you would like to soak your own beans, be my guest. Couldn't be me! These weights are for chickpeas and kidney beans already soaked, cooked, and ready to eat.

You can fiddle around with the proportions of these herbs, depending on what is in your fridge, but do not skip the dill. The dill is important!

This is a fantastic 'new baby' gift.

The Chicken Matrix

A roast chicken is the ultimate low-effort high-reward dinner, but it is also the ultimate thing to have in the fridge at all times. I like to make one on Sunday nights, sometimes for eating in a fancy way, sometimes just for having around. Sandwiches! Salads! Pies! Soups! Pasta bakes! Pancakes! What is best is when you can make a chicken, and have one fancy meal, and then another, *also fancy but completely different meal* with it the next night. It's a double win!

I really am not great at leftovers: I get bored, I get sad. I like food and cooking so much it makes the evening feel sort of shapeless to me if it's the same thing as the day before. I know I'm alone in this – everyone else I've ever lived with has been delighted by the fact I won't touch the Tupperwares in the fridge – but I must speak my truth: I love to repurpose, but I hate to reuse as is. I hate to eat the same thing twice! This is why chicken is a perfect week-ahead thing: you can transform it fully, totally, into something else.

So. Spatchcock your chicken (see opposite). Stick it in a heavy skillet, if you have one, or a plain old roasting dish if not.

Pick a flavour; pick a matching side, or sides; pick a matching carb. Chicken in the oven. Make your sides; buy your carb.

Chicken fully cooked? Juices running clear? Inside temperature at 75°C? (Get a meat thermometer, it will change your life.) Feast. Leftovers in the fridge.

Feast tomorrow as well.

HOW TO SPATCHCOCK A CHICKEN

The reason it is vitally important that you know how to spatchcock a chicken is that it means you can make a delicious roast chicken in *under an hour*. I think 'under an hour' is the key to making a recipe feel like your friend. The ratio of stress to time in cooking is not linear – I don't think they will let me put a graph in here, but basically 15–45 minutes is the sweet spot. Things that take one minute? Stressful, weirdly, often involves hot oil. Things that take three and a half hours? Stressful in a whole new way: it's not enough; it's too much; it's a big chunk of your day! (There's another sweet spot where something takes, like, ten hours, because then you really have to commit.)

So the basic sweet spot, for regular cooking, is under an hour. Which means that in order to eat the best, low-effort, high-reward dinner in said sweet spot, you have to get the backbone out of the chicken and flatten it down in a skillet.

Very easy to spatchcock: pair of big kitchen scissors (or poultry shears, to which I have recently upgraded – and it is truly an upgrade), and flip the chicken over. Cut neatly down one side of the little spine – through the skin and bone! – until your scissors come out the other end. Now cut down the other side of the little spine. Remove spine, possibly to make stock with, possibly just to the bin.

Turn right way up, and put into, ideally, a cast-iron skillet. Press down hard. You want the legs kind of splayed, and then folded outwards to mostly fill the skillet, and have maximum contact with hot iron.

Fifty-five minutes; 190°C.

Flavour	Side	Carb
Honey Butter: mix 2 tablespoons salted butter with 1 tablespoon honey + 1 tablespoon honey to drizzle.	**Sharp green salad**, lots of rocket, big handful of flat-leaf parsley, toasted walnuts, sweet white balsamic drizzle. (Buy the drizzle.)	For the **crispiest, tiniest, butteriest potatoes**: chicken in the skillet; the smallest new potatoes you can get all around, underneath, cubes of extra butter tucked in the pan with rosemary sprigs, plenty of sea salt.
Buttermilk Americana mix: 2 tablespoons buttermilk or thin plain yoghurt; 1 teaspoon MSG, 2 teaspoons salt, 1 teaspoon celery salt, 1 teaspoon onion powder, 1 teaspoon garlic powder, 1 teaspoon ground ginger, 3 teaspoons paprika, 2 teaspoons white pepper, 2 teaspoons black pepper.	**Corn on the cob:** daub with jalapeño butter – mash 2 tablespoons butter into 1 tablespoon finely chopped pickled jalapeños – wrap each buttered cob in foil and bake for 30 minutes alongside the bird. For impeccable **KFC-vibes gravy:** 1 tablespoon butter, 2 tablespoons flour for a roux, plus all the juices from the chicken, plus a tablespoon of honey.	**Mustard mash:** normal mash, extra butter, plus 1 heaped tablespoon Dijon mustard. Stir until smooth. You're welcome.
Sticky Gochujang: use the glaze from Sticky-Crispy Tofu (p. 45): mix 50g gochujang, 50g dark brown soft sugar, 50ml rice wine vinegar, 2 tablespoons soy sauce, plus 4 garlic cloves + 30g ginger, all peeled and grated.	**Pickled cucumber:** slice in half lengthways; de-seed; slice thinly; half-fill a little Tupperware or jar with rice wine vinegar, 50g caster sugar, and 2 tablespoons fine salt. Shake. Add cucumber slices, set in fridge until chicken is ready. Kimchi from a shop.	**Coconut rice:** 400ml tin coconut milk, 1 coconut-milk tin chicken stock, 1 coconut-milk tin jasmine rice. Cook 15 minutes, low heat, lid on.
Miso Butter: 4 tablespoons unsalted butter + 2 tablespoons white miso + 3 crushed garlic cloves	**Roasted onions:** quarter 3 big red onions. Tuck around chicken in skillet before roasting.	**Stock-braised butter beans:** 700g best-quality jarred butter beans, 4 sprigs thyme, 500ml chicken stock, 4 garlic cloves, peeled but not chopped; cook over a low heat until the stock is all evaporated(20 minutes?), and blob of crème fraîche. Black pepper.

Leftovers

Chicken soup, a universal good: especially when it's a leek, potato and rocket chicken soup. If you kept the chicken spines, this is the place to deploy them. If you didn't (hello, welcome, this is your book too), then it's fine too. Either way, take 1 litre of very good chicken stock, 4 rosemary sprigs, 6 garlic cloves and a glass of white wine. Parmesan rind if you have it. Simmer for 30–60 minutes. Fish out the chicken spine if you used it. Sauté 4 finely chopped shallots, 2 finely chopped garlic cloves and 2 big leeks, also finely chopped, in some butter. Chop the leftover potatoes in half, and add them and any leftover shredded chicken to the pan. Five minutes, until piping hot. Pour over the broth. Five minutes more. This keeps the vegetables tender and with texture, not just mush. Just before serving, wilt any leftover rocket directly into the broth. Grate over Parmesan and lots of black pepper.

Potato and sweetcorn fritters with crispy chicken: mix leftover mash and corn kernels with an egg and a spoon of flour to make a soft batter. Heat 1 tablespoon of oil in your biggest pan over a medium heat and fry leftover shredded chicken until crispy and hot through. Set aside. Add another tablespoon of oil and, when shimmering, dollop in the batter in tablespoon-sized dollops. Cook for 3 minutes, or until brown-y golden, then flip. Serve with crispy chicken, reheated gravy, a drizzle of honey and a sprinkling of sea salt.

Korean 'pasta' bake: mix leftover juices with 1 big glug of chicken stock, handfuls of shredded chicken, handfuls of grated mozzarella, 4 finely chopped spring onions; and 500g little rice noodles. Normal pasta is good too, but you'll need a bit more stock. More cheese on top. Sesame seeds. Bake for 15 minutes at 180°C.

Pot pie: warm leftover beans with leftover chicken juices. Lightly crush butter beans to thicken the sauce. If you need to feed more, fold in a second jar of butter beans. Leftover chicken, shredded, leftover onions. Check for seasoning – more miso? more thyme? Little enamel dish; little shop-bought puff pastry lid. Brush with beaten egg; sprinkle with sesame seeds. Bake for 25 minutes at 180°C.

Flavour	Side	Carb
Ginger Soy: take all the trimmings from the ginger you used for scallion sauce, or about 40g ginger, peel and all. Blitz with 30ml light soy, 20ml dark soy, 20ml rice wine, 2 peeled garlic cloves, 1 tablespoon brown sugar until smooth.	**Wilted greens:** wash well, tuck into skillet in the oven when you turn off the heat – let chicken rest and greens steam for 15 minutes – scallion sauce (p. 239)	**Brown rice:** more water than you think, more salty than you think.
Garlic Rosemary: 4 tablespoons roasted garlic purée, 2 tablespoons olive oil, black pepper, 4 sprigs of rosemary tucked around and underneath.	**Roasted lemon Tenderstem:** packet of Tenderstem, roughest ends trimmed. Zest and juice of 1 lemon. 1 tablespoon olive oil. Lots of black pepper. Stick in alongside the chicken for his last 15 minutes.	**Focaccia:** focaccia (buy this from a bakery, for God's sake).
Smoky Cumin: 2 tablespoons cumin, 2 tablespoons smoked paprika, 1 tablespoon brown sugar, 1 tablespoon sunflower oil, 1 tablespoon smoked water.	**Fajita traybake:** 3 red onions, 4 peppers, both thinly sliced, ½ tablespoon chilli powder, ½ tablespoon coriander powder, 1 tablespoon garlic powder, 1 tablespoon oregano, ideally Mexican, no worries if not. Baking tray. Last 15 minutes of chicken. Coconut yoghurt, plus a big pinch of salt, 1 clove of grated garlic, a drizzle of avocado oil: crema for lazy lactose-intolerants. Salsa (p. 164, p. 295, out of a jar.) Guacamole.	**Little tacos** (p. 166), or buy from shop.
Classic MidChick: ginger, garlic, lemon juice, Dijon, olive oil, herbs, chilli flakes. You know this song.	**Bag of salad**, don't bother with dressing, just chicken juices.	**Baguette, butter.**

Leftovers

I am insanely picky about **egg-fried rice**. This is the only good one: cold rice, hot pan, sesame oil, stir lots, shredded chicken, frozen peas, heat down, egg in middle, beat with chopstick, serve, and don't skimp on soy and sweet chilli sauce if you have it.

Crispy broccoli, reheated in a dry frying pan, is spectacular on toast. Rub focaccia toast with garlic, drizzle with olive oil, shreds of cold chicken, top with crispy broccoli and shaved Parmesan.

Green chickpea quesadillas (p. 107), souped up! Shred the chicken, spoon in any leftover peppers and onions, dip into guacamole and crema.

Caesar salad: leftover salad leaves, leftover chicken, p. 98, for dressing, plus baguette croutons: thin slices, drizzled with olive oil, rubbed with garlic, baked in the oven at 150°C for 20 minutes.

Coconut Breakfast Bars

What if a cereal bar, but good for you, and also nice? What if something that can be eaten with joy and wholesome feelings at 8am, but also at 4pm with a cup of tea? What if a lunchbox treat, or a pocket picnic? What if something actually nice to tide you over to the next thing? What if a snack, but the kind of snack that makes you feel better instead of my usual fare of 40 olives eaten straight out of the jar?

I am fussy on cereal bars. I like what I like! I don't like it any other way! I don't like a cereal bar to be cake-y or stodgy or too sweet – it's not pudding, it's breakfast or a 4pm lift – and I want it to have plenty of texture but not to fall apart when you bite into it. I don't want to be picking bits of oatmeal out of my own hair in a meeting at any point in the day. I don't want there to be any dairy or any pure sugar that makes me feel bad about eating it at 8am. This means no golden syrup, my otherwise most treasured friend, or I will feel like it's too much treat for so early in the day.

I googled around a bit, read a few cookbooks, tried a few, threw a lot out or gave them to my partner, a much less picky eater.

Then I remembered. Back in the olden days, when my life was quite a lot worse than it is now (see books passim for details), and I had to leave the house in darkness most mornings to go somewhere very depressing with limited snacks…I made these all the time. They were lodged in a folder on an old laptop for a cookbook I never wrote – *Hospital Food Done Better* – and I had let them drift away from me as a relic of the horror, but now they came back to me with hope in my heart.

The original idea was a Nigella one from about twenty years ago – maybe *Nigella Express*? – but they are probably the most adaptable things I know. The Nigella trick, which I assume she doesn't do any more as a sophisticated person, is condensed milk. (She has an updated version online with chia seeds instead.)

I swapped the condensed milk for condensed coconut milk – easy to buy online, phenomenally delicious – and flipped back through my lists of nuts and seeds and berries. I had made them every which way, and I was delighted to find that they were still as adaptable as ever. As adaptable, and as delicious, and as perfectly suited to my fussy list of demands as I could wish. We were off to the races. They are the perfect cereal bars, in my opinion: dense but not heavy, chewy without being sticky, snackable but not too filling, full of nuts and fruit and seeds. They improve with age, if you keep them in a big tin, and if you can stop eating them. Wrapped up, they slip perfectly into a pocket or a lunchbox. They can suit basically any need, any time, any cupboard. Whatever you have.

This makes 2 big jars, but we get through them. Halve this recipe if there's fewer of you eating snacky-type breakfasts.

☞

PLAIN FLOUR

MAKES 24

75g almonds + 75g hazelnuts (150g total nuts)
300g rolled oats
50g desiccated coconut
150g dried cherries
150g mixed seeds
1 teaspoon fine sea salt
1 teaspoon ground ginger
420g condensed coconut milk (2 small tins, available online)

Carefully line one big, or two normal sized, baking dishes. I use two Pyrex dishes that measure 21cm x 21cm, but truly whatever you have will be fine. Just line with baking parchment. Pre-heat the oven to 150°C.

Roughly chop, or blitz briefly, the almonds and hazelnuts (or whatever nuts you have). You're not looking for a nut flour here; just, maybe, halfway to nut flour.

Stir the chopped nuts with the oats, the coconut, the dried fruit and the seeds. Add a good pinch of salt, and the ground ginger. Stir.

Warm the condensed milk in either the microwave or a sturdy saucepan. (It's kind of a weird consistency if you're expecting coconut milk or condensed milk, but warming it brings it more in line with what we need.) Tip warm condensed milk into lovely cereal mixture. Stir.

Tip into prepared trays, and press down very nice and flat. The thicker they are, the denser they are. If you do it thin on a baking tray, it's like a Nature Valley bar, if that's not too dated a reference. If you do it thick, it's like a flapjack from a whole foods café. For me, somewhere between the two is perfect. Try it! See what you like!

Bake for 15 minutes, then turn the heat down to 130°C, and bake for another 35 minutes. Let cool in the dish for 15 minutes; then slice into bars with your sharpest knife. Eat one warm – crumbly, it's true, but so delicious – and put the rest into a tin for the week ahead.

Notes and Queries

150g mixed nuts, as you please.

150g of any dried fruit! 130g! 170g! Use up what you have in random bags and jars.

I buy the 150g bag of mixed seeds, but you can use a truly random assortment. Mega flexible! Pumpkin seeds are great.

Cinnamon, cardamom, mixed spice – all good swaps for ginger here.

397g tin of regular condensed milk is an easy swap if you want something you can find in any supermarket, but I love, love, love condensed coconut milk. Buy it online! Buy it next-day delivery!

I have done this with one tin of condensed coconut milk and two big apples cooked down into applesauce. A little more crumbly, but completely fine and quite good! I suspect you could also do banana. Let me know!

Tony's Treacle Anzacs

Drinking a proper mug of tea outside – actual mug, not from a Thermos – is one of life's genuine pleasures. Bonus points if it's not just in the garden: drinking a mug of tea from a mug on the beach, for instance, is an exquisite smugness known only to people who live on the seafront. It's like camping, but with none of the indignity. It's like the world belongs to you.

My absolute favourite place in which to drink a mug of tea outside, if you would like to know, is along the little path that winds down the valley of the Afon Dwyfor, in Gwynedd, north-west Wales. You climb down the mossy little steps on the side of the green grave of David Lloyd George, and you hold your tea carefully in both hands so it doesn't spill, and you fish in the pocket of your anorak for an Anzac biscuit, and you walk and you think and you drink your tea and eat your treacle, and the birds are singing and the river is rushing and everything is as it should be. I feel extremely happy whenever I am in north-west Wales. One of the times I am really happiest – in that bit of north Wales, but also in my entire life – is when I am at Tŷ Newydd, which is the National Writing Centre of Wales, and is on the banks of the Afon Dwyfor.

Tŷ Newydd is a beautiful old house that is full of books, and you can see the sea from the library window, and you can go and stay there and study and write and – sometimes – teach. In between bits of teaching, or writing, you can make yourself a cup of tea and Tony, who is the cook at Tŷ Newydd, may be persuaded to make a tray of Anzac biscuits. An Anzac biscuit, the way Tony makes them, is a flat, chewy, crispy disc of oats and coconut and treacle. I find them absolutely irresistible. I could eat ten thousand of them.

This recipe only makes about 24. Luckily, they are extremely easy, so you can make batch after batch after batch. I hope you find somewhere beautiful to eat them out of doors.

140g plain flour
50g golden caster sugar
80g dark brown soft sugar
110g rolled oats
80g desiccated coconut
125g salted butter
2 tablespoons black treacle
½ teaspoon bicarbonate of soda

Pre-heat the oven to 180°C. Line a couple of baking sheets with baking parchment.

Weigh out the flour, sugars, oats and coconut into a big bowl.

Melt the butter in a saucepan over a medium heat. Run a tablespoon under the hot tap (I just use a big metal tablespoon here, not the formal kind of tablespoon) to warm it up a bit, for the treacle. Spoon the treacle into the melted butter and stir. Dissolve the bicarb in 1 tablespoon warm water and stir that in too.

☞

Pour the wet into the dry, and stir to form a scoopable dough. Tablespoon-sized scoops, six to a tray. Bake for 15 minutes then gently flatten each risen cookie with a spatula to form a squashed, crispy, chewy disc.

Cool on a cooling rack, but eat one warm. At least one.

Cendrine's Cannelés

As Nigella to Henry James and mayonnaise,[†] so me to cannelé.

Cannelé are those little dark brown, hyper-shiny, frilly-topped cakes you get in expensive cafés and patisseries. They have a crispy, chewy outside, and an inside best described as 'squishy delicious honeycomb custard'. They are very sophisticated and elegant, etc., and are often the kind of *restrained-lady* option in a coffee shop. The recipes always say things like 'worth the effort' and 'practice makes perfect' and 'complex' and 'traditional' and this all, frankly, came as a deeply unwelcome surprise to me.

When I found this out I had been making and eating them for a year! I thought it was a normal and easy thing! I was an au pair in Paris with my best friend and we would make the batter on a Friday; our boss would bake the cannelés on a Saturday morning; they would eat them for breakfast; and then we would go off into the city, pockets full of still-warm cannelés, hoping to fall in love or make some great art or at the very least get invited to a cool party. Mostly we just wound up eating cannelés by the canal with a bottle of very cheap pink wine, inventing stories and drawing each other. It was probably better than any party to which we could have ever been invited, but that's the kind of thing you only realise in hindsight.

If we did get to a party, we could eat the cannelé on the night bus back to the suburbs. Then we could eat any cannelé still in the tin when we got home! Then we would make an enormous batch of cookies out of guilt for eating all the cannelés, and as a kind of I guess cultural exchange. The cookies would be consumed through the week, and then it would be Friday again, and it would be cannelé day.

Anyway, I came back to England and found out all this was not possible because cannelés are a complex and traditional dessert that take much practice and effort. I read a lot of recipes and felt too small and humble to even try. One million chefs, one million beeswaxed copper moulds.

Then I had an idea, and Googled the recipe in French. Joy of joys: not a chef in sight. Instead, early-internet-type forums full of helpful and officious middle-aged housewives vying to write the shortest and easiest cannelé possible. 'Mix wet into dry, let rest, bake 1h.' This? This I could do. I ordered a cannelé mould off the internet – silicone, £10, dishwashable and easy release – and set to.

Unbelievable. Unbelievable! Crisp, chewy, shiny, glossy, a little sticky, flecked with vanilla and dense with custard and kept like a dream. Not, perhaps, as unimpeachably elegant and stiff-shelled as if I had dipped the copper into beeswax, but easy like Sunday morning. Or, perhaps, easy like Saturday morning.

This makes 16 – a neat 5x3 row on the rack, plus 1 for the cook.

[†] *(How To Eat, p. 13, vital reading.)*

☞

50g butter + 20g extra for buttering
500ml whole milk
1 vanilla pod
2 tablespoons rum (optional)
1 egg + 2 egg yolks
250g caster sugar
120g plain flour

Melt the 50g butter (leave the 20g for now!) in a large saucepan. It needs to be big enough to also hold the milk and the eggs, so don't skimp.

Whisk the milk into the melted butter and scrape in the seeds from the vanilla pod. Vanilla extract will also work here, which I accept that you are much more likely to already own. But a vanilla pod is so nice and complex, no? Tip in the rum, if using, and turn the heat down very low. Simmer for 30 minutes until completely infused. Beat in the egg and yolks, and cook, whisking continuously, for 5 minutes.

Mix the sugar and plain flour together. Tip wet into dry, and stir to make a smooth batter: it's basically just custard. Cover tightly with cling film and put in the fridge until the morning.

Pre-heat the oven to 240°C. It's hot, I know! But worth it.

Melt the remaining butter (microwave ideal, otherwise sorry about making you wash up another pan) and coat the inside of your cannelé moulds. Swirl gleefully. Put buttered cannelé moulds into the fridge to chill while the oven comes up to temperature.

Batter into moulds, leaving space at the top for them to rise. Bake for 5 minutes at 240°C, then turn down to 210°C and cook for a further 40 minutes. Let cool for 15 minutes in the moulds, then turn out onto a cooling rack. You're looking for a burnished, almost burnt top, and a golden-brown bottom. They will get more solid and more squidgy as they cool. They will, in fact, only get better with time.

Velvet Ribbon Peach Cake

One of the most humbling moments of my life was explaining to my accountant just how much I had accidentally spent on velvet ribbons the previous year. Turns out? Velvet ribbons, not tax-deductible. Worth it though, to own such beauty. 'Velvet ribbon' might, to me, be the most beautiful words in the English language: either one alone carries more birthday-party-in-the-past magic than any other word, no? And together? Forget about it! How could I resist? Decadence in dusky pink and deep ochre. Sunset orange. Peach colours, in other words. How could anyone resist? Anyway, this cake is like velvet ribbon to me. Metaphorically, and in homage.

Please consider: a soft, vanilla-scented, lemon-hinted brown-butter batter. A ribbon of sunset-coloured peach jam. More soft crumb. A nubbly, biteable cardamom streusel, American coffee-cake style. A loaf tin for easy lunchboxes or late-night stress snacking. Cheaper and easier than the haberdashery aisle, and ten times more useful. Same feeling.

It takes a while, but it's not complex at all, and for a cake with components, it's surprisingly light on washing up. (You make the streusel in the brown-butter pan.)

Peach jam makes it a year-round cake (who, for the love of God, outside of, like, the American South, has so many perfectly ripe peaches they can bake with them?). It smells so, so good, this one. I find it very hard not just to eat the batter, especially at the crumble stage. Please don't flinch at the amount of butter and sugar. It's a cake. It's a joy. Either do it properly, or don't do it.

(Consider also: wrapping this in baking parchment, then brown paper, then tying with sunset-orange ribbon. Housewarming gift? Birthday present from afar? Either way: chic and delicious.)

250g salted butter
150g golden caster sugar
2 eggs
1 teaspoon vanilla extract
zest of 2 lemons, optional
80g yoghurt (thick sour cream is good too)
200g + 200g plain flour
1 ½ teaspoons baking powder
1 teaspoon + 1 teaspoon fine salt
150g soft brown sugar
1 tablespoon ground cardamom
200g peach jam

Before you do anything else – before you even think about baking – brown the butter. 250g salted butter, straight out of the wrapper, into a heavy-bottomed saucepan over a low heat.

Leave it alone. This is not a faff, just takes time. It melts; it browns; you pour it into a bowl and put it in the fridge or the freezer to stop being quite so liquid. It doesn't need to be set, you understand; just not hot, spitting fat. You can either wash up the saucepan, or you can cool the butter in a big bowl and make the streusel crumble topping in that. (I put the bowl in the dishwasher, so make it in the butter pan.)

Pre-heat the oven – only once the butter is cooling – to 180C. Line either a 2lb (1kg) loaf tin, or two 1lb (500g) loaf tins with greaseproof paper. I honestly just shove the paper in. It's fine. This recipe responds very well to being made as one enormous cake (takes ages but looks amazing), or two smaller cakes (more practical, less silly). It also freezes well, if freezing cake is in your wheelhouse.

Cream together the golden caster sugar, and 85g of the brown butter. I do this in the stand mixer with the paddle attachment. You're after light and fluffy, but it may just go lighter and fluffier. Beat in the two eggs; and the vanilla. If you would like to, you may zest in the zest of two lemons here. I love to put lemon zest in everything, but I understand that not every cake in this book can be a lemon cake.

Tip in the yoghurt, and beat well. It will look disgusting at this point, like it's not working, but that's fine. It's working. Add 200g plain flour, and the baking powder, and the salt. Beat until it looks – and tastes – like delicious cake batter.

Take your remaining brown butter, and mix in the soft brown sugar, the cardamom, the other teaspoon of salt. Add the flour slowly, and stir to form a crumble topping. You might need a little more flour; you might need a little less. It will depend how brown you took your butter. If you form big clumps with your fingers, then break them apart, you will get an excellent texture.

In (each of) your prepared loaf tin(s), layer as follows: half the cake batter, all the jam (big dollops, spread to cover the batter), the other half of the batter, the streusel.

Bake for 50 minutes (smaller) or a full hour and 20, if you went for the big guy. You will know it is done because a) your house will smell amazing and b) a skewer poked into the middle will come out clean. Don't worry if little caramelised bits of peach jam are finding their way to the surface, lava- style.

Caramel peach jam is illegally delicious, all smoky and burnt, like a late summer bonfire.

Lift out onto a cooling rack, and let cool completely before cutting into it. Or almost completely. The appeal of a warm slice of peach cake and a cup of coffee cannot – and must not – be denied.

On the Floor

Marmite and Rosemary Chicken Broth

Dumpling Omelette

Green Dumpling Soup

The Rice Bowl Matrix

Salmon and Jasmine Tea Rice

Sausage and Rocket Gnocchi

Cacio e Kimchi

Fish Finger and Smoked Sweetcorn Tacos

Spelt with Beans, Greens and Berries

Honey-Chorizo Jacket Sweet Potato

Miso and Peanut Burnt Aubergine

Carbonara Risotto and Friends

Almond and Cherry One-Bowl Cake

The Cookie Matrix

Lowest ebb.
Lowest effort.

Does thinking about cooking make you want to lie on the floor and sink into the earth? Is the thought of the shop just one thing too many today? Yeah, ok, you're in the right place. Here are the fastest dinners I have with the least washing-up and most likely to already be composed of something that is in your fridge or cupboard at this time *that are also really delicious and feel fancy*.

I have compiled them here because I fully believe that you will be able to accomplish at least one of these things tonight. And if you can't, *chapeau*, it's time for toast! You win the game! (But, listen: I do think you can. And I will be here to help. This is the point of this book. I really really think you can, and I have been at least as sad as you are right now – no, truly! – and I think you will feel better if you do. Ok? Ok. We will find a way!)

Marmite and Rosemary Chicken Broth

You know those nights when you really can't, but really should? Maybe this is what you need for those nights: cold, knackered, but still – somehow – determined to eat something that isn't just four crumpets and a packet of Hobnobs.

I never want to stand between a person and a packet of Hobnobs, and I never want to be on the side of should. But here I am anyway, because I think you need to know about this soup.

This takes half an hour from the moment you open the kitchen door to the moment you sink onto the sofa clutching your new best friend (soup). That's a real thirty minutes, by the way, not a chef thirty minutes: I am a slow cook at the best of times, and also I have timed this one with a stopwatch.

It will bend itself willingly to what you can get your hands on, but you can probably get your hands on everything you need pretty easily. You might want to grab one of those really good jars of beans, because that will elevate it a whole level, but fuck it: you'll be fine with the regular tins if that's what's in your cupboard. You will also be fine if you never soak beans in your life. I hate to soak a bean.

See also: this soup is made with chicken stock from a packet. *See also:* we're not even going to grate or mince the garlic. *See also:* Marmite instead of depth, time, or anything you'd need to go out and buy. You can't really taste the Marmite: you can just taste oomph.

This soup takes a good handful of shortcuts in order to take one liberty – toasting the rosemary – and I swear to you, it is the most hands-off five-minute liberty you will ever encounter. You merely shove the rosemary sprigs (with a few garlic cloves) into some nice olive oil. You do it in the pan you will use for everything, and you do it while you're doing the five-minute chopping of cabbage and shredding of chicken. (That's it; that's your whole job here.)

The crispy rosemary doesn't add any extra time or extra washing-up, but it makes it all feel – somehow, magically – extra special.

Crispy rosemary, to me, always feels like a treat. Whenever I get it on focaccia or garlic bread I'm always eyeing it up to make sure I've got the same (or more!) as the people around me, like a jealous kid with a bag of sweeties. I love it – and also, you need an extra texture with soup or you get sad. So you have crispy rosemary, and you're five minutes down; and then in the rosemary-garlic oil left in the pan, you throw in half a head of chopped cabbage, for health, and cook that until it's blackened and crispy, about another ten minutes; and then you put the rosemary and cabbage to one side, and add warm chicken stock, a spoonful of Marmite, and a jar of beans to the same rosemary-garlicky pan. You toss in some supermarket rotisserie-type chicken. You make some Marmite toast.

This is fancy café food: please imagine paying £9 for this somewhere in East London, ladled out to you from a vast tureen by a heavily pierced rockstar moonlighting as a waitress. Except, no: please imagine eating this exactly thirty-five minutes after you get home tonight. Five minutes to take off your coat and plug your phone in; thirty minutes to dinner.

☞

SERVES 4, GENEROUSLY, WITH LEFTOVERS

4 tablespoons extra-virgin olive oil
4 sprigs rosemary
4 fat garlic cloves
½ sweetheart cabbage
4 pre-roasted chicken thighs
750g cooked white beans (from a jar or tins)
750ml chicken stock
1 tablespoon Marmite
4 slices sourdough bread

Take off your coat; pour the olive oil into a big sauté pan with high sides, and set it over a medium heat to warm. Put your four rosemary sprigs into the oil.

Grab a chopping board and a knife. Peel each garlic clove and slice each one in half. Toss them into the oil too. This will infuse the oil, and in four minutes – when we're done chopping – we will turn up the heat to blister them and add an extra depth of flavour.

Shred your sweetheart cabbage (cut in half; one half in the fridge for tomorrow; other half cut side down on the board; thin slices horizontally, and the cabbage will just fall apart very neatly).

Turn up the heat on the sauté pan and cook the rosemary and garlic for another 90 seconds until it starts to blacken and crisp; the garlic, partially submerged in delicious oil, will kind of confit a little.

Yank out the rosemary, and throw in the cabbage. Stir to coat in the rosemary-garlic oil, and cook for ten minutes until blackened in places and a very bright green. You may need to turn down the heat a little, but just keep an eye on it.

Shred the chicken. Lift out the cabbage (I usually put it in a big glass Tupperware with the rosemary, because I know I will have leftovers from this soup for tomorrow and why dirty two dishes when you could use one?). Turn the heat down to a simmer.

Open the jar of beans, and tip the beans into the pan. Use the bean-jar (or a jug with a handle if you're worried) to measure out 750ml of chicken stock. (For me, that's two chicken stock pots and 750ml of hot water, YMMV.)

Stir your tablespoon of Marmite right into the hot chicken stock and tip the whole lot over the beans. Add the shredded chicken. Stir all together. A big twist of black pepper.

Simmer for 10–15 minutes; in that time make and Marmite some toast. Divide the cabbage between bowls. Ladle beany broth over cabbage. Serve with a drizzle more olive oil, the crisp leaves of rosemary. Bingo.

Notes and Queries

Don't use garlic purée here. The whole cloves are good and slicing them takes no time.

Any green will do.

I usually use those supermarket chicken thighs here because I can get them on the way home; if you live somewhere where they still have rotisserie chickens, please, please use them. Then again, if you live somewhere where they still have rotisserie chickens, why are you even reading this? You could be eating rotisserie chicken for dinner right this second!

Dumpling Omelette

If you have freezer dumplings, you don't really need this chapter. Freezer dumplings! Soy sauce! That's all a human being could ask for in this life!

And yet, and yet: what if dumplings, but more? What if dumplings, but more filling, more wholesome, and more of a meal? What if dumplings, but an omelette?

I kept seeing videos of people making their freezer dumplings with crispy little skirts - you just make a cornflour slurry and pour it around the dumplings as they pan-fry - and it looked to me like a crispy fried egg. Intriguing, I thought. Eggs and dumplings? Egg-fried dumplings? Omelette dumplings? Fluffy soft golden eggs, spiked with soy and chopped chives, set with crispy fat little dumplings, splashed liberally with chilli crisp? It seemed like a no-brainer, and indeed, it is.

This one is ideally for one, maybe two people. More than that and you would need such a big pan and so many eggs that the thing would cook in a strange way: you need a small frying pan, about the size of a side plate.

My friend Fiona described this as the most important culinary innovation since salted caramel and while I don't think it's my sole innovation, I did come by it honestly, and now I give it to you. I am eating a dumpling omelette as I type this and already I am sad that it will soon be over.

SERVES 2

2 tablespoons neutral oil
8 frozen dumplings
4 eggs
2 tablespoons soy sauce
2 tablespoons chopped chives
1 teaspoon butter
10g Cheddar (optional)
a big handful of pea shoots (rocket?)
2 tablespoons chilli crisp (optional)

Heat the oil over a medium heat in a little frying pan with a lid. Chuck in the dumplings. They will spit, so cover with the lid fast, and leave for 5 minutes to brown and crisp. In this time, beat the eggs with the soy sauce, folding through the chopped chives.

Return to the dumplings. Add the butter, and swirl. Flip the dumplings over, so that the crispy bit is on top, and arrange in a kind of flower shape, with corners pointing in.

Pour the egg mixture between the dumplings, as if you're filling in the background. Cover, and cook for about 2 minutes. If you're using: grate over the cheese. Lid off, and start to swirl the pan, so that the egg mixture creeps up the sides, forming a pretty kind of almost lattice.

Slide onto a plate; fill the spaces between dumplings with a bag of rocket. Spatter with chilli crisp. Maybe a splash more soy? Maybe a drizzle of Kewpie mayo? Devour.

Notes and Queries

I tend to use the pork and chive dumplings for this. Pork and eggs and green onion, it's a classic winner. Leek also good. Have not tried with kimchi.

As I am constantly saying to people, in Korea they put cheese in ramen. Which makes this a fun and legitimate twist rather than the actions of a lunatic.

Pea shoots are the best thing here because they are so pretty. Will you be able to get pea shoots on the kind of night you're on the floor? Absolutely not. Rocket is really wonderful too.

You may need slightly less egg, depending on your pan. Try it and see.

鮮蝦豬肉
衝擊味蕾
只愛功夫
BEST BEFORE
21.11.2026
Frozen At
Boil
8 Minutes

Green Dumpling Soup

The concept is very simple and yet, somehow, worth writing down: you know those shop-bought dumplings (or tortellini, or whatever)? *You should make them into soup.*

Furthermore, you can use that soup as a vehicle for every kind of green leaf or brassica you can imagine, or, more pertinently, every kind of green leaf or brassica you currently have taking up space in your fridge.

You can go cheat's *tortellini in brodo*. You can go cheat's *wonton soup*. You can make something like a cheat's hybrid cross between those two things, if you want, and if you do I recommend you choose a tortellini with pancetta in it for maximum joy.

You need not even trouble yourself with a knife or a chopping board, if you don't want to, and you can have a fully acceptable and wholesome and delicious dinner ready to go in sub-15 minutes from the moment you start thinking about it.

You simply take your stock – chicken stock, for us, but bouillon also slaps, and you could probably get a lot of mileage out of a high-end beef guy – and bring it to a simmer.

You add a few – very few! – extras: two garlic cloves, unpeeled. Fish sauce and a whole bit of ginger for dumplings, black pepper and a splash of olive oil for pasta. You simmer while you do everything ('everything') else.

You wash a lot of spinach. A lot of spinach: it will wilt right down.

If you want to involve a knife, you could chop a head of broccoli? You could slice up any other greens you've got going on? You could consider, if you like, herbs: basil and chives work in both cases. Maybe you want some spring onions for dumplings; maybe a sprig of rosemary for pasta? It's not strictly necessary but we love a flourish. You chop the herbs, if you want herbs, and if you're involving that knife.

You throw your dumplings-slash-pasta, frozen or straight from the fridge, into the simmering broth. You cook them for 2–4 minutes, depending on initial temperature. You chuck in lots of spinach. You chuck in the herbs. If it's pasta, you top the broth with more olive oil and grated Parmesan. If it's dumplings, you top the broth with chilli crisp and sesame seeds.

Here's why it's worth writing down: the first time I made this someone said 'I actually didn't know this...would be allowed'. Listen: it's allowed. It's actively encouraged.

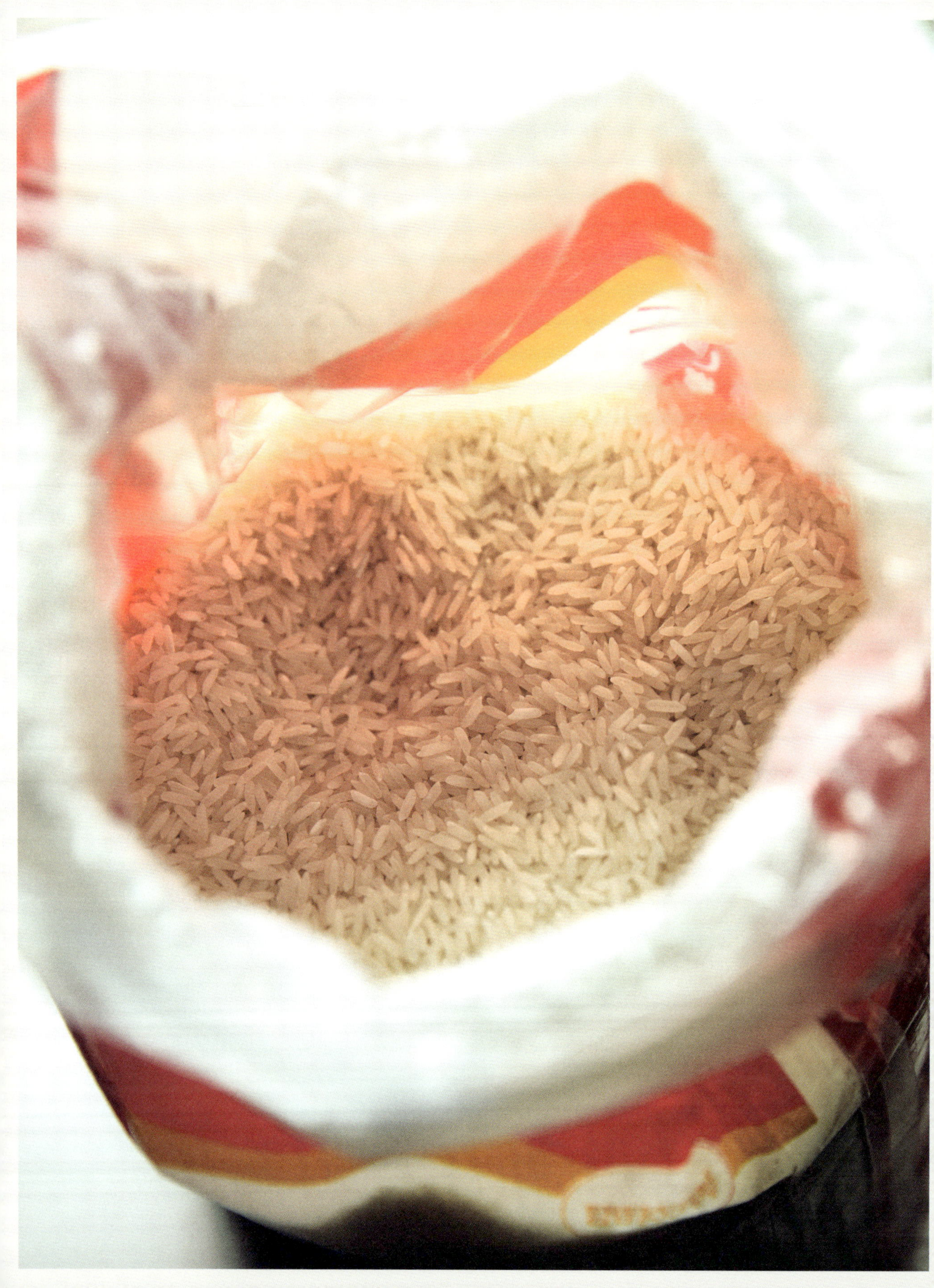

The Rice Bowl Matrix

A friend of a friend of a friend once started a new job at a marketing agency. Pencils sharpened, face shining, there he was: keen as a knife and new as a needle. New desk, new laptop, enormous sack of rice. Enormous sack of rice? Enormous sack of rice.

'We have engraved our client's logo on every single one of these grains of rice,' the new boss told him, proudly. 'And what we want is for you...to tell us.... why we've done that.'

What?

'What we want is for you to tell us why we've had the logo of our client engraved on all this rice. That's why we hired you. We need someone to tell us why we've done that. So we can tell the client.'

And that's marketing, baby. And that's late-stage capitalism.

And that's what I think of every single time I open up a big sack of rice: someone painstakingly engraving a client logo on hundreds, thousands, of perfect white grains and having no idea why they were doing it.

I buy my rice in these big five-kilo sacks because rice is, pound for pound, my favourite food. Like Madame Bollinger, I eat it when I am happy and when I am sad, etc. There are quite literally one thousand ways to eat a bowl of rice, including plain, each one of which is perfect. I love it hot, I love it spicy, I love it cold, I love it drowned in tea or broth or stock, I love it saffron-scented or turmeric golden or olive-oil glossy. I love it with peas (fresh) and peas (dried). I love the smell of cooking rice; I love the way a clean napkin folded over a pot of steaming rice breathes the cleanest and most soothing scent in the world. I love the way it steams.

Unlike capitalism, some things tell their own stories. A bag of rice – a bowl of rice – is one of them. And I will never be tired of hearing it.

If someone wanted to engrave my logo on every grain of a five-kilogram bag of rice, I would be delighted. I don't have a logo. But it would be appropriate all the same.

☞

Rice	Protein	Vitamin
Butter miso: 1 tablespoon white miso, 2 tablespoons butter, 2 mugs boiling water, 1 mug basmati rice	**...prawns**, made crispy quickly in a pan with yet more butter and a garlic clove left whole...	**...edamame beans**, tossed in the same pan to warm through...
Butter stock: 1 chicken stock pot, 2 tablespoons butter, 2 mugs boiling water, 1 mug basmati rice	**...roast chicken leg**, slathered in Dijon mustard and a slab more butter, 20 minutes at 190°C...	**...broccolini**, tossed in alongside the chicken leg, and drizzled with white balsamic...
Butter stock: as above	**...pan-fried rump steak** (see p. 188), left to rest 10 minutes then sliced across the grain...	**...cavolo nero**, tossed in the steak juices and crisped for 3–5 minutes...
Garlic coconut: 400ml tin coconut milk, 200ml boiling water, 4 peeled whole garlic cloves, 1 teaspoon salt, 250g jasmine rice	**...fish fingers...**or, for sophisticates, white fish, wrapped in parchment, drizzled with oil and soy, and roasted for 7 minutes at 170°C...	**...steamed pak choi...** (pak choi under tap; wet pak choi in pan; pan on heat; lid on pan. Maybe a splash of oil. 3–5 minutes.)
Seaweed: 1 sachet/2 teaspoons dashi, 200ml fish stock, 200ml boiling water, 200g short-grain rice	**...crispy smoked tofu** (p. 45, without the sauce, and without pressing)...	**...spinach**, cooked down with garlic and sesame oil, 5 minutes in a frying pan on a medium heat...
Tea and lemongrass: 1 stick of fresh lemongrass, 1 jasmine teabag, 2 mugs boiling water, 1 mug jasmine rice	**...whipped tofu:** 300g firm tofu, blended with 2 tablespoons rice wine vinegar and 1 tablespoon white miso...	**...400g mushrooms**, roughly torn, and fried in the pan for the tofu with 2 tablespoons rice wine vinegar, 1 tablespoon fish sauce and 1 tablespoon light soy...

Bonus

...crispy shallots (p. 241)...

...Kettle Chips: trust me on this...

...salsa verde (p. 247)...

...chilli-crisp vinaigrette (p. 90)...

...sesame seeds and nori sprinkles...

....coriander micro-green, ideally, but what an ask...

Salmon and Jasmine Tea Rice

This is my secret weapon weeknight dinner. Now it can be yours too. There is one pan to wash up – a rice pan – and everything else can go in the dishwasher. It takes 20 minutes, start to finish. It is nourishing and it is delicious. It is better than it has any right to be! It feels kind of fancy? Butter, soy, rice, tea.

The simplest way to cook rice is by volume: I use American cup measurements for rice because, I don't know why. It just works for me. Take ½ cup, or about 100g, of jasmine rice per person; and 1 cup (200ml) of boiling jasmine tea per person. Leave the teabag in. Ideally, you will also throw in a stick of lemongrass, if you have it, but I'm not picky. Pour the tea, with teabag and lemongrass stick, over the rice into a small pan with a lid. Set over a low heat, and cook for about 10 minutes.

Ten minutes is enough time to sort the fish: turn the oven to 180°C. Then you line a baking tray with foil. You line it completely with foil, tucking the foil down around and under the lip of the tray. This is a very important step. Do not skimp on the foil. If you skimp on the foil you will find that you have to do proper washing-up – as in, scrubbing hard – and it will negate the ease of the dinner. This way, we're talking a quick rinse in the hot and soapies, and you're done.

Take your ordinary block of butter. Cut a thickish slice from the end – maybe, like, pound-coin thickness, although can you remember when you last held a pound coin? It's starting to feel like telling someone to measure in cubits. Let's say half a centimetre. You will want one piece of butter per fillet of salmon and one fillet of salmon per person.

Arrange the butter pats on the foil; pop a salmon fillet over each butter pat. Grind black pepper generously – really generously – over the salmon fillets. You can add other peppers – white pepper, Szechuan pepper – if you have them! What's important is to make a kind of gentle crust over the top.

Slide the salmon into the oven. Set a timer for 6 minutes. Check on the rice. Has it mostly absorbed the tea? Fantastic. Turn off the heat. Throw in a big handful of greens – cavolo nero, kale, some chopped broccoli – and wrap the lid tightly in a clean tea towel. Press the lid back over the pan, and set aside. The steam will cook the greens gently.

Remove salmon from oven. Pour over 1 tablespoon soy sauce (light is better; we for some reason usually have dark?) per person. Swirl to combine with melted butter to make salty, rich, delicious sauce. Fluff the rice.

Tea rice into bowl. Steamed greens on top. Salmon on top of that. Pour over butter-soy mixture. Chilli crisp to finish if you have it.

Sausage and Rocket Gnocchi

A simple question of gnocchi, broccoli, rocket and sausage. (A frog he would a-wooing go.)

Plus, little hoops of red chilli! A drizzle of honey! Parmesan on top! You can't miss. This is loosely based on my favourite pizza – white pizza, sausage, friarielli, chilli, salad – but in quick wholesome dinner fashion. I love it. Dinner in twenty minutes, coat to pyjamas.

Cooking gnocchi on a baking tray, in the oven, results in crispy chewy delicious little nuggets. I would describe them as, like somewhere between a roast potato and a noodle. Unsurprising, I suppose! But very, very nice.

Toss the gnocchi in olive oil; shove them in the oven with some chunks of sausage and purple sprouting broccoli and chopped red chilli. A splash of red wine vinegar! A drizzle of honey! Twenty minutes; a bag of rocket tossed through to wilt once you pull it out, and top with a grating of Parmesan. Dinner. Protein! Veg! Carbs! Salty, sweet, spicy, bitter, and umami for *days* and one pan you can shove in the dishwasher. If you chop the sausage with scissors, directly into the pan, it's not even a knife and it's not even a board.

You can be eating this in twenty minutes from now, and you will be cooking for maybe four of those minutes.

SERVES 2–4

6 sausages (400g)
2 red chillies
200g long-stem broccoli, washed and trimmed
500g fresh gnocchi
2 tablespoons olive oil
2 tablespoons red wine vinegar
1 tablespoon honey
2 tablespoons fennel seeds
60g bag rocket
30g Parmesan

Pre-heat the oven to 190°C.

Scissor open the sausages, and crumble onto a baking sheet. (Just do this with your hands if you can.) Scissor the red chillies into hoops, and cut off any knobbly ends of the broccoli.

Toss the broccoli, chilli hoops, gnocchi and sausage together on the baking sheet, drizzle with olive oil, red wine vinegar and honey. Season generously. Scatter over the fennel seeds.

Slip into the oven for 20 minutes, while you slip into something more comfortable (pyjamas).

Remove from the oven; toss the bag of rocket with everything, directly on the baking tray, until the rocket turns just a little brighter green and starts to wilt. Grate over Parmesan. Serve direct from the tray.

☞

Notes and Queries

This is a real case for a 400g six-pack of supermarket sausages, in whatever flavour you lay hands on first. I'm voting for something spicy, but *not* fruity. Skip the apple in favour of pepper or fennel – if you can get Italian sausage, my God, you're on a roll.

Skip the chillies! If you want to add dried chilli flakes instead, go wild.

Purple sprouting broccoli is great, but harder to get hold of and always needs a trim. The fastest possible answer here is the packets of washed, trimmed, Tenderstem broccoli. Proper broccoli works ok, but is very much not as good. Use it if you have to!

Skip the fennel seed!

Buy the pre-washed rocket, save yourself the hassle of washing and drying.

Swap out Parmesan for, well, listen, any cheese you want. A soft goat's cheese? A Taleggio? Even a mozzarella: some kind of soft sharp white to mimic the pizza base will be great here. Use what you have.

Cacio e Kimchi

Here's the thing: when you are very sad or very tired, the best thing to eat is buttered noodles with a small bit of cheese. *Cacio e pepe* is only buttered noodles with a small bit of cheese for grown-ups. The Korean comfort equivalent of *cacio e pepe* is probably something like *tteokbokki*: kimchi, rice dumplings, cheese.

Therefore: kimchi; cheese; spaghetti; toasted sesame seeds like a rich man's Parmesan. Plenty of black pepper to honour the Italian heritage; plenty of chopped kimchi for the Korean side (and my spiritual need to eat a lot of kimchi). A cheerful tablespoon of butter. You can add little crispy lardons – pork belly and kimchi are obvious friends, bacon and cheese ditto – or a swirl of tahini. You don't need either. Spring onions chopped over the top. Serve in, and eat from, the skillet it's made in. No bowls necessary. You're good as you are.

SERVES 2–4

1 tablespoon black peppercorns
100g spaghetti
1 teaspoon fine salt
2 garlic cloves
1 tablespoon butter
4 tablespoons kimchi (chopped if it's the tangly kind)
30g Parmesan
4 spring onions
2 tablespoons toasted sesame seeds

In a large, shallow casserole over a medium-low heat, toast the black peppercorns for a minute. Tip into a pestle and mortar and grind. (This is the most skippable step, by the way, but it does add something.)

In same large shallow pot, spaghetti. Don't be afraid to break it if it won't fit. Add just enough water to cover, the salt, and 2 garlic cloves, crushed but not peeled or chopped. Cook for about 8 minutes, or according to packet directions for al dente; set aside 2 tablespoons of the pasta water, and drain the rest. Return the spaghetti to the casserole, and add the butter and kimchi. Cook for about 3 minutes.

Turn off the heat: add a splash of pasta water, the pepper, and grate in all the Parmesan. Stir to smooth creaminess, adding a splash more water if you need until all the cheese has melted.

Using scissors, chop over the green parts of the spring onions. Scatter over the sesame seeds. Eat with chopsticks from the casserole.

☞

Notes and Queries

Squid ink spaghetti is absolutely knockout here, should you happen to have any. (Get some! It's such a fanciness!)

If you have no kimchi, a spoon of gochujang thinned with pasta water, and a handful of prawns, will do something phenomenal.

Fish Finger and Smoked Sweetcorn Tacos

The fish finger taco is, by now, old hat. Sorry to tell you! Everyone knows about the fish finger taco. You can buy it at Wahaca! The Tesco app has a recipe! *The Guardian* has a recipe! Ottolenghi has a recipe! But...do *you* have a recipe? More to the point, do you have *this* recipe?

The fish finger taco is the grubby descendant of Bajan fish tacos, and *tacos de pescado*. Both of these are beautiful and elegant things; and many fish finger taco recipes begin with having you painstakingly replicate the original shatteringly crisp batter and fishmonger's counter fresh-caught fillets, etc. Nori sheets! Deep-frying! Fantastic stuff. Couldn't be me.

Instead, we are of course talking regular fish fingers, from a regular shop, or your regular freezer. Zero faff required. Then we jazz it up with avocado (sliced), coriander (picked), mayo (bought), and, of all things – tinned sweetcorn. The sweetcorn is the star of the show. Unexpected!

It's fish fingers! It's tinned sweetcorn! It's a taco that takes those beloved things and transforms them into something beyond comprehension: something subtle, sophisticated, and eat-ten-thousand-right-now-able. This really makes me laugh, but it's also really, really good. It's crunchy; it's vibrant; it's sweet and sharp and addictive.

We're talking 12–15 minutes to grill the fish fingers, as per packet directions; we're talking 15–20 minutes on the salsa; we're talking 2 minutes to slice some avocado. And these things are concurrent! We're talking 20 minutes from zero to taco. That's 20 minutes to a full crowd-pleaser dinner.

SERVES 4

12 fish fingers
1 garlic clove
1 tablespoon sunflower oil
340g big tin sweetcorn
12 mini tortillas, flatbreads, wraps, whatever
1 avocado
1 teaspoon ground cumin
2 teaspoons roasted garlic purée
1 teaspoon smoked water
4 tablespoons chopped sweet pickled jalapeños

Fish fingers on, immediately. Before the coat comes off! Packet directions.

Smash the garlic clove, leaving the skin on is fine, and let sizzle with the oil over a low heat until golden. Swirl around sauté-type pan. Cook on low for 5 minutes, then remove the garlic.

Drain and add sweetcorn; turn heat up to medium-high. Put the extractor fan on. Cook for 10–15 minutes until the sweetcorn blisters and burns. Leave the kernels alone to catch and char. We are trying to make tinned sweetcorn taste like something fresh and new and just picked, or at least, like something delicious. Burn the corn on both sides, shaking the pan after a few minutes to get it blackened all over.

☞

zest and juice of 1 lime
2 tablespoons sunflower seeds
mayo, ideally squeezy
sriracha, always squeezy
small handful coriander, leaves picked from the stems

This is a good time to warm through some little wraps or tortillas, whichever you can get hold of, and thinly slice the avocado.

Fish fingers out. (Probably.)

Shake the cumin into the sweetcorn. Stir in the roasted garlic purée, the smoked water, and the chopped jalapeños. Add the lime juice, the lime zest, and the sunflower seeds. Stir.

Assemble tacos and eat as you go. Eat standing up if you need to. Taco; spoon of salsa; fish finger; drizzle of mayo; drizzle of sriracha. Coriander leaf. Fold taco and eat.

Notes and Queries

In terms of tortillas, there is a recipe for making exactly taco-sized tortillas on p. 166. Alternatively buy some small, soft tortillas. Or wraps. Or even flatbreads, though it will be less like a taco and more like a really fantastic sandwich.

I think sliced avocado works better here than guacamole, but if you want to buy a little tub of guacamole so you don't have to slice a single thing, please: be my guest.

Ideally, keep roasted garlic in your fridge at all times for just such an occasion. If not, you'll be ok with a couple of grated cloves of fresh garlic: wait until the sweetcorn has blackened; turn the heat down; let the pan cool off; and add the fresh garlic and a splash of olive oil. You will lose the amazing depth from the roasted garlic, but, like: still fine. Still nice dinner!

I love a hot, sweet jalapeño relish-type thing; if you can only get regular pickled jalapeños, like from a corner shop, that will be fine too. Chop them fine; add a teaspoon of honey to balance it out.

If you have 10 more minutes, I think you should make a cabbage salad for authenticity and also deliciousness. It is very simple. Ok: take half a sweetheart cabbage, and slice it thinly into a bowl. Sprinkle over a teaspoon of salt, and massage in. Massage cabbage vigorously for several minutes until it becomes soft and yielding. Add 2 teaspoons of Mexican oregano, and the juice of a lime. Voilà! Cabbage salad!

Spelt with Beans, Greens and Berries

I knew I was going to make this the moment I found out that borlotti beans are also called *cranberry* beans. I love a little wordplay, and also I love borlotti beans (the only bean I have ever successfully grown!). Borlotti beans are creamy and pretty, and dried cranberries are sharp and sweet and sour, and I hopped about with various greens and grains before landing on this particularly addictive combo. Two kinds of cruciferous vegetable! Wholesome spelt! Balsamic glaze, which feels lightly dated but in a way I am gently charmed by. Don't forget balsamic glaze!

I'm calling this a pilaf, which it isn't, but it's got pilaf vibes: soft grains, sweet berries simmered in stock, little treats (crispy baby Brussels sprouts) tucked in among the spelt. It's got that spoon-in-pan niceness that a pilaf has, and I love it.

It pretty much suits every diet; is accidentally vegan – it truly, truly doesn't need anything else, not even crumbled feta, although do knock yourself out if you want to give it a whirl – so it packs well into lunchboxes. It keeps well for a side/leftover lunch. It's got texture and flavour and salt and dark and sweet. It will work with basically any dried fruit, any bean, and any grain.

In a total pinch, you can skip the whole 'cooking grain' step and buy them in a pouch if you are truly, truly at the end of your tether and need it to be a one-pot wonder. A pouch of beans stirred through a pan of grains, greens wilted in, seasoned well, and eaten with a spoon and even just like that, it's still so, so nice. It's grains, greens and berries, like what a bear might eat. A wholesome bear!

If you *can* find it in you to boil a pan of water – truly all it is! – the simmer in stock is incredibly low-effort and adds a bunch of nice flavours and textures. Crisp! Crunchy! Soft! Slippery! Sharp! Sweet! The fastest and most wholesome dinner in the West! It takes *literally* 30 minutes from the second you open the door to your house for dinner to be on the table and you to be eating it.

It will take you less than 5 minutes to wash up afterwards, also: one pot, one tray, no knife, no chopping board, bowls, cutlery (or possibly just spoons from the common dish, pirate style).

SERVES 2–4

200g ready-trimmed baby sprouts
2 tablespoons extra-virgin olive oil
4 tablespoons balsamic glaze
400ml bouillon or stock
250g spelt grains
100g dried cranberries
2 big handfuls cavolo nero, leaves stripped from the stem
400g borlotti beans (jarred or tinned)

Sprouts onto a baking tray, ideally a deep one. Drizzle with 1 tablespoon olive oil and 2 tablespoons balsamic glaze. Shake to coat. Season generously. Put into the oven; turn the oven to 200°C. Roast for 20 minutes.

Bring the stock to a simmer, and tip in the spelt. Cook for 20 minutes, until almost all the stock is absorbed. Toss in the cranberries, stir, and add the cavolo nero. Cook for 5 more minutes until all the stock is fully absorbed. Fluff with a fork.

Drain and rinse the beans. Sprouts out of the oven, ideally crispy and blackened in places. Tip the beans onto the baking tray, and stir.

Combine beans and sprouts with spelt and berries and greens (either on the baking tray, or in the spelt pan, depending on which is better suited for serving). Check for seasoning. Drizzle with remaining olive oil, balsamic glaze.

Honey-Chorizo Jacket Sweet Potato

As simple as it gets, and yet so astoundingly effective. Are you already making jacket sweet potatoes? You should be. All the correct comfort/effort ratio of a regular jacket potato, plus anti-oxidants (whatever they are). It does take, basically, an hour, but you will be cooking for almost none of that time.

Chorizo and sweet potato are a truly perfect pairing; chorizo and roasted red peppers, ditto. You can, obviously, do this with a red pepper cut into strips – I do! Often! – but jarred red peppers are such a good and joyful shortcut it seems a shame not to use them on a night where you need things to be low-key.

You can use crumbled chorizo – still nice! But there is something specifically delicious about thick coins of chorizo, crisp on all sides and tender and impossibly juicy within. It is probably one of my favourite ways to eat meat of all the ways to eat meat: rich, spicy, golden oil and scarlet smoked paprika. It feels more decadent, somehow, than a standard issue sausage. I recommend it *so much.*

SERVES 2

2 big sweet potatoes
4 fresh chorizo sausages (or 150g chorizo crumbs)
2 garlic cloves
2 teaspoons red wine vinegar
2 tablespoons honey
250g jarred roasted red peppers
1 bag rocket or other sharp salad
2 tablespoons sour cream
1 teaspoon chilli flakes

Flick the oven on to 190°C. Prick the sweet potatoes with a fork, and sprinkle liberally with sea salt. Bake for 45 minutes, or until the skin is crisp and the insides fluffy.

Slice your chorizo into coins, about 5mm thick. If you want to be really fancy, slice these coins on the diagonal. Coins into a cold pan, over a medium-low heat. If you put cold cured meat (like bacon or sausage) into a cold pan, and bring it all up to temperature together, you render the fat – it keeps the meat crisp and we can use all that lovely scarlet oil to make a sauce with the peppers. Crush the garlic cloves, discarding the papery outside, and using the flat of the knife to expose the inside. Toss the garlic cloves into the oil.

Cook slowly, for about 20 minutes, flipping the coins over halfway through. Add the red wine vinegar, a tablespoon of the honey, and the peppers, and cook for a further 10 minutes, stirring occasionally. Set aside until the sweet potatoes are ready.

A handful of rocket on each plate. Split the potatoes and divide the chorizo and pepper mixture between the two. Add a substantial dollop of sour cream, and drizzle with the remaining honey. Sprinkle with chilli flakes. Season generously.

Miso and Peanut Burst Aubergine

How can something this simple be *this* good? I don't know, but I suspect the answer lies in taking three of the world's most delicious things (butter, miso, garlic) and jamming them into a single aubergine.

The best thing about this is that you can put the aubergine in the oven as soon as you get home (no messing about with ingredients, only an aubergine, a splash of oil, and a baking sheet) and know you're already on top of dinner. Sure, you've to whisk up a quick miso-butter dressing; sure, you've to bash up a bag of shop-bought roasted peanuts; but the main bit, the key element, is already underway and you've barely even got your coat off. And what better feeling could there be? You can put your softs on, get the laundry out of the dryer, listen to a little bit of a nice podcast or whatever. Oh, if you want to, you can make a salad, or cook some rice. But the aubergine sings pretty sweetly all by itself.

Those two accompaniments, if you can be bothered: jasmine rice lightly spiked with a teaspoon of rice wine vinegar, and a rocket/coriander salad with lime and chilli oil spooned over.

Rice on plate. Salad on top of rice. Whole burst aubergine atop the salad. That's it – and both of these are optional. You could just grab a pitta bread and dredge it through the buttery aubergine, like a lazy baba ganoush. You could just shove it into a part-bake baguette. You could just sit and spoon it into your mouth, and feel safe.

SERVES 2–4

2 aubergines
1 tablespoon sesame oil
2 fat garlic cloves
2 tablespoons unsalted butter
1 tablespoon white miso
4 tablespoons shelled, roasted peanuts
coriander leaves, to garnish (optional)

Flip the oven to 200°C, and brush the aubergines with the sesame oil. Toss them onto a baking sheet, and put the baking sheet in the oven. (Don't worry that it's not at temperature yet – we'll get there.) Cook for about 40 minutes, or until the aubergines split and the whole thing is soft and blistered.

Crush the garlic cloves into a small heatproof bowl and add the butter. Microwave in 10 second bursts until the butter is melted. Stir in the miso until smooth. (Easy, also, in a pan.)

Bash the peanuts to powder with a rolling pin – still in the bag is fine.

Take the blackened, burst aubergines from the oven. Fork the flesh to break it up. Drizzle over the butter, and fork it right through. Sprinkle with peanuts. Maybe garnish with a coriander leaf? But you don't have to. All you have to do, now, is eat.

Carbonara Risotto and Friends

Here is the easiest possible dinner that still feels like dinner: cook a cup of rice in two cups of double-strength chicken stock (lid on; low heat; steam 16 minutes) with 2 teaspoons olive oil.

Spoon into bowl; use an uncracked egg to make a hollow in the centre of the bowl. Separate the egg; tip the white into one bowl and put it in the fridge; slip the yolk into the *perfectly-sized* hollow in the rice. Crack plenty of black pepper over the top.

Take chopsticks. Stir yolk into rice; hot rice cooks the egg, like carbonara. Be comforted above all things.

Carbonara Rice with Peas

As above, but fry 30g pancetta cubes in another pan. Sprinkle over the pancetta; grate over Parmesan to taste.

Asian-ish Carbonara Rice

As above, but add 2 tablespoons soy sauce, and a teaspoon brown sugar to the pancetta in the pan. Skip the cheese and peas in favour of 1 teaspoon crispy chilli oil. Top with sesame seeds.

Sudden Burst of Energy Rice with Greens

Start with 2 teaspoons sesame oil and a handful of pre-chopped spring greens/kale/leafy vegetable. Pan. Lid on; high heat; cook until crispy. Lift out, and put in the bowl you're going to eat from. Into the sesame oil goes about 2cm grated ginger, 2 grated garlic cloves, your cup of rice, two cups of chicken stock and a splash of rice wine if you have it. Cook as above; stir through a teaspoon of rice wine vinegar when done. Crispy soy pancetta as above. Egg yolk as above. Chilli oil and sesame seeds as above. Crispy greens on top. Chopsticks.

Almond and Cherry One-Bowl Cake

This is the perfect cake for emergencies. I don't know how many cake-based emergencies you have, but let me tell you: this cake is here for all of them. It needs very little from you, and will give you so much. Do you have the kind of life where people pop round for coffee and cake? I don't, but I'd like to cultivate one, and this feels like a promising first step.

Dairy-free, gluten-free, one bowl, one spatula, no need to line anything properly, five minutes tops to stir together, forty minutes to bake, a little bitter from the olive oil, sweet with cherries and vanilla, caramel-crisp-topped, moist, squidgy, rich without being heavy, makes the house smell like marzipan, needs basically zero specially-bought ingredients, and tastes unbelievable: you need this cake in your life, and I do too.

SERVES 8–12

200g ground almonds
150g golden caster sugar
1 teaspoon salt
2½ teaspoons baking powder
200ml extra-virgin olive oil
3 teaspoons almond extract
1 teaspoon vanilla extract
3 eggs
200g frozen cherries
2 tablespoons demerara sugar

Pre-heat the oven to 190°C. Roughly grease and line a 20cm circular cake or flan tin. I literally just tear off a big strip of baking parchment, oil the tin a bit, and press it roughly down so it basically assumes the shape of the tin. Don't worry. Rustic is good.

In a big bowl, weigh out and whisk together the dry ingredients, except the demerara sugar. Make a well in the centre of the dry ingredients; pour in the olive oil, the almond extract, the vanilla extract and crack in the eggs. Whisk the wet ingredients together in the little well; when the eggs and oil have come together, make your whisk-strokes bigger to bring in the dry ingredients too. Whisk to form a smooth batter.

Pour the batter into the lined tin and cover with the frozen cherries. Sprinkle with the demerara sugar, and slide into the oven (you will probably want to put it on another baking sheet for ease). Bake 40 minutes, or until a skewer comes out clean.

The top will look a little burnt. You will think it's gone wrong. It hasn't. That burnt top is the best part: caramel-deep, fudgy, chewy. Serve with tea, or coffee, or a little cloud of fluffy white crème fraîche.

The Cookie Matrix

This is the base recipe from which every cookie I make is derived. The formula has yielded the best cookies of my life, and some cookies that were pretty good; and I thought about just writing out the recipe for the best cookies of my life – which is, of course, usually how cookbooks work.

But I think this is more useful to you: this is the formula for pretty much being able to make a genuinely very nice cookie, whatever you have in, whenever, wherever, and without having to go to the shops or leave the house. In this way, you will, broadly speaking, always be able to make a passable cookie. Not every cookie will be the greatest cookie you have ever made, but every cookie will be better than a cookie from a shop and probably from a bakery too.

Do not try to halve this recipe. Make the full thing; bake two; freeze the rest. Some other day, when you are once again on the floor, you will be unbelievably grateful: fresh-baked cookies? Right now? Minimal effort?

The formula:

[250g sugar]

+

[1 egg + 1 yolk]

+

[170g wet]

+

[250g dry + 1/2 teaspoon bicarb]

+

[150g fun mix-ins]

Dry is flour, or flour-adjacent: oats, finely ground nuts, that kind of thing. Be careful with desiccated coconut, which is amazing, taste-wise, but drinks up liquid in a funny way so you might need to add a bit more fat than otherwise. You want at least some flour, of some kind, in there.

Wet is mostly melted butter, oil, or other fat, like tahini or peanut butter. Could be some – like, up to a quarter weight? – coffee in there. Could be a good splash of milk or alt m*lk or booze to make it up to the number. You want at least some butter or oil, of some kind, in there. (Don't worry about the weight of extracts and essences, not that you would.)

Mix-ins: we're talking chocolate chips, ideally chocolate cut diagonally from a big bar to make lovely uneven splinters and pools; we're talking nuts; we're talking sour cherries, raisins, caramel bits, pretzels, crisps... Listen. If you think it might be delicious in a cookie, this is the very definition of risking it for a biscuit.

Salt the tops lightly with flaky salt. (*Smoked* salt?)

Six, tops, to a lined baking sheet. 180°C; 9 minutes from fridge; 9 minutes 30 seconds from frozen. Lift up the baking parchment to about 10cm; drop it back down hard on the cooling rack. Good cracks.

You can play with this. You *must* play with this. Otherwise you have to leave the house and buy stuff. Nope!

So, for example, these are the cookies I just made this evening following this formula:

I melted 200g of salted butter and let it foam up until it became about 170g brown butter. (Actually, it came to about 180g brown butter, but I wasn't going to waste any, so I knew I would add an extra tablespoon of flour to balance that out a bit, depending on how it looked.)

☞

Into the bowl of the stand mixer, I measured out 250g of sugar: we had about 110g golden caster sugar and 100g soft light brown sugar, and then I made up the remaining 40g with soft dark brown sugar.

I shook in about a teaspoon of vanilla. I usually use vanilla as a base, but I could have used almond extract, or even coffee extract. As above: I do not weigh these because I have a life.

Butter into sugar until the butter cooled and the sugar dissolved; egg and yolk into the butter-sugar. Shiny! Gloopy!

For the dry, I used up the end of a packet of rolled oats, the end of a packet of desiccated coconut, and a couple of tablespoons of plain flour. (Plus my extra tablespoon, to balance out the fact that the wets went over. So, about 270g dry, in the end.) A half-teaspoon of bicarb.

Dry into butter-sugar-egg until stickily combined. You're looking for a texture you could pick up with your fingers and roll into a ball. If it's too sticky, a teaspoon of flour. If it's too dry, a splash of water or milk or coffee or rum.

When I think coconut, I think white chocolate. Fortunately, we had some white chocolate chips. When I think coconut and white chocolate, I think dried cranberries, and we had some of those too. Plus some walnuts. I didn't measure: I guessed. I used all the little bag of walnuts, crushed, and the half-bar of white chocolate, chopped, and a big generous shake of cranberries for some sourness to balance out the sweet. If you pick up a teaspoon of the dough, you should have some of everything in it.

I froze 18 balls of dough; baked 6. Sprinkled with smoked salt. Nine minutes at 180°C; dropped onto a cooling rack from 10cm. Best cookies of my life. Until next time.

Once you know this, you will be able to make any cookie.

☞

	250g sugar	170g wet
Sophisticated!	200g soft dark brown sugar + 50g golden caster sugar	150g salted butter, reduced to 120g brown butter + 50g tahini + 2 teaspoons good vanilla extract
Birthday party!	100g soft light brown sugar + 130g golden caster sugar + 2 tablespoons coconut sugar	170g salted butter
Sexy lemon!	150g soft light brown sugar + 100g golden caster sugar, mixed with the zest of 2 unwaxed lemons	150g olive oil (less, to compensate for the fat in the pistachio!)
Wholesome!	150g soft dark brown sugar + 100g demerara sugar	50g mashed banana + 50g peanut butter + 70g butter
Chaos!	100g soft dark brown sugar + 25g golden caster sugar + 25g demerara sugar	150g salted butter, reduced to 120g brown butter + 3 tablespoons coffee grounds

250g dry	150g mix-ins	Top with…
170g spelt flour + 50g rye flour + 30g plain flour	150g plain dark chocolate: chop bar diagonally into fragments	Smoked salt and sesame seeds
200g plain flour + 50g desiccated coconut	100g milk chocolate chips; 3 tablespoons pretty sprinkles	More pretty sprinkles!
150g plain flour, 100g blitzed pistachios	**Lemon curd!** Take about 100g lemon curd; freeze it in little quarter-teaspoon drops; mix into the batter once frozen. 100g chopped pistachios	Flaky sea salt
100g plain flour + 150g oats	50g walnuts; 50g darkest dark chocolate; 50g raisins	–
100g spelt flour + 100g rolled oats + 50g desiccated coconut	50g lightly bashed salty pretzels; 1 packet plain crisps, ideally ridged; 50g mixed chocolate chips; 2 digestive biscuits, smashed up	Whole pretzel pressed into the centre of each one

Acknowledgements

This book was written in five kitchens, tested in a further seven, and shot in two more, over the course of three fairly wild years. I owe many people thanks. First thanks, as always, to my agent Daisy Parente, and all at L&R, without whom I would never publish anything again.

Thank you to the subscribers of *You Get In Love And Then;* and everyone who has supported my work over the last few years. When you pay an artist directly, you let them make the work of their heart. Writing to you is the work of my heart. This book, which grew from those letters, is the work of my heart. Thank you for your love; your support; your profoundly moving sense of community; the stability, continuity and creative freedom you bring to my life; and all the soup recipes. I am unbelievably grateful. Thank you for eating my food; testing my recipes; reading my writing; and bringing your whole hearts to the party, always. You have changed my life.

Thank you to Louise Haines, Vic Pullen and all at 4th Estate. I am so happy to be here. I have loved making this book with you. What an amazing team: creative, collaborative, and willing to go off on a tangent to make the thing perfect. Special thanks to Luke Bird, who managed to translate many meetings full of pre-Raphaelite calligraphy, gravestones, Delft tiles and 1940s manuals for housewives into something beautiful, useful, and – dare I say it – chic. Thank you, Luke.

Working with Kate Young and Yuki Sugiura is one of the great joys of my job. I can't believe we get to do it again. Yuki took the pictures in this book without a single artificial light source and a great willingness to play, and I love them; so thank you, Yuki, for your ability to follow a dream and find the light in the dark.

To my right hand woman, in food, life, love, death, taxes and all things in between, it's true what they say: Kate Young Solves Everything. Without you I am just a regular medieval knight, and I know a lot less about beauty and a lot less about food. Also, without you, I am in prison for failing to do my tax return. Thank you for keeping me out of prison. And everything else, which is everything.

Thank you to Patrick from the Tinned Fish Company, who met me in a carpark in Bermondsey to hand over fifty tins of tinned fish at absolutely no notice. Lending a stranger fifty tins of precious octopus is no small thing. Thank you also to Sea Sisters and Canny Mushrooms. Thank you to Jay of Jay's Budgens, famously the best Budgens in England, and Jones of Brockley, the deli of my dreams, for letting us shoot in your shops. Thank you to our London neighbours, Paul, Katya and the boys, for bringing us branches of rosemary and their black cast iron pots.

Thank you very much to Queen Monica Heisey of the High Ceilings for her exquisite taste in everything and abundant generosity. Anything that looks extremely perfect was shot at Monica's house.

Everything else was shot at our house. I am very lucky to have in my entire life lived only with the best people in the world, and to cook for these people is the joy of my life. Thank you to Tash and Andy. I love this house, I love every house we live in, and I love our lives. I love every single one of the apes. Thank you is not a big enough word.

Thank you to Katya and Ben for testing the recipes, the heart-shaped cookie cutters, and the most beautiful babies in the world. Thank you to my friend SHZA for coming to our party. We really loved having you! Thank you to my friend E for being such a nice guy. Thank you to Gav for wise counsel and weird art; thank you to Caro for being the person I most want to impress with my cool new Barbie. Thank you to everyone who sends me a four-minute voice note when they eat something good. Thank you to all my friends and family who tested the recipes as well; especially my parents, my most reliable recipe testers and constant champions. Thank you to my sisters: I wrote this book for the three of you.

Thank you to R. People are always telling you that you are very lucky to live with a cook. Not enough people tell me – maybe they don't know? – that I am actually the one who is lucky to live with a great cook. I love to be cooked for by you more than almost anything in the world, and it happens to me almost every day. I am lucky for many reasons, but sharing a kitchen with you is right up at the top. I wrote this book because of you.

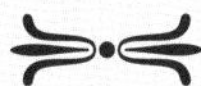

Index

Q

R

S

T

U

V

W

Y

Conversion Chart

UK cups	
¼ cup	62.5ml
½ cup	125ml
1 cup	250ml
1½ cups	375ml
2 cups	500ml

US cups	
¼ cup	60ml
½ cup	120ml
1 cup	240ml
1½cups	360ml
2 cups	480ml

Gas	F°	C°	Fan C°
1	275	140	120
2	300	150	130
3	325	170	150
4	350	180	160
5	375	190	170
6	400	200	180
7	425	220	200
8	450	230	210

I never wanted to write another cookbook. I was so sad when I made the first two. I thought that maybe I would be too sad to try again.

ER
ER
ER
ER
ER
ER
ER
ER
ER